WITHDRAWN

P9-CKP-243

PLANET EARTH!

Senior Editor Georgina Palffy
Senior Art Editor Rachael Grady
Editors Rebecca Fry, Binta Jallow,
Ashwin Khurana, Vicky Richards,
Rona Skene, Anna Streiffert Limerick
Art Editors Sheila Collins, Mik Gates, Jim Green,
Katy Jakeway, Beth Johnston, Kit Lane,
Lynne Moulding, Stefan Podhorodecki
US Editor Jennette ElNaggar
Jacket Design Development Manager Sophia MTT
Jacket Designers Vidushi Chaudhry, Surabhi Wadhwa Gandhi
Production Editor Robert Dunn
Production Controller Jude Crozier
Managing Editor Francesca Baines
Managing Art Editor Philip Letsu
Publisher Andrew Macintyre
Associate Publishing Director Liz Wheeler
Art Director Karen Self
Publishing Director Jonathan Metcalf

Contributors Emma Espley, Dr. Peter Inness,
Dr. Anthea Lacchia, Martin Redfern, John Woodward
Consultants Derek Harvey, David Holmes

Illustrators Andrew Beckett @ Illustration Ltd, Adam Benton,
Peter Bull @ Art Studio, Gary Hanna, Jason Harding,
Stuart Jackson-Carter – SJC Illustration, Jon @ KJA, Arran Lewis,
Simon Mumford, Sofian Moumene, Claudia Saraceni @ Art Agency, Simon Tegg

First American Edition, 2022
Published in the United States by DK Publishing
1745 Broadway, 20th Floor, New York, NY 10019

Copyright © 2022 Dorling Kindersley Limited
DK, a Division of Penguin Random House LLC
22 23 24 25 26 10 9 8 7 6 5 4 3 2 1
001–319142–Oct/2022

All rights reserved.
Without limiting the rights under the copyright reserved above,
no part of this publication may be reproduced, stored in or introduced
into a retrieval system, or transmitted, in any form, or by any means
(electronic, mechanical, photocopying, recording, or otherwise),
without the prior written permission of the copyright owner.
Published in Great Britain by Dorling Kindersley Limited

A catalog record for this book is
available from the Library of Congress.
ISBN 978-0-7440-5625-9

DK books are available at special discounts when purchased in
bulk for sales promotions, premiums, fund-raising, or educational
use. For details, contact: DK Publishing Special Markets,
1745 Broadway, 20th Floor, New York, NY 10019
SpecialSales@dk.com

Printed and bound in the UAE

FOR THE CURIOUS
www.dk.com

Established in 1846, the Smithsonian is the world's largest museum
and research complex, dedicated to public education, national service,
and scholarship in the arts, sciences, and history. It includes 21 museums and
galleries and the National Zoological Park. The total number of artifacts, works
of art, and specimens in the Smithsonian's collection is estimated at 155.5 million.

This book was made with Forest
Stewardship Council™ certified
paper – one small step in DK's
commitment to a sustainable future.
For more information go to
www.dk.com/our-green-pledge

DK SMITHSONIAN

PLANET EARTH!

CONTENTS

LIFE ON EARTH

EARTH AND US

EARTH'S CONTINENTS

Scales and sizes

The data box for each animal includes a scale drawing to indicate its size. These are based on the height of an average adult human male and the hand and thumb tip shown below. The sizes given in this book are **typical maximums**. Unless otherwise stated, the sizes given are the length of the animal, from the front of the head or tip of the beak, to the rear of the body—or tip of the tail or tentacles, where the animal has these. Some animals have shapes that mean width is a more useful measurement than length, so this is given instead.

6 ft (1.8 m)

7 in (18 cm)

PLANET EARTH

In the so-called "Goldilocks zone" in our solar system, our home planet has evolved from its dramatic beginnings to the Earth we know today. During its 4.54 billion years, it has survived meteorite impacts, climate changes, and several mass extinctions, and still spins on.

Land plants
First mosses and ferns grow on land; soon, insects and amphibians follow

Mammals
After the dinosaurs were gone, mammals evolved and prospered.

Prokaryotes
The very first life on Earth—simple bacteria and archaea—appeared quite early.

Dinosaurs
Dinosaurs were dominant for almost 175 million years of the Mesozoic Era—no more than half an hour on this timescale—while birds (avian dinosaurs) lived on!

Humans
Our ancestors were walking upright some 4 million years ago—only around 30 seconds on this clock—but fully modern humans emerged only just over a second before 12.

Early animals
The first evidence appears of animals probably belonging to groups that are around today (sponges and corals).

DEEP TIME

The secret to understanding Earth is understanding time. If the existence of Earth was shown as 12 hours on a clock, your whole life would only represent the last ten-thousandth of a second. For the first hours, Earth was busy taking shape. Then life slowly started to evolve. All along, processes such as the drifting of continents and the rise and fall of mountain ranges and sea levels continually take place.

Multicellular life
The first sign of cells taking on specialized roles in a multicelled organism

Eukaryotes
More complex cells with a nucleus (including protozoans and algae)

EARTH IN TIME

Since it formed from the swirling gas and dust of the solar system, our home planet has been through many changes, affecting its surface, its climate, and the life that has evolved on it. It is still changing today. We are lucky to be here—if the laws of physics were slightly different, stars would not have formed and turned hydrogen into the elements that made Earth and ourselves. If our planet were bigger or smaller, or the sun less stable, we'd have no atmosphere and no water, and without these there would be no life.

EONS, ERAS, PERIODS, AND EPOCHS

Eon, era, and epoch are words often used to convey a very long period of time. In geology, their meanings are more precise. Eons are the longest and are the main divisions of the Precambrian. Eras come next, dividing the last 540 million years into three parts. These eras are divided into periods (such as the Jurassic), subdivided into smaller parts known as epochs.

EON	MYA	
	66	
PHANEROZOIC	252	
	542	
PROTEROZOIC	2,500	PRECAMBRIAN
ARCHAEAN	4,000	
HADEAN	4,600	

ERA	PERIOD	EPOCH	MYA
CENOZOIC	QUATERNARY	HOLOCENE	0.01
		PLEISTOCENE	2.6
	NEOGENE	PLIOCENE	5.3
		MIOCENE	23
	PALEOGENE	OLIGOCENE	33.9
		EOCENE	56
		PALEOCENE	66
MESOZOIC	CRETACEOUS		145
	JURASSIC		201
	TRIASSIC		252
PALEOZOIC	PERMIAN		299
	CARBONIFEROUS		359
	DEVONIAN		419
	SILURIAN		444
	ORDOVICIAN		485
	CAMBRIAN		541

THE DATING GAME

It is one thing to divide geological time into periods, but much harder to put exact dates on those periods. Fortunately, scientists have figured out how to read much of the information hidden in rocks—in the form of rock types, the shapes of layers, type of fossils, or even number of atoms. Organic matter, such as ancient trees, also contains useful clues from the past.

Tree-ring dating

Trees produce annual growth rings, so the number of rings reveals their age. Rings also vary with growing conditions. By comparing ring sequences in very old living trees and ancient trees preserved in bogs, the record can be taken back thousands of years.

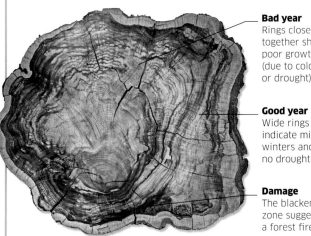

Bad year
Rings close together show poor growth (due to cold or drought).

Good year
Wide rings indicate mild winters and no drought.

Damage
The blackened zone suggests a forest fire.

Looking for layers

Sedimentary rocks are mostly deposited in horizontal layers, or strata, often under water. The layer above is usually younger than the one underneath. In some places, tectonic movements have created diagonal or folded layers.

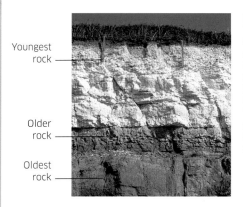

Youngest rock

Older rock

Oldest rock

Horizontal layers
These layers of sedimentary rock at Hunstanton in Norfolk, England, are still much as they were at the time of forming. The youngest, white chalk, settled on top of two older Cretaceous layers.

Folded rock
These swirling layers of Devonian old red sandstone, in Pembrokeshire, Wales, have been folded by tectonic forces into contorted (twisted) shapes. But the stripes of the original layers are still easy to see.

SPACE ROCKS

Meteorites that have fallen down to Earth contain many of the elements found in Earth's rocks, giving hints of how planets formed (see pages 12–13). Meteorites can be dated, too, and most give a date of near 4.6 billion years ago, the age of our solar system.

RARE METEORITE

A stony-iron pallasite with olivine crystals in a once-molten iron base

Old as rock

One way of dating a rock is through the decay of any radioactive atoms (isotopes) it contains. Each has a very precise time over which half of the atoms will decay into another element—known as a half-life. A machine called a mass spectrometer can count the atoms, allowing geologists to figure out the rock's age.

Ancient crystal
As zircon crystals grow, uranium atoms trapped inside them decay to lead atoms. The ratio of lead compared to uranium tells us how many half-lives have passed since the crystal was formed.

1. Newly formed
When it formed, crystallizing from molten rock, this bit of zircon contained plenty of uranium but no lead.

2. 700 million years
Half of the uranium, or U235 (yellow), has decayed into lead 207 (blue): the half-life of U235 is 700 million years.

3. 1,400 million years
Half of the remaining uranium has decayed, so another half-life (700 million years) has passed since the crystal formed.

4. 2,100 million years
Most of the uranium has now decayed. This crystal is very old—it has existed for three half-lives, or three times 700 million years.

Revealing fossils

Rocks can also be dated through the fossils they contain (see also pages 62–63). Species that have existed for a short time (in geological terms, that is a few million years) are particularly useful for matching rock layers in different locations and can indicate when layers are missing.

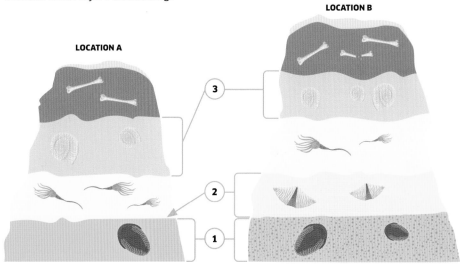

LOCATION A

LOCATION B

1. Oldest layers
The deepest layers in both locations are of different rock types, but the trilobites they contain say both are Cambrian.

2. Missing layer
Location A has no layer with Devonian shell fossils—maybe due to erosion, or perhaps it was above sea level by then.

3. Matching layers
This species of ammonite lived only at a particular stage of the Jurassic, so these layers are the same age.

The expanding universe

The history of the Universe can be shown as a trumpet, with time down its length and space across its width. Using telescopes and satellites, we can look down the 13.77-billion-year length of the trumpet and see how the universe changed over time.

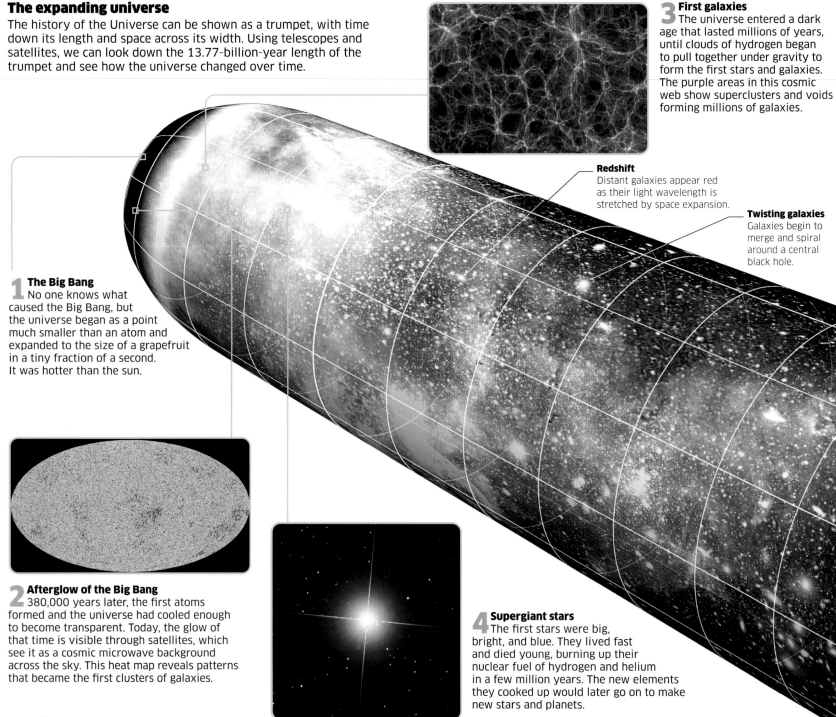

3 First galaxies
The universe entered a dark age that lasted millions of years, until clouds of hydrogen began to pull together under gravity to form the first stars and galaxies. The purple areas in this cosmic web show superclusters and voids forming millions of galaxies.

Redshift
Distant galaxies appear red as their light wavelength is stretched by space expansion.

Twisting galaxies
Galaxies begin to merge and spiral around a central black hole.

1 The Big Bang
No one knows what caused the Big Bang, but the universe began as a point much smaller than an atom and expanded to the size of a grapefruit in a tiny fraction of a second. It was hotter than the sun.

2 Afterglow of the Big Bang
380,000 years later, the first atoms formed and the universe had cooled enough to become transparent. Today, the glow of that time is visible through satellites, which see it as a cosmic microwave background across the sky. This heat map reveals patterns that became the first clusters of galaxies.

4 Supergiant stars
The first stars were big, bright, and blue. They lived fast and died young, burning up their nuclear fuel of hydrogen and helium in a few million years. The new elements they cooked up would later go on to make new stars and planets.

Big Bang

Everything, or at least our present universe, began 13.77 billion years ago. The birth and expansion of the universe was so sudden and fast that it has been called the Big Bang.

The universe didn't expand into a preexisting space. It suddenly appeared from nowhere, and space itself grew with it. At first it was too hot for atoms to exist. As it expanded, hydrogen and helium atoms formed and began to cluster into clouds, out of which the first stars and galaxies emerged. They created new elements and later went on to form new stars and planets. One of those we call Earth.

Key

- Oxygen 65%
- Carbon 18.5%
- Hydrogen 9.5%
- Nitrogen 3.2%
- Calcium 1.5%
- Phosphorous 1%
- Potassium 0.4%
- Sulfur 0.3%
- Sodium 0.2%
- Chlorine 0.2%
- Trace elements such as magnesium, boron, and copper 0.2%

We are all made of stardust

Nearly all the elements that make up the human body were first formed in stars and supernovas over billions of years. After the Big Bang, there was little except hydrogen and helium, the two lightest elements. All the remaining elements have been cooked in the nuclear fusion furnaces of stars and recycled into new planetary systems. They are then found in our solar system, our planet, and within us.

100–400 billion—the estimated number of **stars** in our **Milky Way galaxy**.

3,200 The number of **planetary systems discovered** so far.

11

5 Supernova blast
When a big star runs out of fuel, it can no longer support its own weight. It collapses, creating a supernova—a powerful star explosion—and spews new elements out into space. Elements that we depend on, such as carbon, nitrogen, and oxygen, were all made in stars.

Looking into the past
A telescope is a time machine. Although light travels at 186,000 miles per second (300,000 km/s), it takes millions of years for light to reach us from other galaxies. A "light year" – the distance light travels in a year – is a measure of distance. This image shows Galaxy NGC 5010, which is 140 million light-years away. So we are seeing this galaxy as it was 140 million years ago.

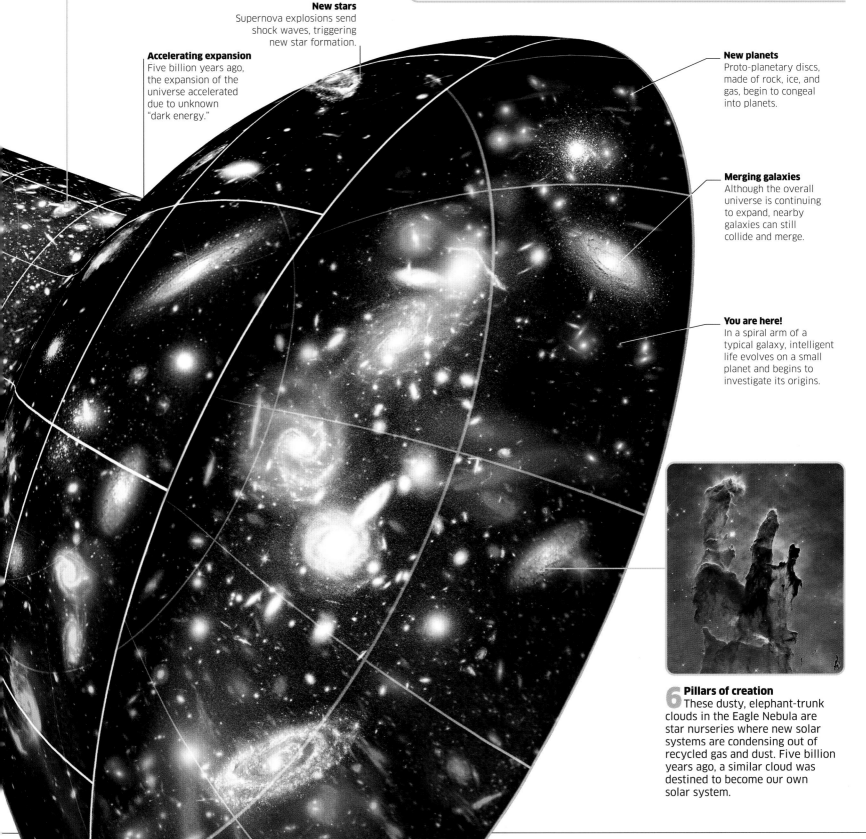

New stars
Supernova explosions send shock waves, triggering new star formation.

Accelerating expansion
Five billion years ago, the expansion of the universe accelerated due to unknown "dark energy."

New planets
Proto-planetary discs, made of rock, ice, and gas, begin to congeal into planets.

Merging galaxies
Although the overall universe is continuing to expand, nearby galaxies can still collide and merge.

You are here!
In a spiral arm of a typical galaxy, intelligent life evolves on a small planet and begins to investigate its origins.

6 Pillars of creation
These dusty, elephant-trunk clouds in the Eagle Nebula are star nurseries where new solar systems are condensing out of recycled gas and dust. Five billion years ago, a similar cloud was destined to become our own solar system.

New planet formation
Planets form in this darker ring toward the center of the disk, where the dust has cleared.

Birth of Earth

Almost 4.6 billion years ago, as the solar system settled into its current pattern, Earth began to form from a giant cloud of swirling gas and dust–the remains of dead stars.

A disturbance, perhaps a nearby exploding star, sent shock waves through the gas and dust cloud and it collapsed into a protoplanetary disc. A new star, the sun, formed at its center. The remaining cloud material slowly came together into a series of planets, one of which we call Earth.

Protoplanetary disc (4.568 billion years ago)

Planets are formed in a rotating ring of dust and gas orbiting a young star. This spinning cloud is known as a protoplanetary disc. The star drives gas and ice outward, where it condenses into giant gas planets like Jupiter and Saturn. Closer to the star are heat-resistant rocks that can form smaller, Earth-like planets.

Forming our planet

After the creation of the solar system, huge clouds of dust and gas collapsed into a dense sphere, which became the sun. Rocks in the region orbiting the sun collided and sometimes stuck together. After millions of years, some formed the beginnings of planets, such as Earth. Gravity held the rocks together, causing them to contract and melt into a sphere. Over time, dense iron sank to form a core.

Floating chunks of rock
There are rocks of all sizes left from the protoplanetary disc – from dust to objects many miles (kilometers) across.

Volcanic eruption
With most of the planet molten, huge amounts of gas and steam escape in tremendous volcanic eruptions.

Crust formation
In places, the surface begins to cool enough for a rocky crust to form.

Sudden collision
When an impact strikes, the rock vaporizes, melting a crater in the new crust and blasting debris back into space.

1 Accretion (4.54 billion years ago)
Dust and chunks of rock in the protoplanetary disc collide and clump together under gravity. This forms a new planet that is mostly molten. Masses of "building trash" are still floating around, including rocks the size of mountains that blast craters in the surface.

30 billion miles (19 billion km) across—**the average size** of a **protoplanetary disc**.

332 million cu miles (1.386 billion cu km)—the total **volume of water on Earth** that emerged from **falling comets** and **volcanic gases**.

13

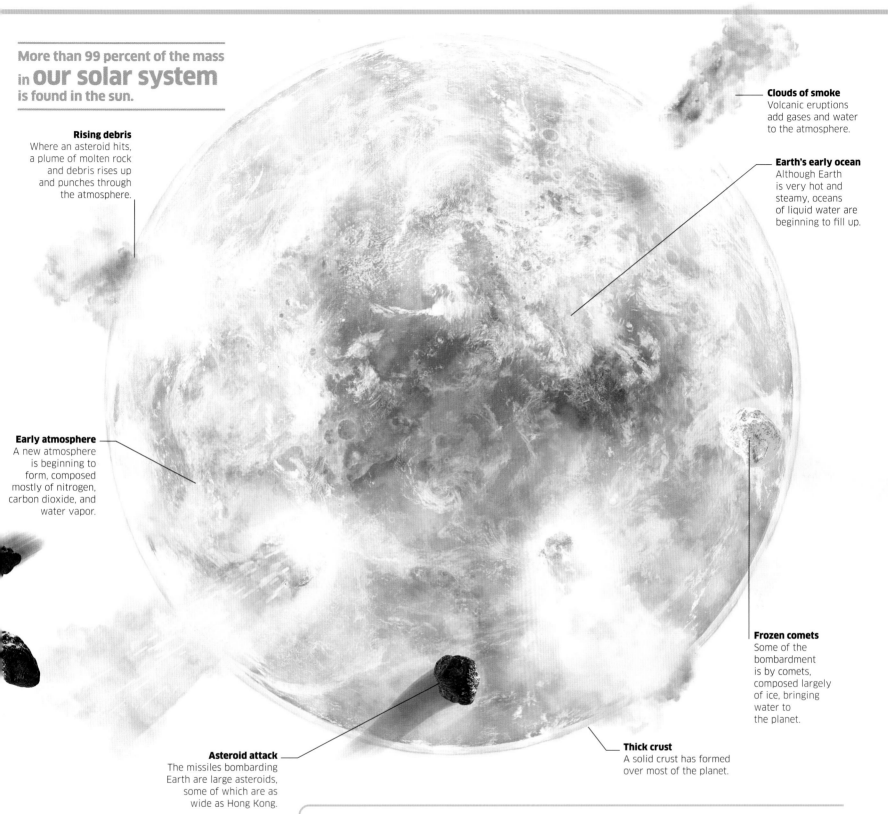

More than 99 percent of the mass in **OUR SOLAR SYSTEM** is found in the sun.

Rising debris
Where an asteroid hits, a plume of molten rock and debris rises up and punches through the atmosphere.

Clouds of smoke
Volcanic eruptions add gases and water to the atmosphere.

Earth's early ocean
Although Earth is very hot and steamy, oceans of liquid water are beginning to fill up.

Early atmosphere
A new atmosphere is beginning to form, composed mostly of nitrogen, carbon dioxide, and water vapor.

Frozen comets
Some of the bombardment is by comets, composed largely of ice, bringing water to the planet.

Asteroid attack
The missiles bombarding Earth are large asteroids, some of which are as wide as Hong Kong.

Thick crust
A solid crust has formed over most of the planet.

2 Late Heavy Bombardment (4 billion years ago)
Many researchers believe that around half a billion years after Earth formed, a barrage of failed planets pummeled its surface. This period, known as the Late Heavy Bombardment, may have lasted between 20 million and 200 million years. Icy comets and asteroids containing large amounts of water in their minerals hit Earth, gradually forming oceans of water and creating the conditions for life.

Earth's first atmosphere (4.2 billion years ago)

When Earth first formed, it most likely formed an atmosphere made up of hydrogen and helium. As the sun began to shine brightly and release nuclear energy, a fierce solar wind of particles blew outward, stripping away Earth's first atmosphere. The air we breathe now came afterward, from comets, volcanic eruptions, and life itself. Although the solar wind still blows gently today, our atmosphere is protected by Earth's magnetic field.

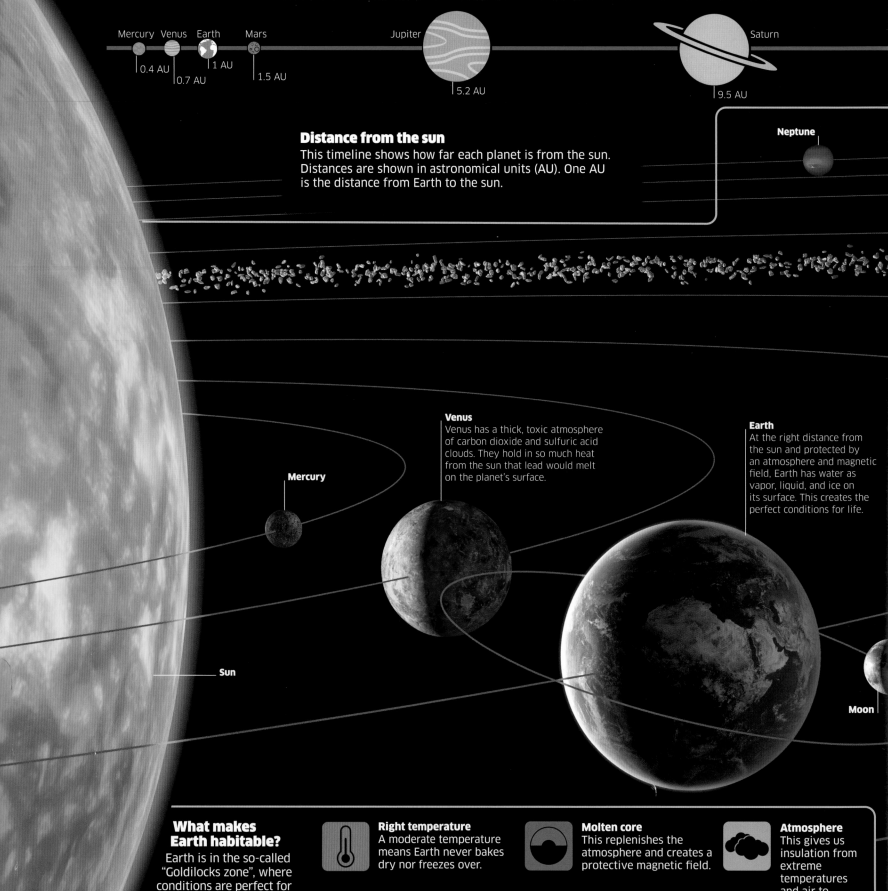

1,113,527 The **number of asteroids** **discovered** so far.

Mercury Venus Earth Mars
0.4 AU
0.7 AU
1 AU
1.5 AU

Jupiter
5.2 AU

Saturn
9.5 AU

Neptune

Distance from the sun
This timeline shows how far each planet is from the sun. Distances are shown in astronomical units (AU). One AU is the distance from Earth to the sun.

Venus
Venus has a thick, toxic atmosphere of carbon dioxide and sulfuric acid clouds. They hold in so much heat from the sun that lead would melt on the planet's surface.

Earth
At the right distance from the sun and protected by an atmosphere and magnetic field, Earth has water as vapor, liquid, and ice on its surface. This creates the perfect conditions for life.

Mercury

Sun

Moon

What makes Earth habitable?
Earth is in the so-called "Goldilocks zone", where conditions are perfect for life. Not only is it the right distance from the sun for liquid water to exist, but as the sun slowly warms, life has consumed insulating carbon dioxide from the atmosphere, preventing overheating. There are eight factors that make life possible on Earth.

 Right temperature
A moderate temperature means Earth never bakes dry nor freezes over.

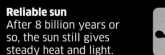 **Reliable sun**
After 8 billion years or so, the sun still gives steady heat and light.

Spin and tilt
Days and seasons prevent any single place from baking or freezing for long.

Molten core
This replenishes the atmosphere and creates a protective magnetic field.

 Surface water
Available as rain, water is essential for the chemistry of life.

 Sufficient mass
Gravity pulls us down and stops our atmosphere from escaping into space.

Atmosphere
This gives us insulation from extreme temperatures and air to breathe.

 Elements
Carbon, oxygen, nitrogen, phosphorus, and other trace elements are essential to life.

1 trillion—the estimated **number of comets** in the **outer reaches of the solar system.**

It takes **Venus longer to rotate once on its axis** than to complete one **orbit of the sun**, meaning **its day is longer than its year.**

Uranus

19 AU

Neptune

30 AU

Uranus

Saturn

Planets in orbit

There are eight planets in the solar system, all of which revolve around the sun. The first four (Mercury, Venus, Earth, and Mars) are terrestrial planets made of mostly rock, while the outer four (Jupiter, Saturn, Uranus, and Neptune) are made of gas. The farther a planet is from the sun, the cooler its temperature. The only exception is Venus, whose surface reaches 867°F (464°C) due to its dense atmosphere.

Jupiter protects the Earth
Jupiter, at more than twice the mass of all the other planets put together, protects Earth from impacts as its gravity sucks in asteroids and comets. Its "black eye" is where the remains of Comet Shoemaker-Levy 9 crashed into Jupiter in 1994.

Mars
This cold, dry, desert planet has a thin atmosphere, which slowly escapes from its low gravity. Its red appearance is due to rusting iron minerals in the Martian soil. Scientists have long believed this planet has the greatest possibility for life.

Earth in space

Earth is one of eight planets that orbit around the sun in our solar system. To the best of our knowledge, it is the only one that is able to sustain life.

Astronomers have discovered more than 3,000 planetary systems (stars with planets orbiting around them) but they are inhospitable environments. Some are icy wastes illuminated by unstable stars. Even in our own system, the outer planets, such as Jupiter and Saturn, are huge, hot bags of gas. Earth is in a privileged position, occupying a stable habitable zone—unlike even our closest neighbors, Venus and Mars. If Earth was where Uranus is, the ocean would completely freeze over. If Earth took Mercury's place, it would be so close to the sun that its water would create a steamy atmosphere.

Asteroid belt
Located between Mars and Jupiter, more than one million pieces of ancient space rubble make up this belt.

16 planet earth ∘ **EARTH AND MOON**

240,000 miles (385,000 km)–the **approximate distance** between the **moon** and **Earth**.

Earth and moon

The moon is our close companion in space. It lightens our nights, gives us our calendar months, and influences our tides.

Moons are natural space objects that orbit planets or asteroids. Earth is unusual in having a single large moon. Venus has none; Mars has two small moons, and Jupiter has about 80. Ours forms a beautiful sight in the night sky and is the only other world so far visited in person by humans, the first time by Apollo 11 in 1969. Without wind, water, or tectonic forces to alter its surface, the moon still carries the ancient scars of its early history and can tell us things about Earth, too.

1 ON TARGET
Just 50 million years after Earth formed (see pages 12-13), our planet is still red-hot. Theia, an object the size of Mars, is on a collision course, traveling at high speed.

2 IMPACT
Theia strikes Earth at a steep angle, largely melting, or even partly vaporizing, both bodies. Most of Theia's core and mantle merge with Earth.

MOON GEOLOGY

Rock brought back from the moon is very similar to many rocks on Earth, suggesting a common origin. The most abundant rock in the darker *maria* regions is basalt, and in the highlands, feldspar-rich anorthosite, a type of ancient igneous rock also found on Earth.

FORMATION OF THE MOON

Different kinds of moons are formed in different ways. Some moons are asteroids captured by a planet's gravity. The rocks of our moon are too similar to Earth's for this to be the case. Some moons are "spun out" from a planet's bulge but do not have an iron core. Most likely, our moon was formed when Earth was hit by an object called Theia, whose core became part of both Earth and moon.

Lunar layers

The early moon was molten. It settled into layers, with denser materials sinking to form a core, giving it a structure like Earth's. The moon's core is small (about 20 percent of its full diameter)–in comparison, the diameter of Earth's core is almost half of Earth's total diameter.

Solid iron inner core

Molten iron outer core

Mantle of solid rock, containing the kinds of minerals found on Earth

Solid crust, on average 31 miles (50 km) thick

MOON GEOGRAPHY

With no atmosphere, no continental drift, and no vegetation, little changes on the moon. The surface we see is ancient and covered in craters from impacts. There are also cracks, probably caused by the moon shrinking as it cools. On the side, we can see large dark blotches resembling a face or a rabbit.

Bombarded moon

The moon had a difficult start in life, suffering bombardment from the rocks and asteroids left over from the formation of the solar system. Some of the craters even have craters on top of them, helping astronomers figure out their relative ages. A few craters, such as the Tycho Crater (see below) are more recent, some with radiating rays of debris still visible.

One of more than 100,000 impact craters on the lunar surface

Moon dust

After 4 billion years of impacts from tiny meteorites, a thick layer of very fine dust, called regolith, has built up on the lunar surface. Rich in a rare form of the element helium, it could be mined for nuclear fuel. In shaded craters at the moon's south pole, it contains water ice.

Footprint on the moon
With no wind, prints left on the moon in 1969 will last for millions of years.

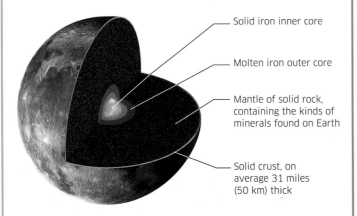

Mare Serenitatis
The "Sea of Serenity" is one of the smaller basalt-filled impact craters formed in the Late Heavy Bombardment.

Montes Apenninus
This rugged mountain range has 16,400 ft (5,000 m) peaks. Apollo 15 landed nearby in 1971.

Tycho Crater
This comparatively recent impact took place about 108 million years ago.

Seas and mountains

The dark areas on the moon were once thought to be seas and named *maria*. In fact, they are vast impact basins, flooded with basalt lava some 3.9 billion years ago, during a period of impacts known as the Late Heavy Bombardment. They are surrounded by the even older lunar highlands, which also cover the far side of the moon.

12 The number of **people** who have **walked** on the **moon**.

842 lb (382 kg)—the amount of **moon rock** brought back by the **Apollo astronauts**.

1.48 in (3.78 cm) per year—the **rate** at which the **moon** is **moving away** from Earth.

17

3 MOLTEN SPLASH
Molten rock fragments are flung out into space. Some fall back but most start to form a glowing hot ring around Earth.

4 THE MOON GROWS
The thickest part of the ring begins to coalesce (come together) and eventually forms a small single body of molten rock that sweeps up the remaining ring material.

5 HEAVY BOMBARDMENT
Earth and moon cool down, but 3.9 billion years ago, asteroid impacts form craters on the moon that flood with molten basalt.

6 EARTH AND MOON TODAY
Today, the moon looks much as it did billions of years ago, while on Earth, continents, oceans, an atmosphere, and life have evolved.

LOCKED IN ORBIT

Earth and moon are held together in orbit by gravity. The strong gravitational pull between them has striking effects. It causes the tides on Earth (see page 87) and moon quakes. It also slows the rotation of both. The moon is "tidally locked" to Earth. This means that it rotates in the same time it takes to orbit Earth—so one side permanently faces Earth. The "lock" has slowed Earth down— 4.5 billion years ago, it spun so fast a day lasted just a few hours!

Moon's orbit

The moon orbits Earth, but not in a perfect circle. At its closest, it is more than 31,000 miles (50,000 km) nearer than at its farthest point. It takes the moon the same time to spin around its own axis as it needs to orbit Earth—about 28 days.

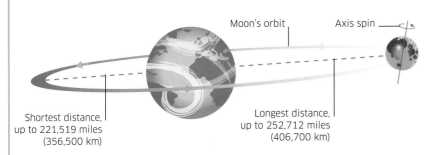

Moon's orbit

Axis spin

Shortest distance, up to 221,519 miles (356,500 km)

Longest distance, up to 252,712 miles (406,700 km)

Earth without moon

The gravitational pull of the moon stabilizes the axis of rotation of Earth. Without it, the North Pole might swing through up to 85 degrees, plunging half the world into millions of years of freezing darkness while the other side bakes in sunlight.

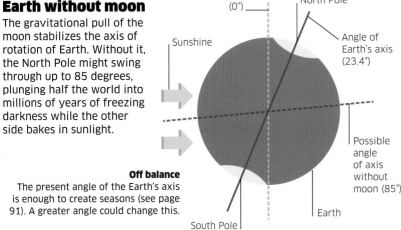

(0°)

North Pole

Sunshine

Angle of Earth's axis (23.4°)

Possible angle of axis without moon (85°)

Earth

South Pole

Off balance
The present angle of the Earth's axis is enough to create seasons (see page 91). A greater angle could change this.

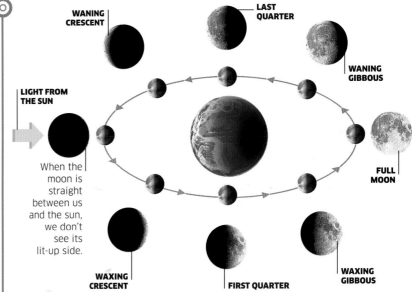

WANING CRESCENT

LAST QUARTER

WANING GIBBOUS

LIGHT FROM THE SUN

FULL MOON

When the moon is straight between us and the sun, we don't see its lit-up side.

WAXING CRESCENT

FIRST QUARTER

WAXING GIBBOUS

PHASES OF THE MOON

The inner circle of this diagram shows the moon orbiting Earth, lit by the sun. From Earth, we see it illuminated from different angles as it goes through its 28-day cycle—changing from "new moon," or waxing crescent, to full moon, and then waning again, as shown in the outer circle. We see only one side of the moon, but the other side is not dark, except when the moon appears full to us.

Lunar eclipse

In a total lunar eclipse, when the Earth shades the full moon from the sun, the only light reaching the moon is the red glow from Earth's dusty atmosphere, causing a "blood moon," like the one seen in this photograph. When the moon comes between Earth and the sun, it creates a solar eclipse.

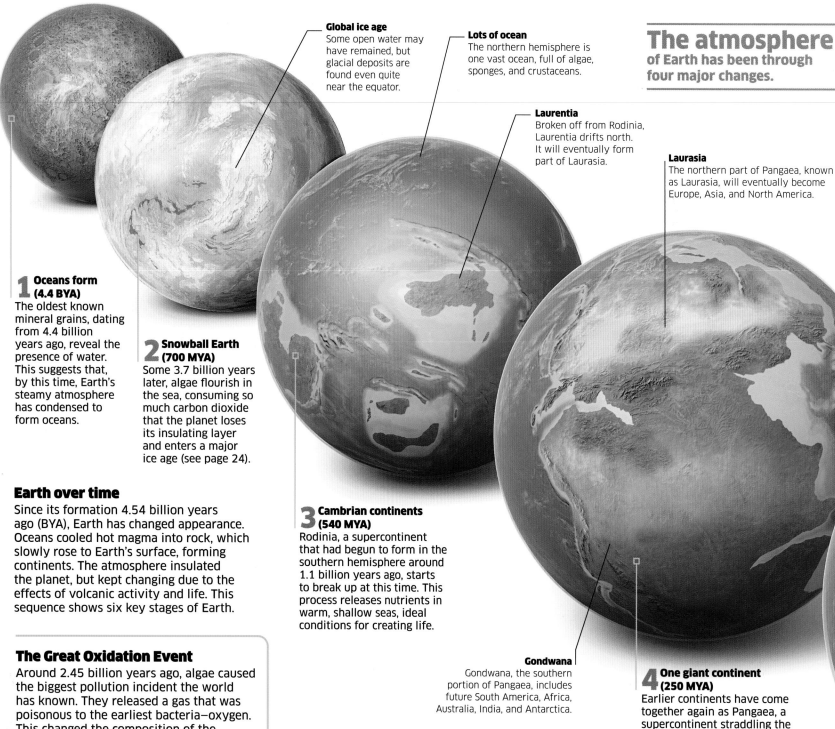

Global ice age
Some open water may have remained, but glacial deposits are found even quite near the equator.

Lots of ocean
The northern hemisphere is one vast ocean, full of algae, sponges, and crustaceans.

The atmosphere
of Earth has been through four major changes.

Laurentia
Broken off from Rodinia, Laurentia drifts north. It will eventually form part of Laurasia.

Laurasia
The northern part of Pangaea, known as Laurasia, will eventually become Europe, Asia, and North America.

1 Oceans form (4.4 BYA)
The oldest known mineral grains, dating from 4.4 billion years ago, reveal the presence of water. This suggests that, by this time, Earth's steamy atmosphere has condensed to form oceans.

2 Snowball Earth (700 MYA)
Some 3.7 billion years later, algae flourish in the sea, consuming so much carbon dioxide that the planet loses its insulating layer and enters a major ice age (see page 24).

Earth over time
Since its formation 4.54 billion years ago (BYA), Earth has changed appearance. Oceans cooled hot magma into rock, which slowly rose to Earth's surface, forming continents. The atmosphere insulated the planet, but kept changing due to the effects of volcanic activity and life. This sequence shows six key stages of Earth.

3 Cambrian continents (540 MYA)
Rodinia, a supercontinent that had begun to form in the southern hemisphere around 1.1 billion years ago, starts to break up at this time. This process releases nutrients in warm, shallow seas, ideal conditions for creating life.

The Great Oxidation Event
Around 2.45 billion years ago, algae caused the biggest pollution incident the world has known. They released a gas that was poisonous to the earliest bacteria—oxygen. This changed the composition of the atmosphere and, eventually, led to many new oxygen-breathing species.

Gondwana
Gondwana, the southern portion of Pangaea, includes future South America, Africa, Australia, India, and Antarctica.

4 One giant continent (250 MYA)
Earlier continents have come together again as Pangaea, a supercontinent straddling the equator. It is surrounded by the vast Panthalassa Ocean.

Banded ironstone
The first free oxygen left its mark in thick layers of banded ironstone, formed as the iron-rich mud reacted (was oxidized) and went rusty.

Evolving Earth

Some 4 billion years ago, Earth would have been unrecognizable. But our planet took shape as the climate changed and continents moved. Chemical reactions created the minerals in rocks, and the conditions were right for the first life on Earth.

In the beginning, Earth was seemingly lifeless. Meteorites rained down on it, volcanoes erupted, and its atmosphere was unbreathable. Slowly, the planet cooled enough for oceans to form. Earthquakes and erosion covered the scars of its violent formation. Single-celled bacteria began using sunlight to consume carbon dioxide and release oxygen, making the air breathable. But carbon dioxide was the blanket that kept the planet warm and with less of it in the air the seas froze over. Eventually, the climate stabilized and the continents drifted to produce the globe we know.

66 million sq miles (170 million sq km)—the land area of the supercontinent Pangaea.

4 billion years—the length of time before large animals appeared on Earth.

19

First life

We do not know exactly where, when, or how life began on Earth. Perhaps in hydrothermal systems underground or under the sea; perhaps in shallow ponds, or even seeded from space on meteorites. We do know that first life is at least 3.7 billion years old and did not evolve beyond microscopic bacteria and algae for the next 3 billion years.

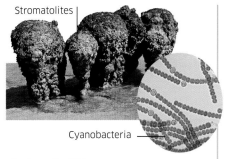

Stromatolites

Cyanobacteria

Single-celled life
Resembling pond slime, strands of single-celled cyanobacteria floated in the sea or built up in layers to form stromatolites, the oldest known fossils.

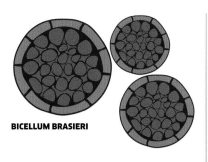

BICELLUM BRASIERI

Multicellular life
The trace of a billion-year-old blob found in Scottish sandstone is the first evidence of specialized cells forming a single organism.

Sponges
The tiny Eocyathispongia, 0.04 in (1 mm) across and 600 million years old, represents one of the earliest known fossils of a present-day animal.

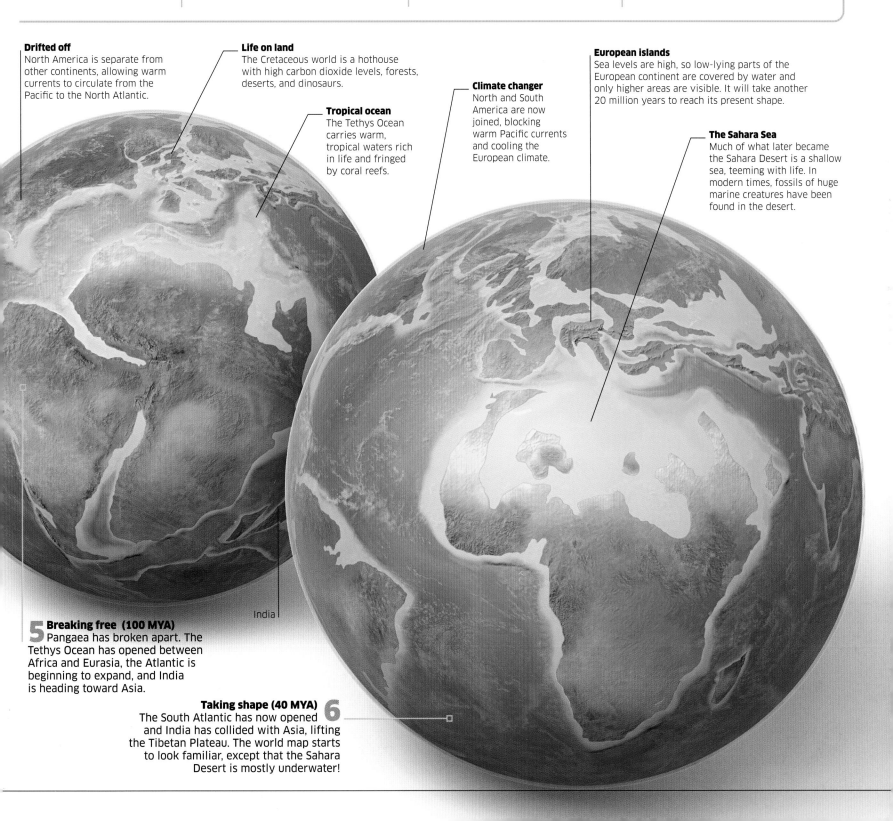

Drifted off
North America is separate from other continents, allowing warm currents to circulate from the Pacific to the North Atlantic.

Life on land
The Cretaceous world is a hothouse with high carbon dioxide levels, forests, deserts, and dinosaurs.

Tropical ocean
The Tethys Ocean carries warm, tropical waters rich in life and fringed by coral reefs.

Climate changer
North and South America are now joined, blocking warm Pacific currents and cooling the European climate.

European islands
Sea levels are high, so low-lying parts of the European continent are covered by water and only higher areas are visible. It will take another 20 million years to reach its present shape.

The Sahara Sea
Much of what later became the Sahara Desert is a shallow sea, teeming with life. In modern times, fossils of huge marine creatures have been found in the desert.

India

5 Breaking free (100 MYA)
Pangaea has broken apart. The Tethys Ocean has opened between Africa and Eurasia, the Atlantic is beginning to expand, and India is heading toward Asia.

Taking shape (40 MYA) 6
The South Atlantic has now opened and India has collided with Asia, lifting the Tibetan Plateau. The world map starts to look familiar, except that the Sahara Desert is mostly underwater!

Out of the more than **4 billion species** that have ever **lived** on Earth, **99.8 percent** are **extinct**.

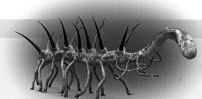

575 MILLION YEARS AGO

Ediacaran period
Newly thawed shallow seas opened the way to the first multicellular animals. Stationary sea pens (Charnia) filtered food while crawlers (Dickinsonia) grazed on bacterial slime.

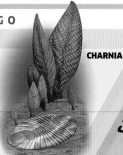

CHARNIA

DICKINSONIA

541 MYA

CAMBRIAN

Cambrian period
Around 541 million years ago, there was an explosion in the variety of life. Predatory crustaceans developed jaws, so others needed shells or spines to survive.

Hallucigenia
This wormlike creature had protective spines and tube feet like a starfish.

Pikaia
The pikaia, ancestor of all vertebrates, had a spinal cord but no bones.

Timeline of life

Divided into geological periods (see page 8), this timeline shows only a few examples of the wonderful diversity of species that have evolved and died out over the last 600 million years.

Edaphosaurus
This large, plant-eating reptile was in a group known as therapsids, probably the ancestors of mammals.

299 MYA

PERMIAN

Permian period
Much of the supercontinent Pangaea was desert. A new group of reptiles evolved, but huge volcanic eruptions ended the period, causing the biggest extinction event ever.

Meganeura
As oxygen levels in air rose from 20 to 35 percent, dragonflies evolved and grew into giants.

TRIASSIC

Triassic period
Extinction left the world open to new life. Coniferous trees replaced the coal forests, and dinosaurs gradually took over from therapsids. More volcanic eruptions eventually ended the period.

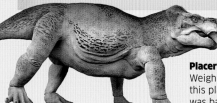

Placerias
Weighing around a ton, this plant-eating therapsid was barrel-shaped, like a hippopotamus.

Nothosaurus
This marine reptile had needle-sharp teeth for catching fish.

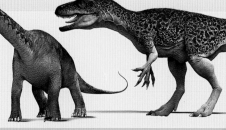

▶ 252 MYA

Long-necked dinosaurs, known as sauropods, were huge, slow-moving vegetarians.

145 MYA

CRETACEOUS

Cretaceous period
Plants and animals prospered in this stable, warm period and chalk formed in shallow seas. Dinosaurs were common; some developed feathers and took to the air.

Diplodocus
Feeding on leaves, this large sauropod could weigh up to 16.5 tons (15 metric tons).

Allosaurus
Walking on two legs, this 39 ft (12 m) long dinosaur had lots of serrated teeth for tearing meat.

Argentinosaurus
One of the largest land animals ever, this sauropod from Argentina could be 115 ft (35 m) long.

Pterosaurs
The Cretaceous period saw many different flying reptiles, some with 23 ft (7 m) wing spans.

Confuciusornis
One of many species of feathered dinosaurs and primitive birds from China, this was the first to have a toothless beak.

Extinction
The dinosaurs came to an abrupt end when a meteorite crashed into Earth (see pages 22–23).

PALEOGENE

8.2 ft (2.5 m)—the **size** of a fully grown **giant sea scorpion**, the **largest arthropod** that ever lived.

90 percent of **marine species** and 70 percent of **land species** perished in the Permian/Triassic **extinction** around **250 million** years ago.

21

485 MYA

Ordovician period
Abundant life in warm, shallow seas included shellfish and jawless fish. Primitive plants moved up on land. The period ended in an ice age that resulted in mass extinctions.

ORDOVICIAN

Astraspis
This primitive fish lacked jaws and was covered by star-shaped scales.

Red lines indicate mass extinctions.

444 MYA

Silurian period
Warming, shallow seas filled with coral reefs and the first fish with bones and jaws. Vascular plants (that can draw up water) colonized the land, along with fungi, millipedes, and spiders.

SILURIAN

Guiyu oneiros
Known from fossils in China, this is one of the first fish with a bony skeleton.

HALYSITES CHAIN CORAL

DEVONIAN

359 MYA

Devonian period
Fishes dominated the sea and crawled onto land. The first trees appeared, but deserts spread near the equator. The period ended with a mass extinction.

419 MYA

Coal swamp
Lepidodendron and calamites grew tall, fell in the swamps, and eventually turned to coal.

Carboniferous period
Plants removed carbon from the air, over time deposited as limestone under the sea and as coal on land. Giant insects, amphibians, and reptiles roamed the swamps.

CARBONIFEROUS

Eurypterids
Giant sea scorpions were abundant in the Devonian seas.

Tiktaalik
This fish could pull itself onto land.

Strong front fins for moving on land

201 MYA

Megazostrodon
Nocturnal and fast, this small, furry creature was one of the first true mammals.

Jurassic period
Pangaea split into two continents and a warm climate allowed forests to grow near the poles. Dinosaurs ruled the land and marine reptiles and pterosaurs the sea and air.

JURASSIC

Liopleurodon
This species of pliosaur was the top marine predator of the late Jurassic.

Stenopterygius
One of a large group of marine ichthyosaur reptiles up to 13 ft (4 m) long with sharp teeth, it fed on fish, squid, and ammonites.

Belemnite, an early type of squid

Life story

Life on Earth has a history of at least 3.7 billion years, but only in the last 600 million years does it become easy to see in the fossil record.

The earliest animals bigger than a pinhead crawled around on the seafloor eating slime. Then, in the Cambrian period, they developed hard jaws and protective shells and evolution took off. Ever since, it has been a race to colonize new habitats, eat without being eaten, and survive climate change and natural disasters—some of which caused mass extinctions. Along the way, nature has produced some amazing creatures. Most of these are now extinct, while some have close relatives in modern species.

66 MYA

Paleogene period
With a cooler climate and no dinosaurs, warm-blooded mammals and birds rapidly diversified. Grasses and flowering plants spread widely on land.

Mesohippus
Most mammal groups began in the Paleogene. This early horse was just 2 ft (60 cm) tall.

23 MYA

Neogene period
The climate continued to cool; grasslands spread and large mammals evolved. Human ancestors started making stone tools.

NEOGENE

Deinotherium
Similar to elephants in size, these mammals died out as grasslands replaced forests.

2.6 MYA

Quaternary period
The latest geological period saw a series of ice ages, the rise and fall of giant mammals, such as mammoths, and the earliest modern humans.

QUATERNARY

22 planet earth ○ **METEORITES**

160,000 mph (258,000 km/h)—the maximum speed of a meteorite.

Bombardment continues

Rocks continue to fly around the solar system, and astronomers have identified almost 30,000 that cross Earth's orbit. Most of them are less than 0.6 miles (1 km) across and no big ones are currently predicted to hit our planet.

Barringer Crater, Arizona
This well-preserved impact crater was formed about 50,000 years ago by an iron meteorite. It is 0.75 miles (1.2 km) across.

Chelyabinsk Meteor, Russia
On February 15, 2013, thousands saw this fireball fly over Russia. The object was about 98 ft (30 m) across and exploded in the atmosphere.

Meteorites

The solar system is littered with rubble left over from its formation, and space dust is constantly raining down on Earth. Occasionally, a much bigger lump hits our planet.

Look at the moon and you can see that it is pitted with impact craters, and these are billions of years old. The Earth must have been bombarded in the same way, by asteroids, comets, and meteoroids, but the evidence has eroded away over time. Harmless meteorites are still falling today, and every so often a rock the size of a mountain speeds toward us, with potentially devastating consequences.

Asteroid trail
Traveling at 12,500 mph (20,000 km/h), the asteroid leaves a trail brighter than the sun.

The Chicxulub impact

An asteroid 6 miles (10 km) across struck Earth 66 million years ago. It landed near present-day Mexico, forming a crater 12 miles (20 km) deep. Dinosaurs were wiped out and creatures that survived the devastating blast faced forest fires and later global climate change and famine.

2 Moment of impact
The asteroid vaporizes, melting the seafloor and radiating shock waves. Debris from it punches through the atmosphere and circles the globe.

1 Incoming!
An asteroid bigger than Mount Everest hurtles toward an area of land and sea that is now Mexico's Yucatán Peninsula.

Shock wave
The impact creates hurricane winds that strip vegetation from land for hundreds of miles.

Steep descent
The asteroid is heading for Earth at an angle of about 60 degrees, toward a shallow sea.

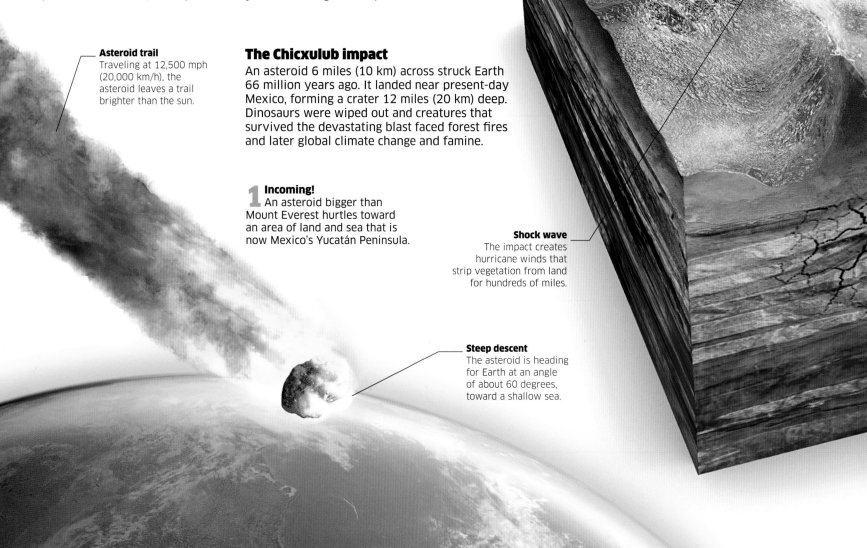

76 percent of **animal and plant species** became **extinct 66 million years ago**.

7,385 tons (6,700 metric tons) of **space dust** can **fall to Earth each year**.

23

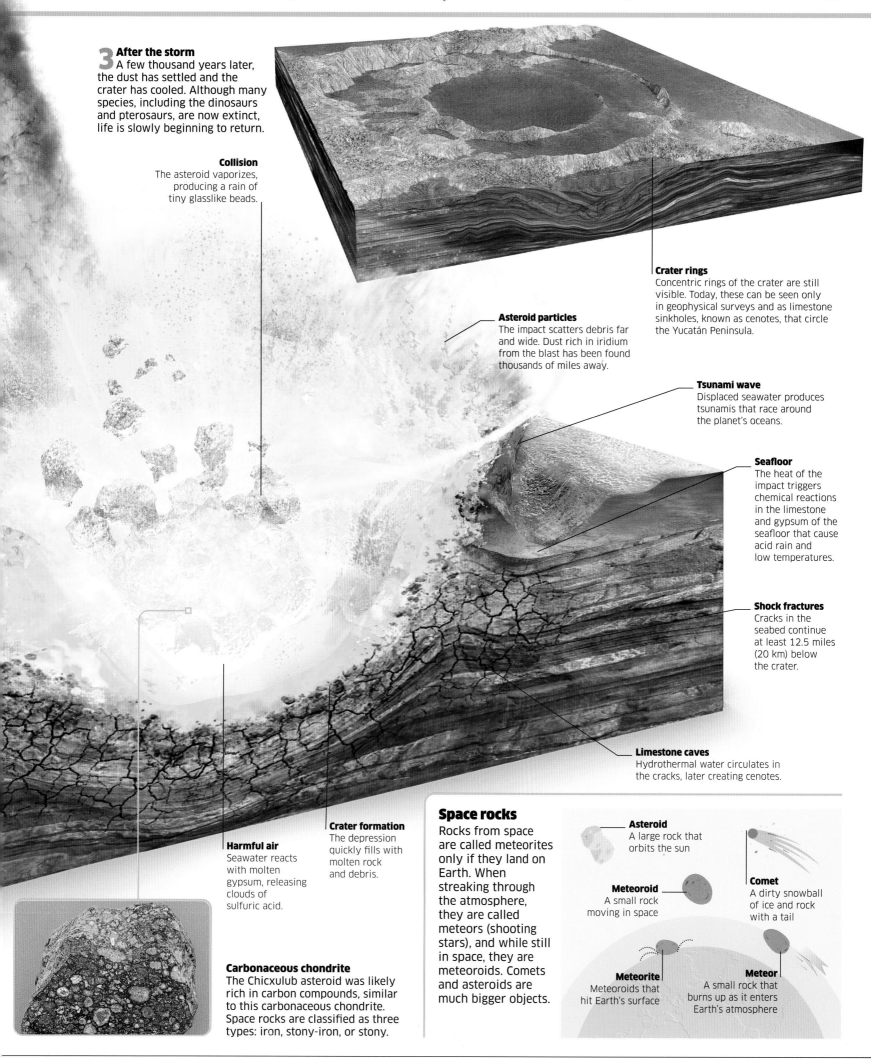

3 After the storm
A few thousand years later, the dust has settled and the crater has cooled. Although many species, including the dinosaurs and pterosaurs, are now extinct, life is slowly beginning to return.

Collision
The asteroid vaporizes, producing a rain of tiny glasslike beads.

Crater rings
Concentric rings of the crater are still visible. Today, these can be seen only in geophysical surveys and as limestone sinkholes, known as cenotes, that circle the Yucatán Peninsula.

Asteroid particles
The impact scatters debris far and wide. Dust rich in iridium from the blast has been found thousands of miles away.

Tsunami wave
Displaced seawater produces tsunamis that race around the planet's oceans.

Seafloor
The heat of the impact triggers chemical reactions in the limestone and gypsum of the seafloor that cause acid rain and low temperatures.

Shock fractures
Cracks in the seabed continue at least 12.5 miles (20 km) below the crater.

Limestone caves
Hydrothermal water circulates in the cracks, later creating cenotes.

Harmful air
Seawater reacts with molten gypsum, releasing clouds of sulfuric acid.

Crater formation
The depression quickly fills with molten rock and debris.

Carbonaceous chondrite
The Chicxulub asteroid was likely rich in carbon compounds, similar to this carbonaceous chondrite. Space rocks are classified as three types: iron, stony-iron, or stony.

Space rocks
Rocks from space are called meteorites only if they land on Earth. When streaking through the atmosphere, they are called meteors (shooting stars), and while still in space, they are meteoroids. Comets and asteroids are much bigger objects.

Asteroid
A large rock that orbits the sun

Comet
A dirty snowball of ice and rock with a tail

Meteoroid
A small rock moving in space

Meteorite
Meteoroids that hit Earth's surface

Meteor
A small rock that burns up as it enters Earth's atmosphere

Ice ages

Earth's climate is held in a delicate balance, but since its beginnings, our planet has experienced a few very cold extremes, known as ice ages.

Ice ages occur when there is less insulating carbon dioxide in the atmosphere, or when changes in Earth's orbit angle it away from the sun so that average temperatures fall and ice sheets expand. The coldest periods of an ice age are known as glacials. During the coldest glacial of the latest ice age, mammoths and other animals roamed near the edge of the ice sheet.

SIBERIA

Bering land bridge, shown in darker tint

LAURENTIDE ICE SHEET

ALASKA

Migration of animals and humans into Alaska

Beringia

During the last glacial period, a lot of water was held frozen in polar caps and ice sheets, resulting in lower sea levels. Siberia (Asia) was connected to Alaska (North America) by a land bridge. This region is known as Beringia. Animals and humans were able to migrate from Asia into North America.

Wall of ice
The ice sheet, here up to 1 mile (1.6 km) thick, towered over the animals on the steppe below.

Woolly mammoth
Weighing up to 6.6 tons (6 metric tons) and with huge curved tusks, woolly mammoths had very thick fur. They were well adapted for life on the vast, cold steppe.

Cave lion
Across Europe, northern Asia, and Beringia, these lions were top carnivores. But they would not have much luck with a mammoth ferociously defending its young.

Timeline of ice ages

The history of Earth's climate is a balancing act between hothouse and icehouse, often depending on what is in the atmosphere. There have been six major ice ages since Earth's formation. We live in the last one, although fortunately in an interglacial period rather than during a glacial peak.

Earth formation, 4.56 billion years ago (BYA)
The lifeless planet was mostly molten, with a thick, steamy atmosphere of carbon dioxide and nitrogen.

Pongola Ice Age 2.9–2.78 BYA
Carbon dioxide reacted with volcanic rocks and was also absorbed by the first cyanobacteria. Earth got very cold.

Huronian Ice Age 2.4–2.1 BYA
After a warmer period, the seas were blooming with algae and bacteria that consumed carbon dioxide and released oxygen, and temperatures fell again.

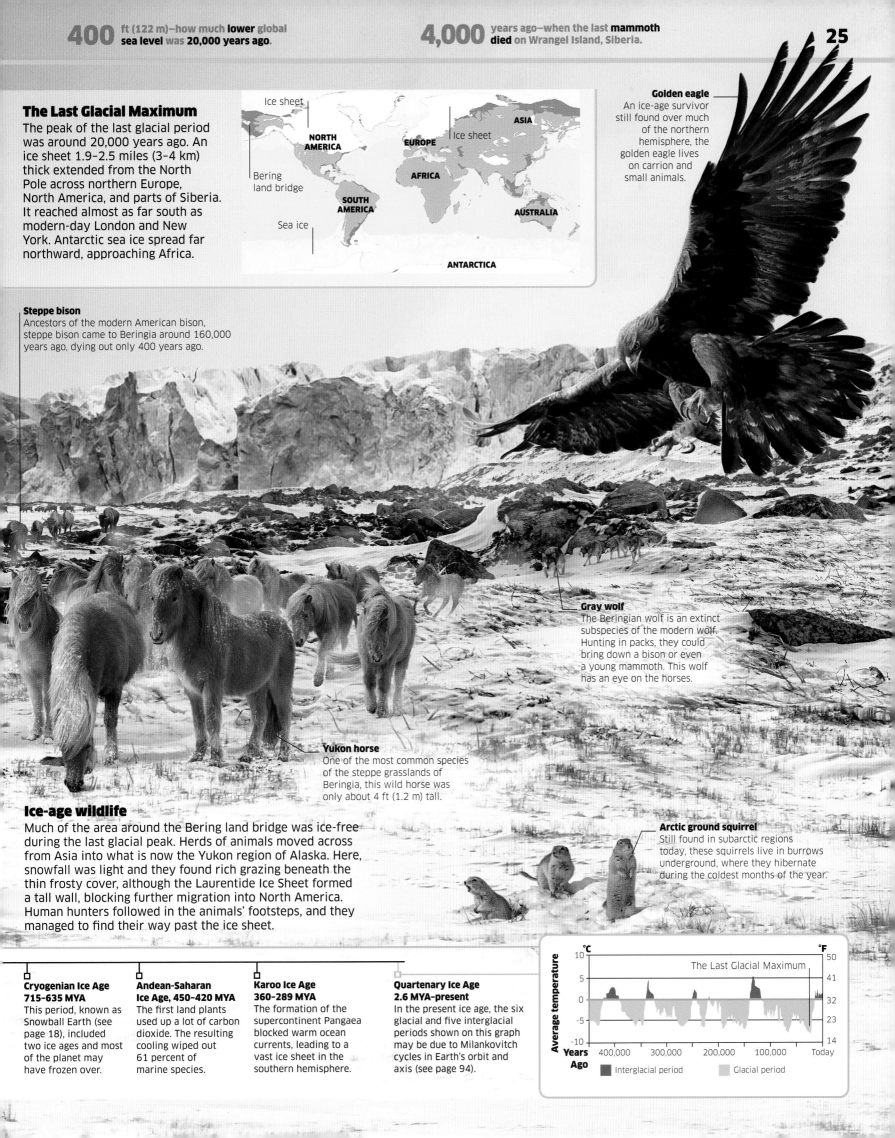

400 ft (122 m)—how much **lower** global sea level was 20,000 years ago.

4,000 years ago—when the last **mammoth** died on Wrangel Island, Siberia.

25

The Last Glacial Maximum

The peak of the last glacial period was around 20,000 years ago. An ice sheet 1.9–2.5 miles (3–4 km) thick extended from the North Pole across northern Europe, North America, and parts of Siberia. It reached almost as far south as modern-day London and New York. Antarctic sea ice spread far northward, approaching Africa.

Ice sheet

NORTH AMERICA

ASIA

EUROPE

Ice sheet

Bering land bridge

AFRICA

SOUTH AMERICA

AUSTRALIA

Sea ice

ANTARCTICA

Golden eagle
An ice-age survivor still found over much of the northern hemisphere, the golden eagle lives on carrion and small animals.

Steppe bison
Ancestors of the modern American bison, steppe bison came to Beringia around 160,000 years ago, dying out only 400 years ago.

Gray wolf
The Beringian wolf is an extinct subspecies of the modern wolf. Hunting in packs, they could bring down a bison or even a young mammoth. This wolf has an eye on the horses.

Yukon horse
One of the most common species of the steppe grasslands of Beringia, this wild horse was only about 4 ft (1.2 m) tall.

Ice-age wildlife

Much of the area around the Bering land bridge was ice-free during the last glacial peak. Herds of animals moved across from Asia into what is now the Yukon region of Alaska. Here, snowfall was light and they found rich grazing beneath the thin frosty cover, although the Laurentide Ice Sheet formed a tall wall, blocking further migration into North America. Human hunters followed in the animals' footsteps, and they managed to find their way past the ice sheet.

Arctic ground squirrel
Still found in subarctic regions today, these squirrels live in burrows underground, where they hibernate during the coldest months of the year.

Cryogenian Ice Age 715–635 MYA
This period, known as Snowball Earth (see page 18), included two ice ages and most of the planet may have frozen over.

Andean-Saharan Ice Age, 450–420 MYA
The first land plants used up a lot of carbon dioxide. The resulting cooling wiped out 61 percent of marine species.

Karoo Ice Age 360–289 MYA
The formation of the supercontinent Pangaea blocked warm ocean currents, leading to a vast ice sheet in the southern hemisphere.

Quartenary Ice Age 2.6 MYA–present
In the present ice age, the six glacial and five interglacial periods shown on this graph may be due to Milankovitch cycles in Earth's orbit and axis (see page 94).

The Last Glacial Maximum

Average temperature

°C 10 5 0 -5 -10

°F 50 41 32 23 14

Years Ago 400,000 300,000 200,000 100,000 Today

■ Interglacial period   ■ Glacial period

Inhabited Earth

Around 300,000 years ago, a new subspecies emerged in Africa, later spreading around the world. This was *Homo sapiens*–modern humans.

These humans were thoughtful, developed language, and made tools–and art. This painting in Sumpang Bita cave, Sulawesi, is one of many found in Indonesia. Some of them date back 45,000 years, making them the oldest cave art in the world. This one shows a dwarf buffalo called an anoa, unique to island, together with hand prints made by holding a hand against the rock and blowing paint at it.

ROCKY EARTH

Seemingly solid beneath our feet, our planet is in constant motion. Occasionally, we feel and see evidence of its inner workings, in volcanic eruptions and earthquakes, but plenty more is going on. Rocks are continually being recycled and pieces of crust move around the surface.

FIELD WORK

The starting point for much of geology is going out in the field with a hammer and notebook to examine the rocks and collect samples. A trained eye can learn much about what lies beneath. A handheld lens shows the minerals and fossils in a rock, suggesting how it formed and its approximate age. The angles of layers and cracks show the history of folding and mountain building. The first geological maps were made in this way.

Whatever it takes
Geologists will go wherever they can to sample the rocks—up mountains and deep underground. A small hammer reveals the minerals in a fresh surface. A compass and what is called a clinometer can measure the angle and direction of the strata (layers).

TAKING A CLOSER LOOK

If you bring a rock sample back to the lab, it will reveal more secrets. By shining light vibrating in a certain direction through a thin, polished slice of rock, each mineral grain or microfossil becomes visible. A powerful electron microscope allows even closer inspection, and, by vaporizing the sample with a laser beam in a device called a mass spectrometer, the smallest individual particles can be counted.

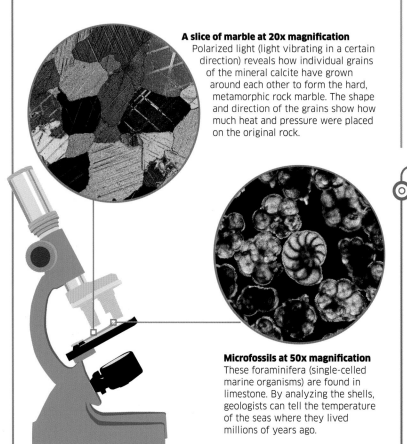

A slice of marble at 20x magnification
Polarized light (light vibrating in a certain direction) reveals how individual grains of the mineral calcite have grown around each other to form the hard, metamorphic rock marble. The shape and direction of the grains show how much heat and pressure were placed on the original rock.

Microfossils at 50x magnification
These foraminifera (single-celled marine organisms) are found in limestone. By analyzing the shells, geologists can tell the temperature of the seas where they lived millions of years ago.

REVEALING EARTH

Geology is the study of Earth's history and structure as recorded in the rocks. Humans may never be able to travel to the center of the planet, but geologists can tell a lot by studying rocks on the surface or viewing Earth from space. Rock and mineral samples brought up to the surface by volcanoes, as well as simulations in laboratories, can reveal surprising details about our planet's inner workings.

SEISMIC WAVES

When the ground shakes from an earthquake, what we feel are seismic waves. Near the site of the earthquake, the waves can be damaging, but their arrival times at places further away help geologists figure out the types of rocks that they have passed through on the way.

P and S waves

There are two main types of seismic waves, known as P and S waves. P, or pressure, waves cause the rocks to be compressed and stretched in the direction of travel. P also stands for primary, as these waves travel faster and arrive first. S stands for secondary or shear waves, which move the rock up and down. S waves can only travel through solid rock.

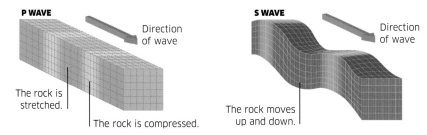

P WAVE
Direction of wave
The rock is stretched.
The rock is compressed.

S WAVE
Direction of wave
The rock moves up and down.

THE MOHO DISCONTINUITY

In 1909, during an earthquake in Croatia, local seismologist Andrija Mohorovičić noticed that seismic waves arrived at earthquake monitoring stations in two stages, suggesting that some waves had traveled faster than others.

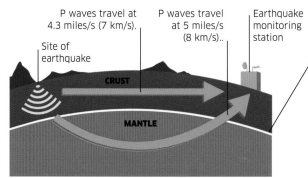

P waves travel at 4.3 miles/s (7 km/s).
P waves travel at 5 miles/s (8 km/s)..
Earthquake monitoring station
Moho discontinuity
Site of earthquake
CRUST
MANTLE

Boundary revealed
Mohorovičić concluded that the different speeds of the P waves meant they had traveled through rock of different densities. Thus, the boundary between Earth's crust and mantle (the Moho discontinuity) had been discovered.

Whole planet body scan

Just as doctors use X-rays to see inside the human body, so geologists use seismic waves to "see" inside Earth. P waves reflect off some layers, move quickly through hard rock, and move more slowly through softer rock. Meanwhile, S waves cannot pass through molten (liquid) rock at all.

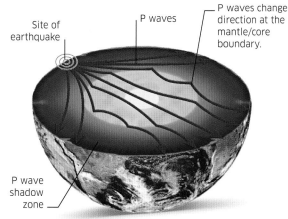

Site of earthquake

P waves

P waves change direction at the mantle/core boundary.

P wave paths
P waves traveling through Earth will pass through the molten outer core, but they change direction suddenly when they meet a boundary between rock in different states. This creates shadow zones, where no P waves are detected.

P wave shadow zone

Site of earthquake

S waves do not pass through the liquid outer core.

S wave paths
S waves from the same earthquake will not pass through the molten outer core, leaving a much wider shadow zone across half of the planet.

S waves

S wave shadow zone

P wave changes direction at solid inner core

Weak P wave in shadow zone

Site of earthquake

Solid inner core
In 1936, the Danish seismologist Inge Lehmann detected very weak P waves in the P wave shadow zone. She figured out that they must have reflected off something inside the core of the Earth. This was the first evidence of a solid inner core.

P wave

UNDER PRESSURE

Scientists cannot directly study the extreme heat and pressure that exist deep inside Earth. Instead they try and replicate these conditions in a lab, using hard materials such as diamond, which can withstand lots of pressure. By applying pressure to a mineral sample between two small diamonds (each less than the width of your fingernail), geologists can recreate pressures deep inside the Earth and work out their effects.

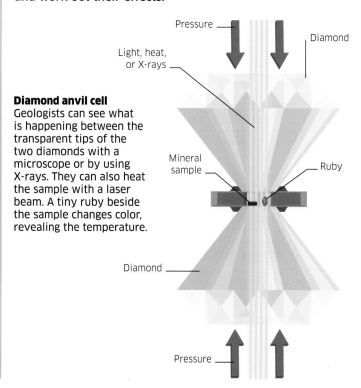

Pressure

Diamond

Light, heat, or X-rays

Diamond anvil cell
Geologists can see what is happening between the transparent tips of the two diamonds with a microscope or by using X-rays. They can also heat the sample with a laser beam. A tiny ruby beside the sample changes color, revealing the temperature.

Mineral sample

Ruby

Diamond

Pressure

EARTH FROM SPACE

To see the bigger picture, you sometimes need to stand back. Observing Earth from space brings new perspectives, not only on surface features but also on the interior. The space agency NASA produced this map of our planet's gravity by measuring the pull of Earth from two satellites. Variations in gravity are often due to changes in a region's mass. For example, mountains, which increase gravity, or ocean trenches, which reduce it.

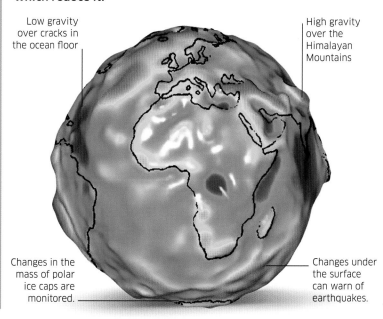

Low gravity over cracks in the ocean floor

High gravity over the Himalayan Mountains

Changes in the mass of polar ice caps are monitored.

Changes under the surface can warn of earthquakes.

DRILLING DOWN

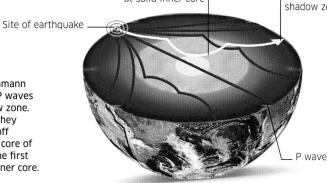

Taking a core sample gives direct evidence of the rocks below us. Mining companies do this regularly to prospect for new reserves, and scientific drilling projects have also probed the ocean floor. There have even been attempts to drill down to the Moho discontinuity, but this is expensive and, so far, they have failed. The record depth reached is about 40,000 ft (12,000 m).

Earth's structure

Our planet is like a giant onion made of layers of solid and semisolid rock or metal. It is a dynamic, living globe, and motion deep within it supports life on the surface.

A journey to the center of our Earth would take you first through a thin veil of atmosphere and ocean into solid rock. As you burrowed down, the heat and pressure would rise. After an average of 22 miles (35 km), you would be through this outer crust and into denser rocks known as the mantle. Here, almost solid, hot rock rises and cold rock sinks. At 1,796 miles (2,890 km) down, you would come to a churning core of molten iron, slowly crystallizing to form a solid inner iron core.

Onion planet
Earth came into being approximately 4.54 billion years ago, but it took hundreds of thousands of years for it to cool and separate into distinct layers. There are six main layers: the solid inner core, the liquid outer core, the semisolid mantle, a hard crust, covered largely by liquid oceans—all enveloped in a gaseous atmosphere.

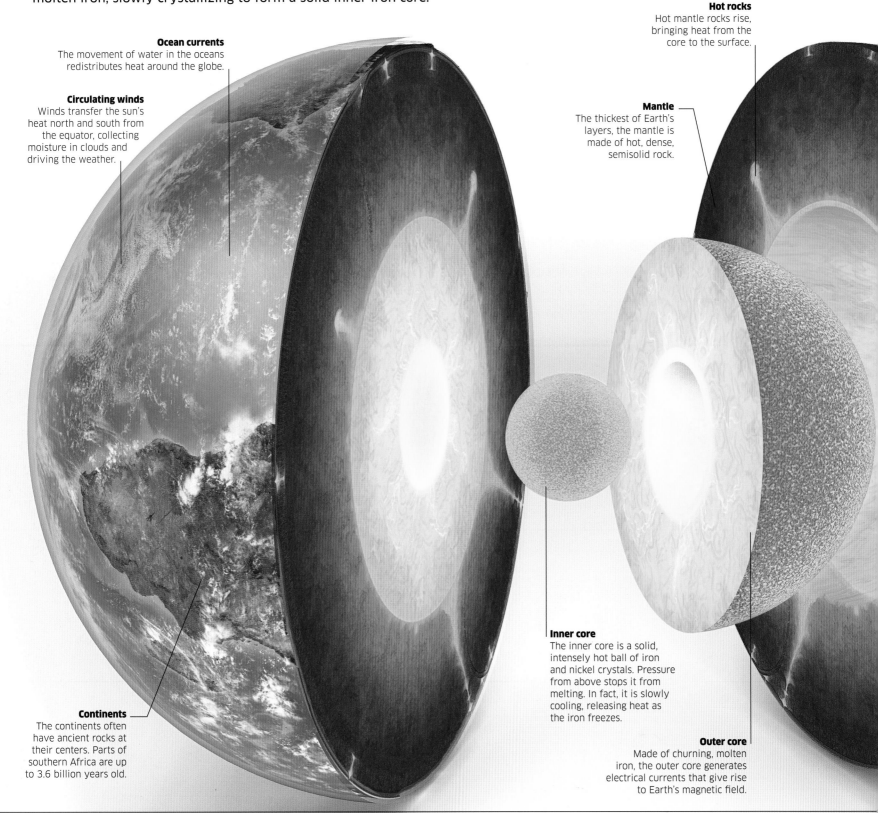

Ocean currents
The movement of water in the oceans redistributes heat around the globe.

Circulating winds
Winds transfer the sun's heat north and south from the equator, collecting moisture in clouds and driving the weather.

Hot rocks
Hot mantle rocks rise, bringing heat from the core to the surface.

Mantle
The thickest of Earth's layers, the mantle is made of hot, dense, semisolid rock.

Continents
The continents often have ancient rocks at their centers. Parts of southern Africa are up to 3.6 billion years old.

Inner core
The inner core is a solid, intensely hot ball of iron and nickel crystals. Pressure from above stops it from melting. In fact, it is slowly cooling, releasing heat as the iron freezes.

Outer core
Made of churning, molten iron, the outer core generates electrical currents that give rise to Earth's magnetic field.

Continental crust
The continents float like giant rafts above the mantle, drifting about on underlying currents.

Oceanic crust
The crust under the oceans is thinner, denser, and younger than that of the continents. Constantly forming, it sinks back into the mantle after about 100 million years.

Air
Only the lowest part of Earth's atmosphere contains air we can breathe.

Water
Earth's oceans, rivers, lakes, rain, clouds, and underground water are all essential to life.

The biosphere
Known as "the zone of life," the biosphere includes all the microorganisms, plants, and animals in or on land and air and in water. The air we breathe, the crust and upper layer of the mantle, and all water on Earth together create the conditions for life, which is what makes our planet unique in the solar system. Survival of all species depends on a balance between the three.

Earth
The soil and rocks on land and under the sea, plus the uppermost, solid part of the mantle are home to millions of plants, animals, and microorganisms.

Troposphere
The lowest layer of the atmosphere, the troposphere contains the air we breathe and is where clouds and storms make weather.

The atmosphere
A layer of gases, known as the atmosphere, surrounds the Earth. If you try skydiving, it feels like an ocean of air. Seen from above, however, it is just a thin layer, protecting us from the ravages of space and giving us the breath of life.

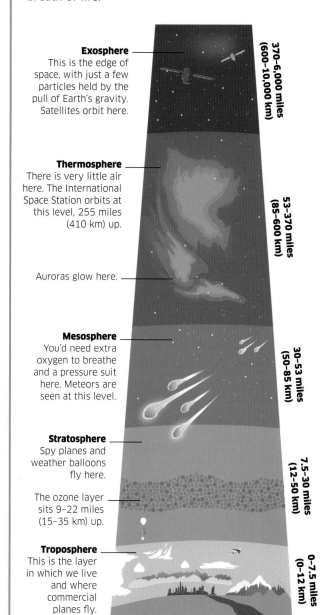

Exosphere
This is the edge of space, with just a few particles held by the pull of Earth's gravity. Satellites orbit here.

370–6,000 miles (600–10,000 km)

Thermosphere
There is very little air here. The International Space Station orbits at this level, 255 miles (410 km) up.

Auroras glow here.

53–370 miles (85–600 km)

Mesosphere
You'd need extra oxygen to breathe and a pressure suit here. Meteors are seen at this level.

30–53 miles (50–85 km)

Stratosphere
Spy planes and weather balloons fly here.

The ozone layer sits 9–22 miles (15–35 km) up.

7.5–30 miles (12–50 km)

Troposphere
This is the layer in which we live and where commercial planes fly.

0–7.5 miles (0–12 km)

Hydrosphere
Oceans cover 70 percent of Earth's surface and average 2.5 miles (4 km) in depth. With lakes, rivers, and rain, they form the hydrosphere.

Lithosphere
The rocky slabs of Earth's crust are fused to the hard upper mantle, which sits on top of the hotter, softer lower mantle.

34 rocky earth ○ **THE CRUST**

4.28 billion **years** is the age of the **oldest** continental **rock** on Earth.

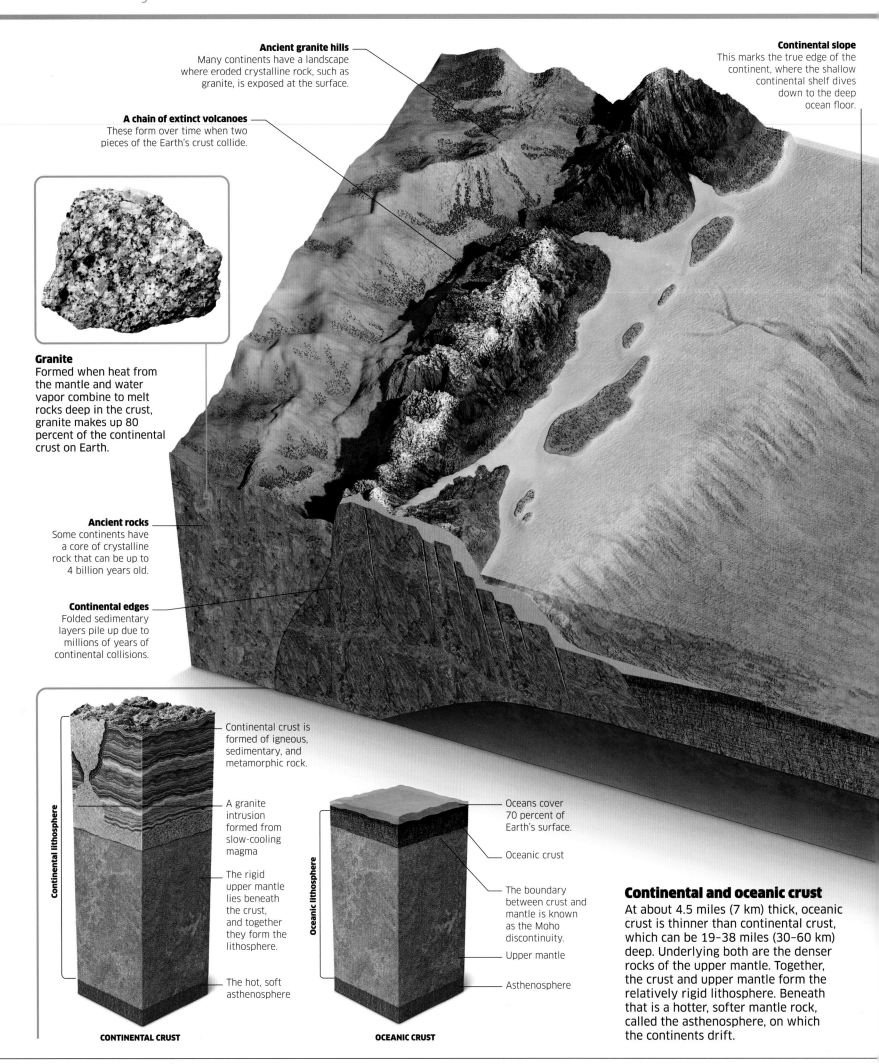

Ancient granite hills
Many continents have a landscape where eroded crystalline rock, such as granite, is exposed at the surface.

A chain of extinct volcanoes
These form over time when two pieces of the Earth's crust collide.

Continental slope
This marks the true edge of the continent, where the shallow continental shelf dives down to the deep ocean floor.

Granite
Formed when heat from the mantle and water vapor combine to melt rocks deep in the crust, granite makes up 80 percent of the continental crust on Earth.

Ancient rocks
Some continents have a core of crystalline rock that can be up to 4 billion years old.

Continental edges
Folded sedimentary layers pile up due to millions of years of continental collisions.

Continental crust is formed of igneous, sedimentary, and metamorphic rock.

A granite intrusion formed from slow-cooling magma

The rigid upper mantle lies beneath the crust, and together they form the lithosphere.

The hot, soft asthenosphere

Continental lithosphere

CONTINENTAL CRUST

Oceans cover 70 percent of Earth's surface.

Oceanic crust

The boundary between crust and mantle is known as the Moho discontinuity.

Upper mantle

Asthenosphere

Oceanic lithosphere

OCEANIC CRUST

Continental and oceanic crust

At about 4.5 miles (7 km) thick, oceanic crust is thinner than continental crust, which can be 19–38 miles (30–60 km) deep. Underlying both are the denser rocks of the upper mantle. Together, the crust and upper mantle form the relatively rigid lithosphere. Beneath that is a hotter, softer mantle rock, called the asthenosphere, on which the continents drift.

Ocean crust is rarely more than 200 million years old.

2,280°F (1,250°C)—the melting point of granite at surface pressure.

1,200°F (650°C)—the melting point of granite with a high water content at deep crust pressure.

35

The crust

It might seem rock-solid, but, on a planetary scale, the ground beneath our feet is just a thin layer of debris that has floated to the surface.

Earth has two types of crust: oceanic and continental. Oceanic crust is being created continually from melted rock that emerges from rifts under the sea. It is made of dense rocks such as basalt, containing lots of iron and magnesium. After about 100 million years, it has cooled and is so dense that it sinks back into the mantle. Continental crust is mostly granite and is lighter. It stays afloat and builds up into great rafts of rock with a deep base.

Undersea volcanoes

Thousands of volcanoes are hidden beneath the sea in volcanic island arcs made by sinking oceanic crust. When the Hunga Tonga–Hunga Ha'apai volcano in the South Pacific Ocean erupted in 2022, the blast could be seen from space.

Ocean trench
Where old ocean crust takes a dive, it can create a deep ocean trench in the seafloor.

Volcanic island arc
A chain of undersea volcanoes forms over the sinking ocean crust in a line parallel to the ocean trench.

Melting rocks
Water within the sinking oceanic crust lowers the melting point of the rock, creating a row of volcanoes on the seabed.

Subduction
Old, cold oceanic lithosphere is too dense to float on the asthenosphere and dives back down into the mantle.

Asthenosphere

Gabbro
The top of oceanic crust is made of basalt. Deeper down, the rocks cool more slowly to make gabbro, with larger crystals of pyroxene and feldspar but very little quartz.

Tectonic plates

The surface of the Earth is not as solid and static as it might seem. The globe is spherical, so its top layer is fractured into curved pieces, known as tectonic plates. There are seven major and eight minor ones—and they are on the move.

Study the Atlantic Ocean on a map and it looks as if South America and Africa could fit together like pieces in a jigsaw puzzle; 110 million years ago (mya), they did. The continents are floating in a slow-motion waltz across the surface of the globe, breaking apart and crashing into one another where the plates meet. All the time, oceans are forming and being destroyed to fill the gaps between them.

Northward bound
Around 300 mya, the British Isles were on the equator. About 500 mya, they were near Antarctica.

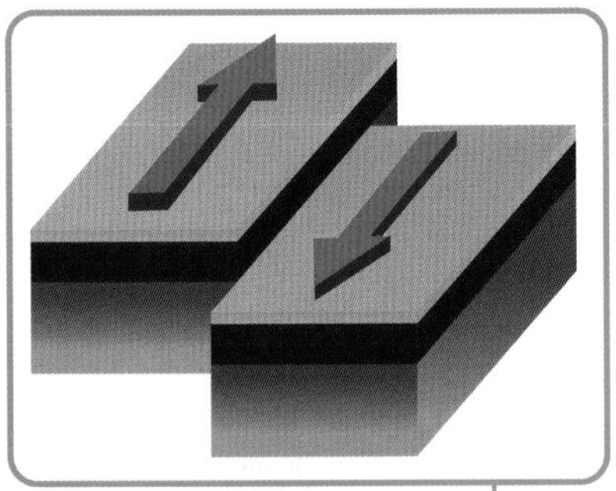

Caribbean island chain
The Caribbean plate is diving beneath the North American plate, causing rock to melt at the top of the mantle and creating a chain of volcanic islands, including Soufrière Hills on Montserrat island.

The Mid-Atlantic Ridge
This is where new ocean crust is created as the continents move apart.

Transform plate boundary
The Pacific plate slides north past California along the San Andreas Fault. It often gets stuck, then jerks forward, causing earthquakes.

NORTH AMERICAN PLATE

AFRICAN PLATE

SOUTH AMERICAN PLATE

CARIBBEAN PLATE

COCOS PLATE

PACIFIC PLATE

SOUTH AMERICAN PLATE

NAZCA PLATE

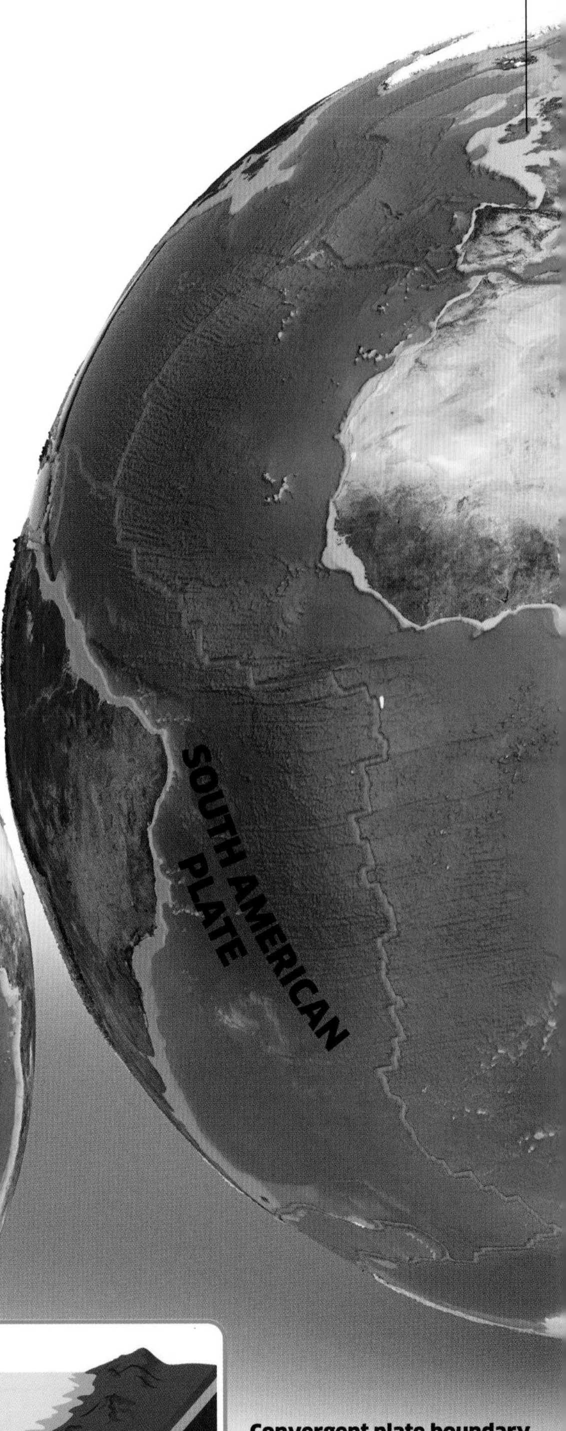

The Pacific plate
This is the largest tectonic plate, at 40 million sq miles (100 million sq km).

Convergent plate boundary
The longest mountain chain on land, the Andes stretch 4,350 miles (7,000 km). As wet oceanic rock from the Nazca plate sinks beneath South America, it melts, creating volcanoes.

1,086 The number of times greater **water pressure** is at the bottom of the **Mariana Trench** than atmospheric **pressure at sea level**.

3 in (7 cm)—the distance **Australia**, the **fastest-moving continent** in the world (today) moves in **a year**.

37

The highest mountain on land
Mount Everest is 29,032 ft (8,849 km) high. It is in the Himalayan mountain chain, which formed 40 mya when the Indian plate crashed into the Eurasian plate (see pages 40–41).

There was once a vast ocean between Africa and Eurasia—the **Tethys Ocean**—now, the Mediterranean Sea.

Japan
Close to the point where four plates meet, Japan is prone to earthquakes, volcanic eruptions, and tsunamis.

New ocean
The Red Sea is one of the youngest oceans. It started opening about 5 mya. Before that, for 20 million years, it was a continental rift.

EURASIAN PLATE

EURASIAN PLATE

ARABIAN PLATE

AFRICAN PLATE

INDIAN PLATE

PHILIPPINE PLATE

PACIFIC PLATE

AUSTRALIAN PLATE

ANTARCTIC PLATE

Antarctica
Connected to South America, Africa, Australia, and India until 45 mya, Antarctica was then isolated by ocean currents and froze over.

Dancing continents
Geologists can track the continents using tiny magnetic particles, trapped pointing North when volcanic rocks hardened. These reveal a complex dance over hundreds of millions of years. The plates they sit on meet up in different ways as they move apart, toward each other, or past each other, causing earthquakes and volcanoes.

Jigsaw fit
The outlines of South America and Africa fit snugly together. Rock and fossil evidence proves they were joined 140 mya.

Divergent plate boundary
Africa is sitting on rising plumes of hot mantle that are stretching it apart along the East African Rift Valley. In the future, it could split the continent and form a new ocean.

Deepest ocean trench on Earth
The Mariana Trench was created by the Pacific plate diving beneath the Philippine plate. It is 1,500 miles (2,550 km) long and up to nearly 7 miles (11 km) deep. If Mount Everest were dropped into the trench, the summit would be 1 mile (1.6 km) under water.

Spreading rifts

Deep under the ocean lies the longest mountain range on the planet. It snakes 40,000 miles (65,000 km) down the Atlantic Ocean and around into the Pacific and Indian oceans, like the seam on a giant tennis ball.

Known as a mid-ocean ridge, this undersea chain has formed over millions of years at a crack in Earth's outer shell where two tectonic plates are moving apart. As the plates move away from each other, semimolten magma pushes up in between them, creating new ocean crust. The plates move very slowly: the Atlantic Ocean is getting wider by 0.8–2 in (2–5 cm) each year (about the rate that your fingernails grow), but over the past 100 million years, it has grown more than 1,800 miles (3,000 km).

Diving between continents
In places on Iceland, the ridge is so deep that it is flooded with crystal-clear water where divers can explore this huge rift between the continents.

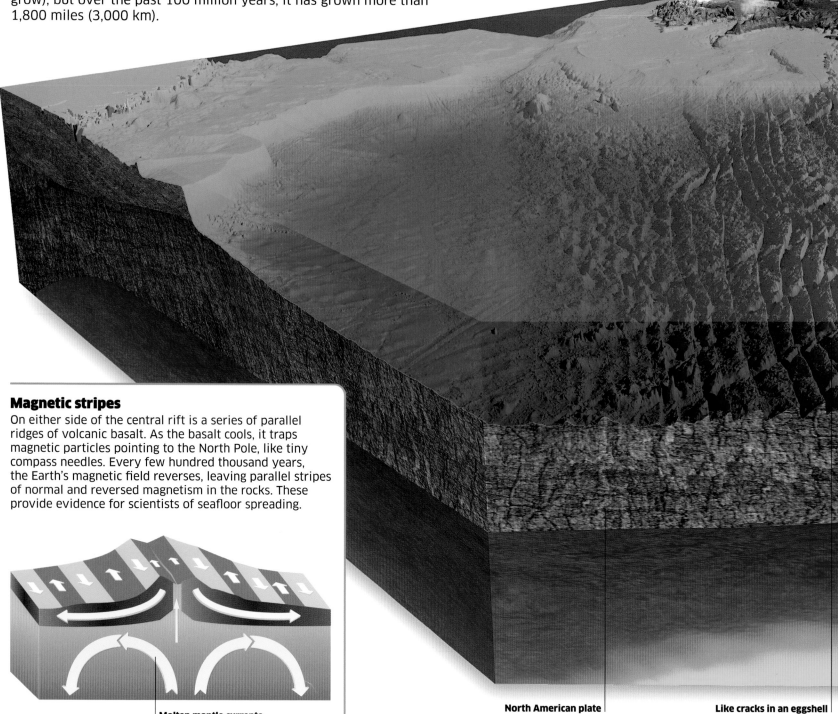

Magnetic stripes

On either side of the central rift is a series of parallel ridges of volcanic basalt. As the basalt cools, it traps magnetic particles pointing to the North Pole, like tiny compass needles. Every few hundred thousand years, the Earth's magnetic field reverses, leaving parallel stripes of normal and reversed magnetism in the rocks. These provide evidence for scientists of seafloor spreading.

■ South
■ North

Molten mantle currents
The tectonic plates are pushed apart by circulating mantle currents.

North American plate
The North American plate continues right across that continent.

Like cracks in an eggshell
The plates on either side of the ridge crack as the flat plates slide across the curved surface of the Earth.

750°F (400°C)—the temperature of water that escapes from vents deep inside the mid-ocean ridges.

1963 The year the island of Surtsey was born, when an undersea volcano off Iceland rose above the surface.

39

The Mid-Atlantic Ridge

The Atlantic Ocean has an average depth of 13,000 ft (4,000 m). Running down the middle of it is the Mid-Atlantic Ridge, which extends from the Arctic Ocean past the tip of southern Africa. The center of the ridge rises 8,000 ft (2,500 m) above the seafloor and has a rift valley along its crest, where the Eurasian and North American tectonic plates are moving apart.

Rising above the waves

Most of the Mid-Atlantic Ridge is under water, but it is clearly visible on Iceland. This is because an additional plume of hot rock rises from deep in the mantle under the island, lifting the ridge above the waves. This volcanic activity also provides geothermal energy that powers Iceland's electrical system.

Volcanic activity
There are more than 100 volcanoes on Iceland. Some are extinct, but more than 30 are still active.

Surtsey
This volcanic island was formed by eruptions between 1963 and 1967.

Ocean sediment
As the new crust moves away from the central ridge, layers of fine sediment build up on the seafloor.

A lost landscape
These sunken valleys and ridges were formed 56 million years ago, when this part of the Eurasian plate sat over the same mantle plume that later created Iceland.

Parallel ridges
As the magma cools on either side, it is pushed away by more rising magma in a series of parallel ridges.

Soft, plastic layer
The hard ocean lithosphere slides over the hotter, softer asthenosphere.

Rising magma
Semimolten magma continuously rises up from beneath the crust to fill the gap between the two plates.

Eurasian plate
The Eurasian tectonic plate extends all the way from the Mid-Atlantic Ridge to Siberia.

Pillow lava
Most volcanic activity along a mid-ocean ridge is quite gentle, with the molten basalt oozing out like toothpaste and being quickly cooled by the sea to form pillows of lava inside the central rift valley.

40 rocky earth ○ **COLLIDING CONTINENTS**

3.6 billion years old—the age of the oldest mountain range in the world (**Barberton Makhonjwa Mountains** in **South Africa**).

Colliding continents

The highest mountains on Earth today, the Himalayas, and Tibetan Plateau, are the result of a head-on collision between India and Asia, around 40 million years ago.

The process of mountain building takes millions of years. Tectonic plates can neither move fast nor brake suddenly. Ocean crust, which is heavy, sinks when it meets continental crust, but if two continents meet, they both crumple and rise, creating a mountain range. The Himalayas are one of the most recent examples of this, but all continents are filled with mountains from past collisions.

1 Breakaway plate (80 MYA)
The Indian tectonic plate breaks away from Gondwana and starts separating from Madagascar—forming a new ocean ridge between them. The floor of the Tethys Ocean begins to subduct (sink) beneath Asia.

Shrinking ocean
The ancient Tethys Ocean starts to close as the Indian plate heads north.

New ocean ridge

Ocean crust sinking beneath Asia

Full-speed ahead
India is now moving rapidly toward Asia at a rate of around 6 in (15 cm) per year.

Hot spot volcanoes
These propel India even faster northward, and their volcanic gases contribute to the death of the dinosaurs.

India heads north

India was slowly drifting northward 80 million years ago (mya) after the breakup of the supercontinent Gondwana (see page 18), when it had a boost from a mantle hot spot that sent it crashing into Asia. In the process, a whole ocean was lost and its sediments scooped up into high mountains. Those mountains altered air circulation across the planet, drying out North and East Africa and giving monsoon rains to India.

Seabed in the sky
We know the ocean floor was pushed up into the Himalayas because marine fossils, such as this ammonite, have been found 16,000 ft (5,000 m) up the mountains.

Volcanic eruptions
A range of active volcanoes rises along the edge of Asia.

Scooped up sediment
As the continents near each other, the shallow sea between fills with sediments from the eroding new mountains.

2 Passage north (65 MYA)
India's passage north is boosted by huge volcanic eruptions. Half of the lava forms a vast volcanic plateau in India, and the other half stays off the east coast of Africa, under today's Comoro Islands.

Slowing down
By this point, India's northward drift has slowed to around 1.6–2.4 in (4–6 cm) per year.

3 Narrow basin (50 MYA)
Only a narrow basin exists where once there was the vast Tethys Ocean. As wet oceanic crust subducts under Asia, the rock partially melts and a line of volcanoes rises above.

Rising magma
Moisture rising from the sinking ocean plate lowers the melting point of the mantle lithosphere and magma arises.

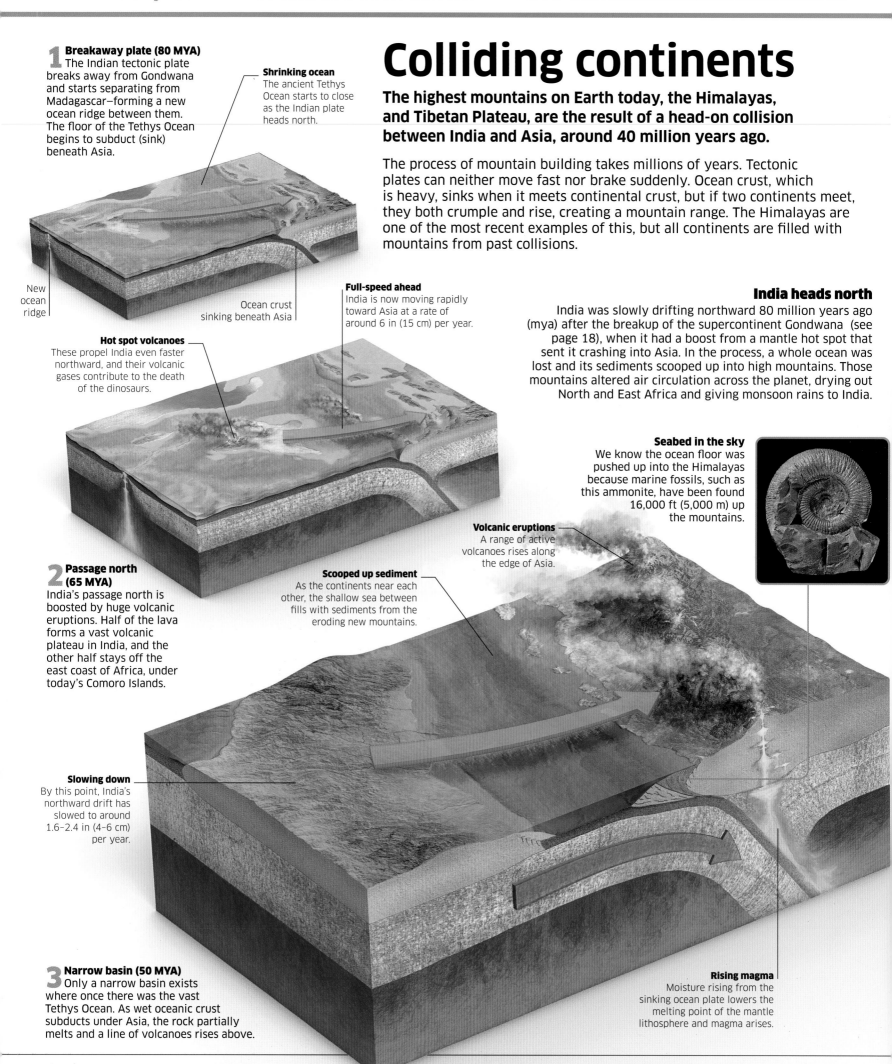

The **Scottish Highlands**, the **Atlas Mountains** in North Africa, and the **Appalachian Mountains** were once all part of **the same mountain range**.

4.4 miles (7 km)—**how much** parts of the **Himalayas** (Nanga Parbat massif) **have grown** in the past **1 million years**.

41

Young and old mountains

Every continent carries the scars of mountain-building collisions (known as orogenies). Comparatively, recent mountain ranges such as the Himalayas (and the Rockies) are still steep and rugged. Older ranges have been worn almost flat. Some mountain ranges have been split apart by later tectonic movements—the Caledonian Mountains in Scotland and the Appalachian Mountains in the US, for example, are now divided by the Atlantic Ocean.

Young mountains
The Himalayas have been rising for more than 40 million years—which is young for mountains—and are still growing by 0.4 in (1 cm) per year. Were it not for erosion, they would be twice as high.

Old mountains
The Appalachians in the US are the result of several continental collisions—one 480 mya, and the other 270 mya. Like all old mountains, they have been eroded into rows of low, smooth hills.

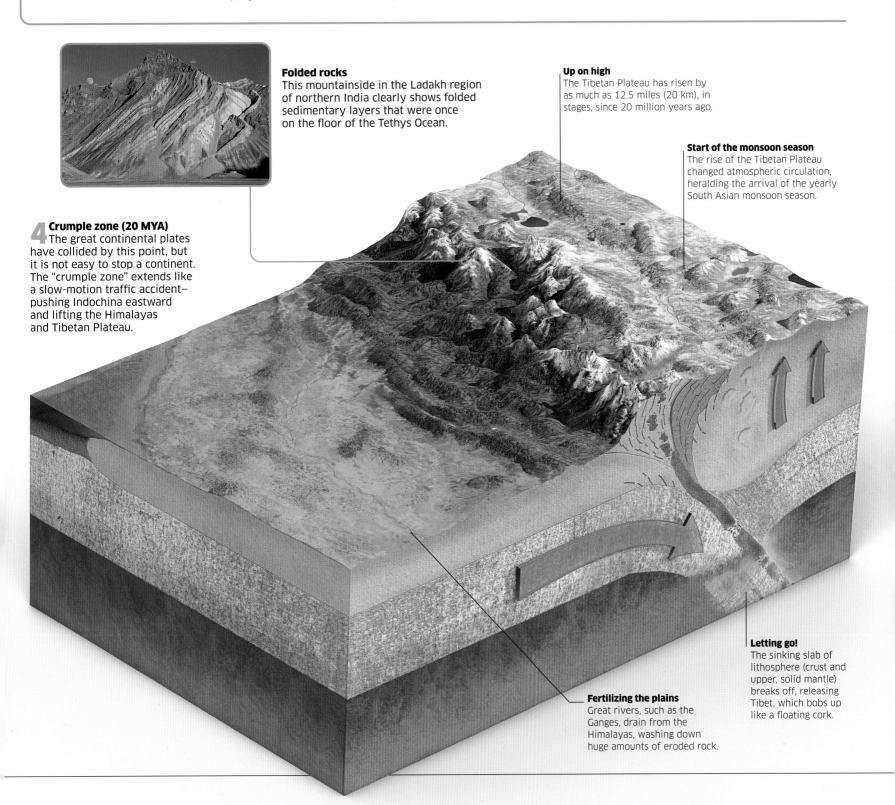

Folded rocks
This mountainside in the Ladakh region of northern India clearly shows folded sedimentary layers that were once on the floor of the Tethys Ocean.

Up on high
The Tibetan Plateau has risen by as much as 12.5 miles (20 km), in stages, since 20 million years ago.

Start of the monsoon season
The rise of the Tibetan Plateau changed atmospheric circulation, heralding the arrival of the yearly South Asian monsoon season.

4 Crumple zone (20 MYA)
The great continental plates have collided by this point, but it is not easy to stop a continent. The "crumple zone" extends like a slow-motion traffic accident—pushing Indochina eastward and lifting the Himalayas and Tibetan Plateau.

Letting go!
The sinking slab of lithosphere (crust and upper, solid mantle) breaks off, releasing Tibet, which bobs up like a floating cork.

Fertilizing the plains
Great rivers, such as the Ganges, drain from the Himalayas, washing down huge amounts of eroded rock.

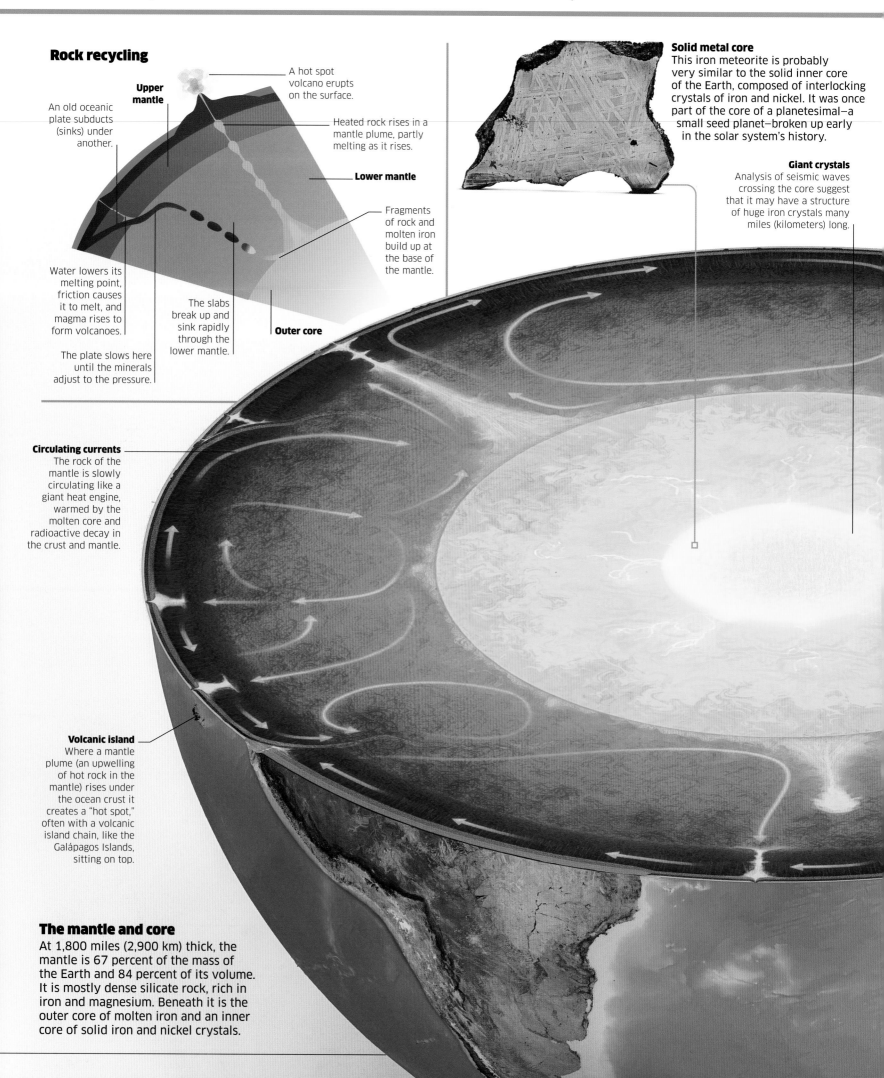

Rock recycling

Upper mantle

A hot spot volcano erupts on the surface.

An old oceanic plate subducts (sinks) under another.

Heated rock rises in a mantle plume, partly melting as it rises.

Lower mantle

Water lowers its melting point, friction causes it to melt, and magma rises to form volcanoes.

The slabs break up and sink rapidly through the lower mantle.

Fragments of rock and molten iron build up at the base of the mantle.

The plate slows here until the minerals adjust to the pressure.

Outer core

Solid metal core
This iron meteorite is probably very similar to the solid inner core of the Earth, composed of interlocking crystals of iron and nickel. It was once part of the core of a planetesimal—a small seed planet—broken up early in the solar system's history.

Giant crystals
Analysis of seismic waves crossing the core suggest that it may have a structure of huge iron crystals many miles (kilometers) long.

Circulating currents
The rock of the mantle is slowly circulating like a giant heat engine, warmed by the molten core and radioactive decay in the crust and mantle.

Volcanic island
Where a mantle plume (an upwelling of hot rock in the mantle) rises under the ocean crust it creates a "hot spot," often with a volcanic island chain, like the Galápagos Islands, sitting on top.

The mantle and core
At 1,800 miles (2,900 km) thick, the mantle is 67 percent of the mass of the Earth and 84 percent of its volume. It is mostly dense silicate rock, rich in iron and magnesium. Beneath it is the outer core of molten iron and an inner core of solid iron and nickel crystals.

47 terawatts—the **heat output of Earth**, which is equivalent to **thousands** of nuclear **power plants**.

200 million years—the **time** it takes for **rock** to **cycle** through **the mantle** from **subduction** to **eruption**.

43

Erupting at the surface
Where the Australian plate dives beneath Asia, the wet ocean crust lowers the melting point of mantle rock, and magma rises and erupts. The 1883 explosion of Krakatoa was one of the most devastating eruptions in history. Now a new volcano is rising above the sea.

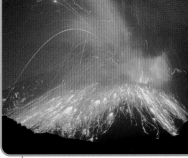

The core
The outer core is made of liquid iron and nickel, around 1,400 miles (2,200 km) thick, but pressure on the inner core keeps it solid.

Hard upper mantle
Beneath the crust is a rigid layer, the mantle lithosphere. Under old continents, it can reach 100 miles (150 km) thick.

D" Layer
At the base of the mantle is a dense, variable layer about 125 miles (200 km) thick, probably of rock infused by iron from the core. It is called the D" (D double prime) layer.

The inner layers

Humans have explored the surface of our planet and even traveled to the moon, but just 30 miles (50 km) under our feet is an unknown world. Recently, however, geologists have begun to unravel Earth's inner secrets.

Beneath the crust lies the mantle. The top layer of it is hard rock and welded to the crust (together, these form the lithosphere), but below that it gets hotter and softer. Although still solid rock, it is soft, like putty, and can flow slowly. The entire mantle is in a continuous circulation, swallowing old, cold ocean crust and regurgitating material heated by the molten core beneath.

Secrets of the mantle
There is no way of sampling the mantle directly, but, occasionally, volcanic eruptions spew out samples from the mantle for geologists to study.

Sparkling treasures
Kimberlite is volcanic rock that erupted in ancient volcanoes at supersonic velocities. It comes from deep in the mantle and can carry tiny samples of a high-pressure form of carbon—diamond.

Rising from the deep
Much of the upper mantle is thought to be made of a rock called peridotite, rich in a dense, green mineral called olivine. When such lumps of rock are found in volcanic magma, they are known as mantle xenoliths.

Continental rafts
Continental crust can build up over billions of years to a thickness of 40 miles (60 km). The oldest rocks on Earth are found in southern Africa, Canada, and Australia.

Oceanic crust
Oceanic crust averages only 4.5 miles (7 km) thick, but attempts to drill through it have so far failed.

1 million mph (400 km/s)—speed of the **solar wind**.

The magnetopause
This is the outer edge of Earth's magnetic influence.

Between the gaps
Where the magnetic lines dip down to the poles, solar particles spiral in toward the upper atmosphere.

Outer Van Allen belt
This spans the orbits of satellites that circle Earth with its spin, which have to be radiation-hardened.

Magnetotail
Magnetic field lines stream out downwind of the sun, forming a comet-shaped tail millions of miles (kilometers) long.

Van Allen radiation belts
These are rings of energetic charged particles, mostly electrons, trapped between lines of the magnetic field. They are a radiation hazard for spacecraft and astronauts.

Auroras
Any solar particles that get through near the poles collide with particles in the atmosphere, creating auroras. The energy released by particles of different gases gives these dramatic bands of light in the sky their colors. Most auroras occur 55–90 miles (90–150 km) up.

Inner Van Allen belt
This is above most satellites on low Earth orbits.

Magnetic bubble

Earth's magnetic field can be visualized as a series of field lines flowing around the globe. A wind of charged particles from the sun bombards this magnetosphere, compressing it on Earth's daylight side; on the far side, it streams away from the sun. The magnetic field deflects electrically charged particles, protecting Earth from harmful radiation.

The solar wind
A constant stream of charged particles blows out from the sun, boosted by solar storms.

Magnetic Earth

Earth has a strong magnetic field, as if it were a giant bar magnet. This field makes magnetic particles and compass needles point north. It also shields the surface from harmful cosmic rays and particles from the sun.

Earth is not a permanent magnet but a magnetic dynamo. Swirling currents of molten iron in its outer core generate an electric current, which in turn produce a magnetic field. This creates an invisible magnetic bubble, known as the magnetosphere, around the planet. For unknown reasons the direction of the field reverses roughly every 800,000 years and north becomes south!

Particle bombardment
Most of the particles are positively charged (protons). They are joined by energetic cosmic rays from distant exploding stars.

Bow shock
The solar wind meets the magnetosphere at supersonic speeds and abruptly slows down.

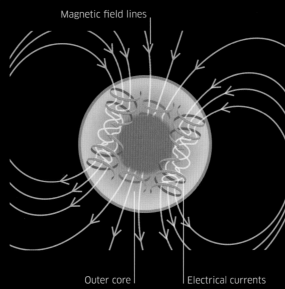

Magnetic field lines

Outer core | Electrical currents

Magnetic North Pole

200 CE   500 CE
TODAY
1000 CE   1250 CE
1800 CE   750 CE
1850 CE

Geographical North Pole

Magnetosheath
Charged particles cannot cross the magnetic field lines and are deflected, forming the magnetosheath.

Giant magnetic dynamo

Molten iron in Earth's outer core is always in motion. This is due to constantly flowing convection currents that transfer heat throughout the core, and also the planet's rotation around its axis. The motion generates electrical currents in the metallic fluid, which create the magnetic field.

Wandering pole

This map shows the location of the geographical North Pole, as seen from above. It also plots the positions of the Magnetic North Pole, which has wandered around the Arctic Circle over the last 2,000 years. Although the inner core and mantle stabilize Earth's magnetic field to some degree, it is not fixed either in strength or direction.

46 rocky earth ○ EARTHQUAKES AND TSUNAMIS

Millions of earthquakes occur around the world every year—but many of them can't be felt.

Earthquakes and tsunamis

The tectonic plates that make up Earth's crust are on the move. They shift slowly, and sometimes get stuck, but they are unstoppable. Stresses build up and, eventually, the plates move, causing an earthquake.

Small tremors are frequent and can happen almost anywhere, but major earthquakes are far more common along tectonic plate boundaries. The places where they are likely can be predicted, but not the time. In spite of that, many cities are built in earthquake-prone regions.

Faults

When tectonic plates of the Earth's crust are stretched, pushed together, or dragged alongside each other, the cracks created are known as faults. There are three main types.

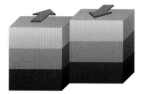

Strike-slip
This is when plates slide past each other horizontally, as at the San Andreas Fault in California.

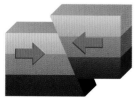

Reverse or thrust
This occurs when plates are squashed and shortened so that one slab rises, as in the Glarus Thrust Fault in Switzerland.

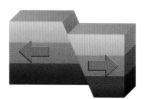

Normal
This occurs when rocks are pulled apart and the crust is stretched, as in the East African Great Rift Valley.

How earthquakes are measured

There are two ways of measuring earthquakes: magnitude (the energy released) and intensity (its effects). The Modified Mercalli Scale measures the intensity of an earthquake.

Intensity	Shaking and Damage
I	Not felt.
II–III	Weak. Felt indoors. Hanging objects swing.
IV–V	Minor damage. Felt outdoors. Standing vehicles rock.
VI–VII	Moderate damage. Felt by all. People walk unsteadily.
VIII–IX	Considerable damage. Visible cracks in the ground. Pipes broken.
X	Total damage. Large landslides. Objects thrown into the air.

A scene of devastation
A severe earthquake has just struck. It has split this street down the middle and caused a huge amount of destruction. The only undamaged building was specially designed for an earthquake zone.

Earthquake-proof building
This building has survived due to its bracing and hydraulic pistons, which reduce swaying.

Crashed cars
Vehicles are thrown off course as the ground shakes, causing accidents.

Gas pipes
If a gas pipe is fractured, there's a serious risk of fire or even explosion.

Epicenter
This is the point on the Earth's surface above the focus.

Rubber mountings
This building can resist shaking due to sturdy rubber foundations.

Plate movement
This is a normal fault. Stresses have built up until the ground moves by several feet..

Focus
This is the point in the Earth's crust where a fault starts to crack.

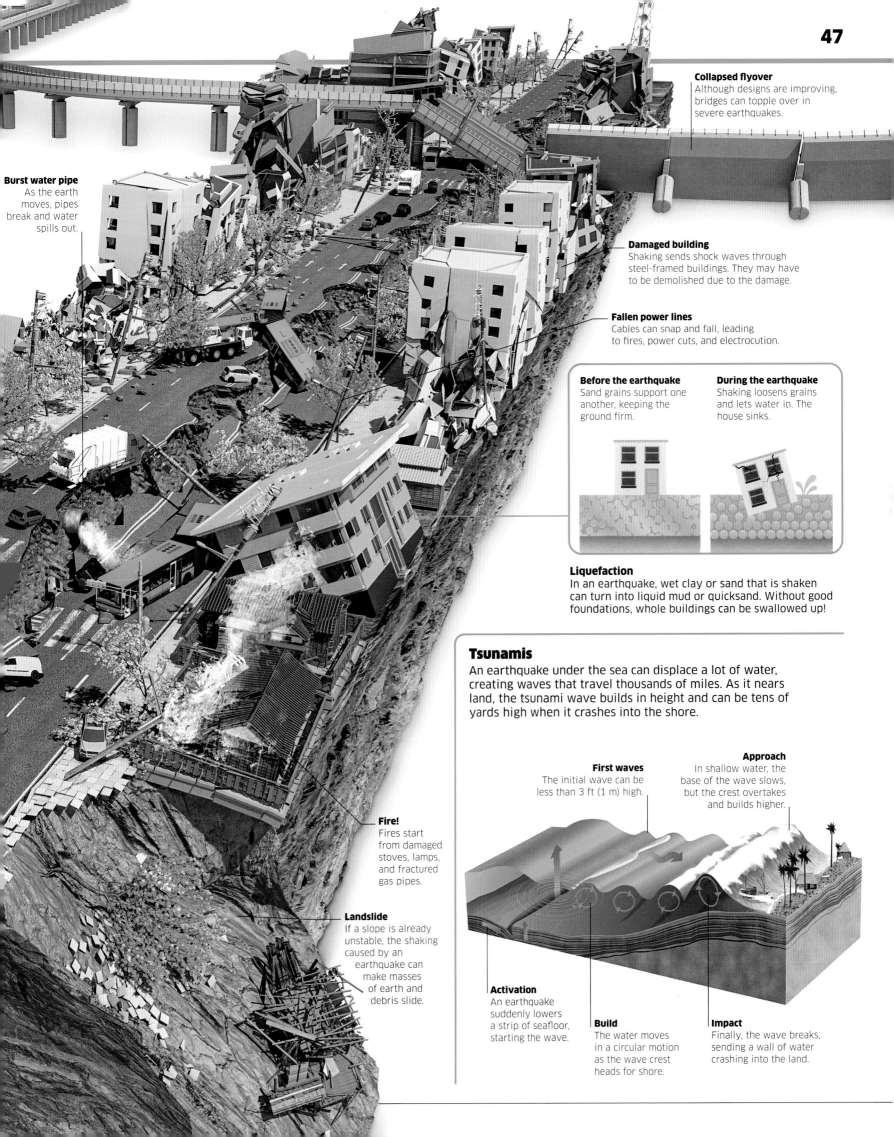

Collapsed flyover
Although designs are improving, bridges can topple over in severe earthquakes.

Burst water pipe
As the earth moves, pipes break and water spills out.

Damaged building
Shaking sends shock waves through steel-framed buildings. They may have to be demolished due to the damage.

Fallen power lines
Cables can snap and fall, leading to fires, power cuts, and electrocution.

Before the earthquake
Sand grains support one another, keeping the ground firm.

During the earthquake
Shaking loosens grains and lets water in. The house sinks.

Liquefaction
In an earthquake, wet clay or sand that is shaken can turn into liquid mud or quicksand. Without good foundations, whole buildings can be swallowed up!

Tsunamis
An earthquake under the sea can displace a lot of water, creating waves that travel thousands of miles. As it nears land, the tsunami wave builds in height and can be tens of yards high when it crashes into the shore.

Fire!
Fires start from damaged stoves, lamps, and fractured gas pipes.

Landslide
If a slope is already unstable, the shaking caused by an earthquake can make masses of earth and debris slide.

First waves
The initial wave can be less than 3 ft (1 m) high.

Approach
In shallow water, the base of the wave slows, but the crest overtakes and builds higher.

Activation
An earthquake suddenly lowers a strip of seafloor, starting the wave.

Build
The water moves in a circular motion as the wave crest heads for shore.

Impact
Finally, the wave breaks, sending a wall of water crashing into the land.

Volcanoes

A volcano is an opening in the Earth's crust through which molten rock erupts. In the mantle, hot rock rises. Near the surface, the pressure drops causing some of the rock to melt, push upward, and escape through a volcano—the most spectacular, and dangerous, expressions of our dynamic planet.

Molten rock is known as magma while it is still underground and lava once it has erupted. The composition of magma is not the same as the rock it comes from, as the rock only partially melts, squeezing magma out from between the grains.

THE RING OF FIRE

Most volcanoes are found around the edges of tectonic plates. A map of the volcanoes around the biggest plate, the Pacific, reveals what is known as the Pacific Ring of Fire.

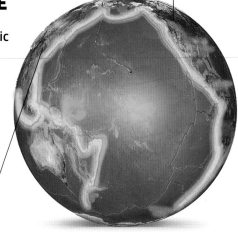

North America

Southeast Asia
Here, the Pacific plate dives beneath the Eurasian plate.

TYPES OF VOLCANOES

The shape of a volcano and the violence of its eruptions depend on the nature of the magma beneath it. If it contains more silica (a compound of silicon and oxygen), it is stickier and does not flow so easily. If there is a lot of water or dissolved gas, eruptions are more explosive, pulverizing the lava to cinders and ash.

Very fluid lava comes from deep within the mantle.

Shield
These volcanoes are broad, with lava flows covering a huge area in all directions. They can also grow tall, although most of their height is often hidden beneath the sea, as in Hawaii.

Built of alternating layers of lava flows, cinders, and ash.

Stratovolcano
These are the classic pyramid shape of volcanoes, such as Mount Fuji in Japan. They are often above subducting ocean crust that carries water, which turns explosively to steam and pulverizes the magma.

The cone is built up of spattered fragments.

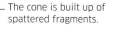

An ash-cinder cone
These are often the first sign of a new volcano, or a new crater on the flank of an old one. They can produce spectacular fire fountains.

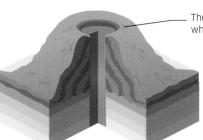

The lava is so sticky that it often cools where it erupts, creating a rounded lip.

A lava dome
Magma that comes from continental crust is high in silica and is very viscous (sticky). So, instead of flowing out, it pushes up in a huge dome, either to burst explosively or to harden where it is.

VOLCANIC ROCKS

Volcanic rocks are known as igneous extrusive rocks as they have been "extruded" from the Earth like from a tube. There are many types, classified by their composition and texture.

This is a dense, dark rock, rich in magnesium and iron.

Usually fine-textured but can contain larger crystals

Basalt
The most common volcanic rock, basalt is produced in huge quantities under the sea and by shield volcanoes.

Rhyolite
A typical rock from continental volcanoes, it is light in color and high in silica (quartz) and feldspar.

Gas pockets make it so light that it can float on water.

Known as "volcanic glass," due to its texture

Pumice
Similar in composition to rhyolite, pumice is blown into a foam by expanding gases and cooled rapidly.

Obsidian
Very high in silica, obsidian cools so quickly that the minerals have no time to crystallize into grains.

CALDERA

A caldera is a large, cauldron-shaped depression in the top of a volcano. It can be caused by an explosive eruption blowing the top off the volcano, or by a collapse into a hollow chamber after the magma has gone. Some are bigger than the volcano they swallowed and some contain lakes.

Located in Lanzarote, Spain, these extinct volcanoes are called Caldereta and Caldera Blanca.

122,750 cu miles (512,000 cu km)—the estimated volume of basalt erupted by the Deccan Traps.

2,650 years—the longest recorded continuous volcanic eruption: Mount Stromboli in the Mediterranean.

49

SHIELD VOLCANOES

These form on "hot spots" above plumes of hot rock rising up through the mantle. The rock starts to melt 95 miles (150 km) down. Only a few percent melts, creating runny lava that can cover a wide area. In Earth's past, shield volcanoes have produced millions of cubic miles of basalt and caused climate changes that may have led to mass extinctions of plants and animals.

The Deccan Traps

This plateau in Western India was created by a giant shield volcano that erupted about 66 million years ago. It covers an area of around 77,000 sq miles (200,000 sq km), with layers of basalt more than 1.2 miles (2 km) thick in places.

Types of lava

There are two main types of basalt lava from shield volcanoes, which look very different in appearance. This is due to the temperature of the lava, the speed at which it flows, and how quickly its surface cools. Both lavas have been given Hawaiian names that describe how they look: 'a'ā means "stony, rough lava," and pāhoehoe translates to "smooth, unbroken lava."

'A'ā lava
Pronounced "ah-ah," this lava flows fast, causing rapid heat loss at its surface, which creates jagged lumps of lava that tumble forward as it moves. These lumps keep the rock underneath hot so that it can flow far.

Pāhoehoe lava
Pronounced "paw-hoey-hoey," this lava erupts slightly hotter and flows faster than 'a'ā lava. It is often called "ropey" lava due to the way its outer layer wrinkles as it cools. Like 'a'ā lava, it can also flow great distances.

Volcanic island chains

Hot spots can occur in the middle of tectonic plates under oceans, creating a chain of volcanic islands. This is because the hot spot is fixed, while the tectonic plate drifts slowly over it at a steady pace. The Hawaiian archipelago is an example of this process in action. Today, Hawaii (or Big Island) sits over the hot spot and has three active volcanoes, but more than 130 older islands, atolls, and seamounts exist in the chain.

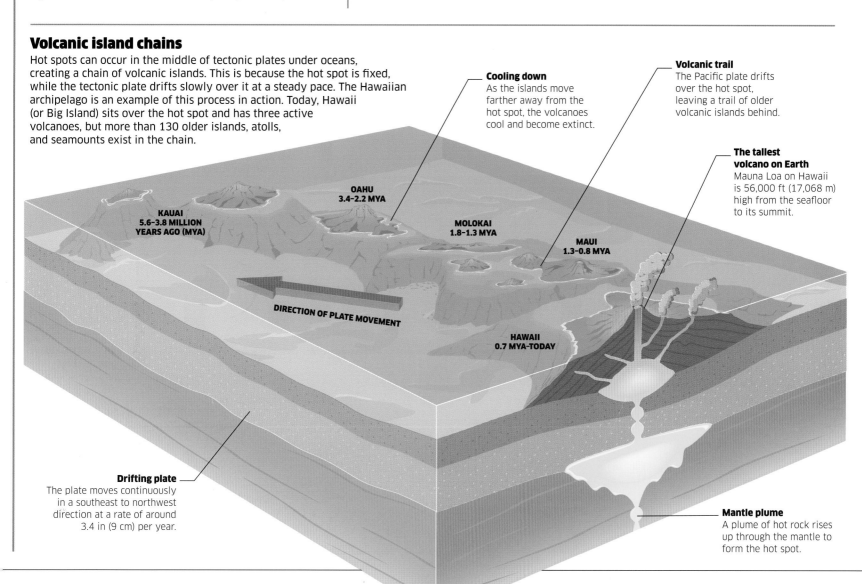

Cooling down
As the islands move farther away from the hot spot, the volcanoes cool and become extinct.

Volcanic trail
The Pacific plate drifts over the hot spot, leaving a trail of older volcanic islands behind.

The tallest volcano on Earth
Mauna Loa on Hawaii is 56,000 ft (17,068 m) high from the seafloor to its summit.

KAUAI
5.6–3.8 MILLION YEARS AGO (MYA)

OAHU
3.4–2.2 MYA

MOLOKAI
1.8–1.3 MYA

MAUI
1.3–0.8 MYA

DIRECTION OF PLATE MOVEMENT

HAWAII
0.7 MYA–TODAY

Drifting plate
The plate moves continuously in a southeast to northwest direction at a rate of around 3.4 in (9 cm) per year.

Mantle plume
A plume of hot rock rises up through the mantle to form the hot spot.

Ash blanket

When the Cumbre Vieja volcano on La Palma in the Canary Islands erupted in 2021, lava flows destroyed more than 3,000 buildings and thick ash covered everything in the area.

The Canaries are a chain of volcanic islands and underwater volcanic mountains off the northwest coast of Africa. Eruptions started about 70 million years ago and are probably due to a mantle hot spot beneath the African plate (which is moving slowly eastward). La Palma is one of the youngest and most active of the volcanic islands.

Stratovolcanoes

Mount Etna in Sicily is Europe's biggest, most active volcano. It is a stratovolcano, made up of multiple layers of lava flows, ash, and cinders, rising to a conical summit towering 11,013 ft (3,357 m) above sea level. Geologists are now discovering its internal anatomy.

Etna is a complex volcano. It probably began as an underwater volcano over a mantle plume 500,000 years ago. It later developed into a stratovolcano, fueled by the old Tethys Ocean plate sinking beneath Europe. Around 8,000 years ago, the eastern flank of Etna collapsed, causing a huge tsunami in the Mediterranean Sea. Historical records document frequent eruptions, sometimes engulfing villages. In 1669, lava reached the walls of the city of Catania, nearly 19 miles (30 km) away to the east of the volcano.

A dangerous job

Vulcanologists monitoring Etna hope to directly sample the volcanic gases for clues about the source of the lava and when the volcano will next erupt. They have to be well prepared—and careful where they tread! Heat-proof boots and suits help, as do gas masks. However, they offer little protection from lava bombs, which can be the size of soccer balls.

Trouble brewing

Magma can pool below the surface without erupting, causing the flank to swell. If the area collapses, it can release the magma, causing a deadly sideways blast.

Living in Etna's shadow

Thousands of Sicilians live in small towns and villages on the sides of Etna. For them, the eruptions, and layers of volcanic ash or rocks on their streets, are a familiar sight.

Ancient origins

Beneath the layered roots of the present-day stratovolcano lies an ancient, broad shield volcano, similar to the island of Hawaii.

Mount Etna

A volcano like Mount Etna is built up of alternating layers of lava flows, ash, and cinders. The underground plumbing is complex. There are many dykes (cutting through the rock layers) and sills (running between the layers) of lava, and it has multiple craters, as the magma tries to find a way out. Eruptions are frequent and can last for months or years but are seldom devastating.

Buried beneath the lava

In 2001, fissures opened above the small town of Nicolosi, which had been totally destroyed in 1669. The lava was unstoppable but moved slowly and halted just before reaching the town. This outlying house was not so lucky.

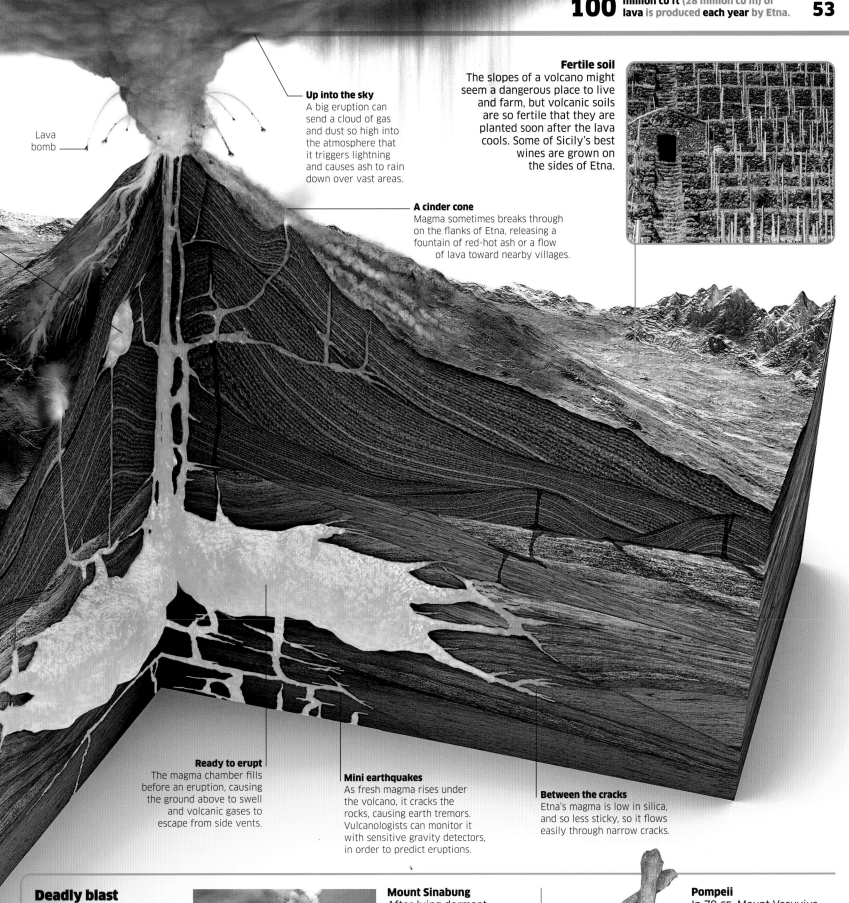

Lava bomb

Up into the sky
A big eruption can send a cloud of gas and dust so high into the atmosphere that it triggers lightning and causes ash to rain down over vast areas.

A cinder cone
Magma sometimes breaks through on the flanks of Etna, releasing a fountain of red-hot ash or a flow of lava toward nearby villages.

Fertile soil
The slopes of a volcano might seem a dangerous place to live and farm, but volcanic soils are so fertile that they are planted soon after the lava cools. Some of Sicily's best wines are grown on the sides of Etna.

Ready to erupt
The magma chamber fills before an eruption, causing the ground above to swell and volcanic gases to escape from side vents.

Mini earthquakes
As fresh magma rises under the volcano, it cracks the rocks, causing earth tremors. Vulcanologists can monitor it with sensitive gravity detectors, in order to predict eruptions.

Between the cracks
Etna's magma is low in silica, and so less sticky, so it flows easily through narrow cracks.

Deadly blast
Ash that is too heavy to rise into the sky can race down the sides of a stratovolcano at speeds of more than 60 mph (100 km/h), accelerated by expanding steam and gas, and at temperatures over 1,470°F (800°C). This is called a pyroclastic flow.

Mount Sinabung
After lying dormant for 400 years, this Indonesian stratovolcano began erupting in 2010. In 2021, it produced a series of pyroclastic flows, leading to the evacuation of 27,000 people from within a 1.2 mile (2 km) radius.

Pompeii
In 79 CE, Mount Vesuvius erupted and pyroclastic flows buried the Roman town of Pompeii under more than 19 ft (6 m) of ash. A plaster cast was made of the shape left by this dog, killed in the hot ash.

Bubbling mud
Frequent features of geothermal areas such as hot springs are pools of fine mud, bubbling with steam and volcanic gases, like giant cauldrons of porridge.

Stone terraces
As hot water saturated with chemicals cools, it deposits terraces of stone—some silica, others calcite (calcium carbonate).

Geyser
A steamy jet erupts when the water reaches boiling point, releasing the pressure.

Geysers and hot springs

Volcanic heat doesn't always lead to fire fountains and lava flows. It can also power an underground boiler, creating colorful hot springs and geysers.

Hot rocks beneath Earth's crust can create geothermal features on the surface. Rain seeping down from above, or existing groundwater, becomes heated as it travels deeper or nears a shallow magma source. Pressure then sends it upward to form hot springs, which can offer a pleasant hot bath or a scalding cocktail of toxic chemicals. One of their more spectacular features can be a geyser, periodically shooting a jet of hot water and steam high into the sky.

Devil's Bath
The fluorescent green water in this pool gets its color from particles of sulfur and iron salts. It also stinks of bad eggs from volcanic hydrogen sulfide gas.

A warm soak

In the snows of a Japanese winter, macaque monkeys enjoy their own hot tub bath in Jigokudani Park, which is named "The Valley of Hell" because of its geothermal springs. Water temperatures average 122°F (50°C), which not only warms the "snow monkeys" but also seems to lower their stress levels.

Building pressure
Water collects in chambers and heats up. Eventually, it starts to boil, sending a pressurized jet up the mineral-lined pipe above it.

Hot-water reservoir
At depths of several hundred feet, the pressure keeps the water from boiling, even though it is very hot.

266°F (130°C)—the **highest temperature** some **heat-loving bacteria** can **survive**.

240 cu miles (1,000 cu km)—the **volume of magma** from the **last big eruption** of the **Yellowstone supervolcano**.

55

Boiling waterfall

Yellowstone supervolcano

Today, tourists flock to the scenery, hot springs, and geysers in Yellowstone National Park, Wyoming. Around 640,000 years ago, however, it erupted as a "supervolcano," thousands of times more violent than any volcanic eruption today. The caldera is still above two magma chambers and rises and falls like the flank of a sleeping dragon that could awake at any moment.

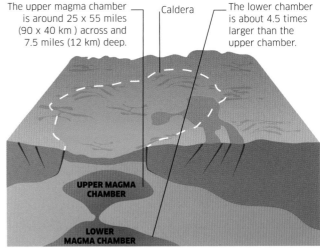

The upper magma chamber is around 25 x 55 miles (90 x 40 km) across and 7.5 miles (12 km) deep.

Caldera

The lower chamber is about 4.5 times larger than the upper chamber.

UPPER MAGMA CHAMBER

LOWER MAGMA CHAMBER

Fumaroles
A fumarole is a volcanic vent emitting steam and volcanic gases. A cone of deposits can build up around it, often frosted with yellow sulfur.

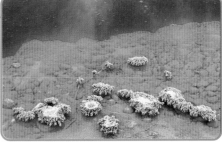

Heat-loving bacteria
Thermophilic bacteria thrive in the 167°F (75°C) heat of the Champagne Pool—so called because it fizzes with carbon dioxide bubbles. The orange edge to the pool is due to a buildup of compounds of arsenic and deposited as the water cools and evaporates.

Cold water
Cold surface water trickles down through cracks in the ground toward the hot, volcanic rock beneath, heating up as it goes.

Rising up
The water rises to the lake above where it cools due to evaporation.

Hot water
The pressurized water is heated to more than 440°F (230°C), dissolving minerals from the rock.

Rotorua, New Zealand
There are hot springs in many parts of the world. Maori legend suggests that the geothermal features around Rotorua, in New Zealand, were left by fire demons on their way to rescue a priest from freezing on a mountain. Maori people are still the guardians of the springs, which are heated by the collapsed caldera (crater) of a huge volcanic eruption that occurred 140,000 years ago.

RECYCLED ROCKS

Even the oldest rocks on Earth are far younger than most on the moon. The reason is that here on Earth we have weather and active plate tectonics (see pages 36-37). Our rocks are constantly pounded by wind and waves, dissolved by acid rain, and washed away. They are buried, cooked, melted, and erupt again in a never-ending cycle over hundreds of millions of years. This is the rock cycle.

The rock cycle

Rocks may seem solid and permanent, but they are constantly changing. Mountains rise and are eroded away; rocks are buried, pressed, and melted deep in the Earth, only to rise again as new peaks.

There are hundreds of different rocks on our planet, but they can be divided into three main types–igneous, sedimentary, and metamorphic–depending on how they were formed. Igneous rocks were once molten. Sedimentary rocks are the dissolved or eroded remains of other rocks. Both can be transformed by heat and pressure into metamorphic rocks.

New rock
Igneous rock erupts from volcanoes, spreading out as layers of ash and lava.

Chemical weathering
Acid rain dissolves some rocks or reacts with them, breaking them into soil.

Mechanical weathering
Wind, ice, and water cause rocks to disintegrate, carrying the debris down to the sea.

Crashing waves
Waves cut into the coast and pound the rocks into fine sand.

Layer upon layer
Sand, silt, and mud are washed out to sea to sink to the ocean floor, forming new sedimentary layers.

Marine sediments
These are scooped into a wedge. One day they will build new mountains.

Melted granite
Heat and moisture melt deep crustal rocks so they rise as a huge mass of magma.

Regional metamorphism
These layers have been squeezed, cooked, and folded into metamorphic rocks.

A laccolith
Rising molten granite forces its way between the layers of rock.

Contact metamorphism
Rocks in direct contact with rising magma are transformed by the heat.

Sinking ocean crust
Ocean crust subducts, recycling basalt back into the mantle.

IGNEOUS ROCKS

Igneous rocks, such as basalt and granite, all start as molten magma. Intrusive igneous rocks rise underground, filling cracks (dykes and sills) and larger chambers (batholiths and laccoliths) but do not erupt on the surface. Extrusive igneous rocks erupt out of volcanoes on land or under the sea. Both sorts can be high in silica (granite and rhyolite) or low in silica (gabbro and basalt).

The Giant's Causeway, Northern Ireland, UK
This is an igneous extrusive basalt flow. As the lava cooled, it contracted and cracked into huge hexagonal columns.

The Sierra Nevada Mountains, California
These exposed granite igneous intrusions were formed about 100 million years ago deep in Earth's crust.

4.374 billion years—the age of the **oldest**-known mineral grain (a **zircon** from **northern Australia**).

790 million tons (720 **million metric tons**) per year—the amount of **sediment** that the **Brahmaputra River**, in **Asia**, can carry.

57

The Painted Desert, Arizona
These colorful layers of sandstone and mudstone were laid down in the Triassic period around 230 mya.

The White Cliffs of Dover, England, UK
Chalk is made of calcium carbonate, the remains of tiny plankton that extracted carbon dioxide from the sea.

SEDIMENTARY ROCKS

Sedimentary rocks are all the products of weathering and erosion, and usually end up at the bottom of lakes or on the seabed. Over millions of years, layers of sediment build up and are pressed together by the weight of the layers on top. Some, such as rock salt and gypsum, are formed from evaporated seawater. Others, such as coal and chalk, are organic (plant or animal remains). Many are ground-up rock fragments, classified by their size, ranging from fine mud to coarse sand and gravel. All can harden to form solid rock.

METAMORPHIC ROCKS

Metamorphic rocks have been through the Earth's pressure cooker—changed by the immense pressure of overlying rock or by subterranean heat, or both. Pressure aligns the grains, and heat makes minerals grow into interlocking crystals. The resulting matrix is often folded and faulted. Rocks at quite shallow depths can be altered simply by contact with an igneous intrusion (contact metamorphism). Whole regions become metamorphic if buried deep enough (regional metamorphism).

Continental pileup

The oldest cores of continents are like giant scrap heaps on which tangled debris has piled up over billions of years. Metamorphism has changed what started out as granite into folded layers of gneiss. Hidden within it are clues to its long and violent history of deep burial, intercontinental collision, and erosion.

Achmelvich Bay, northwest Scotland, UK
These rocks are the remains of the deep roots of a 3-billion-year-old continent.

King Oscar Fjord, Greenland
Some of the oldest rocks on Earth exist in Greenland, often exposed by erosion.

Constantly changing

As hot intrusions of granite (such as this laccolith) intrude between the layers of overlying rock, they change that rock through heat and pressure into metamorphic forms. They also drive mineral-laden, super-heated brine through the cracked rock above, depositing rich mineral veins.

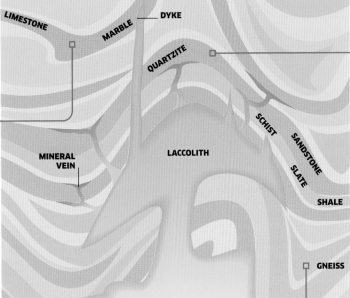

Quartzite
Sand grains are made of quartz (silicon dioxide). With heat and pressure, the grains bind together, forming quartzite.

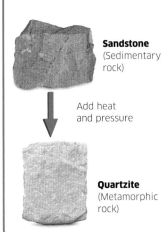

Sandstone
(Sedimentary rock)

Add heat and pressure

Quartzite
(Metamorphic rock)

Marble
Moderate heat and pressure turn limestone into marble. If the limestone is pure calcium carbonate, the marble can be pure white.

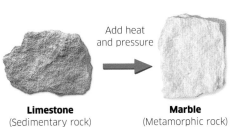

Add heat and pressure

Limestone
(Sedimentary rock)

Marble
(Metamorphic rock)

Gneiss
If the clay minerals in shale (made from mud) are pressed and heated, first they align to make slate, then sparkling crystals of mica grow, forming schist. Finally, as the rock almost melts, it turns into gneiss.

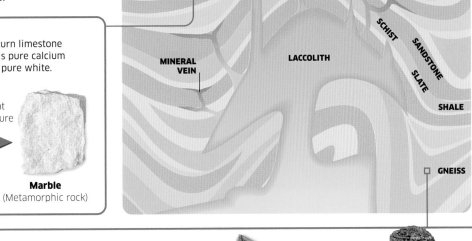

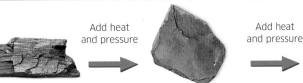

Shale
(Sedimentary rock)

Add heat and pressure

Slate
(Metamorphic rock)

Add heat and pressure

Schist
(Metamorphic rock)

Add heat and pressure

Gneiss
(Metamorphic rock)

Minerals

Our solid planet is made of rocks, and rocks are made of minerals. A mineral is an element or compound with a specific chemical composition and distinctive crystal structure. Many minerals provide the ores and raw materials for human industry.

Mineral grains in rocks can be so small that they are visible only with a microscope, but they can also grow into spectacular crystals, usually deep within the Earth. Minerals crystallize naturally in two main ways: through the cooling of lava and magma; or by evaporation from a solution, either above ground or in cracks and veins between rock layers underground.

The Mohs hardness scale

One way to help identify a mineral is by its resistance to scratching. Geologists use the Mohs scale and special "hardness pencils," but everyday objects are useful too. For example, you can scratch gypsum but not calcite with your fingernail, apatite but not orthoclase with a knife. Nothing can scratch a diamond.

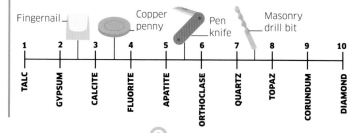

Fingernail | Copper penny | Pen knife | Masonry drill bit

| 1 | 2 | 3 | 4 | 5 | 6 | 7 | 8 | 9 | 10 |
| TALC | GYPSUM | CALCITE | FLUORITE | APATITE | ORTHOCLASE | QUARTZ | TOPAZ | CORUNDUM | DIAMOND |

ROCK-FORMING

Most rocks in the Earth's crust are made out of a few main groups of minerals. The most common of these are silicates (compounds of oxygen and silicon, plus metals such as aluminum and magnesium).

QUARTZ
Hardness: 7

The most abundant mineral in the Earth's crust, quartz is one of the main components of continental rocks such as granite. It is also found in sand and has many uses, including glassmaking.

AUGITE
Hardness: 7

Belonging to a group called pyroxenes, it is a major component of basalt, thus one of the commonest minerals in the Earth's crust.

OLIVINE
Hardness: 6–6.5

A dense, green mineral containing magnesium and iron silicates, it is common in rocks of the upper mantle. In pure form, it is the gemstone peridot.

FELDSPAR
Hardness: 6

Often found in igneous rocks, including granite, its two commonest forms are orthoclase (shown here) and plagioclase.

MICA
Hardness: 2.5–4

Found in igneous rocks and where clay minerals in sedimentary rocks have been metamorphosed, its flat crystal structure makes it a good industrial insulator.

METAL ORES

An ore is a mineral containing enough of a metal to make it worth extracting. After mining, the ore can be concentrated by panning or floating, using chemicals such as solvents, or with heat. Ores, such as gold, tin, copper, and platinum, are found as "native ores," which means the metal is found in its pure, natural state without the need for extraction.

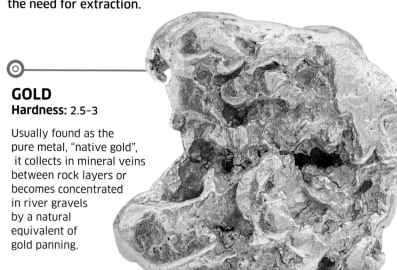

GOLD
Hardness: 2.5–3

Usually found as the pure metal, "native gold", it collects in mineral veins between rock layers or becomes concentrated in river gravels by a natural equivalent of gold panning.

COPPER
Hardness: 3

The most abundant form is copper sulfide, but it sometimes occurs as the "native" metal. Copper is a good conductor of electricity, making it valuable for use in electrical cables.

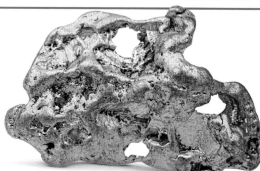

ILMENITE
Hardness: 5–6

A common mineral in igneous rocks, ilmenite has even been found on the moon. The principle ore of titanium, its dense crystals sink to the bottom of magma chambers.

BAUXITE
Hardness: 1–3

Strictly a sort of earth, rather than a pure mineral, bauxite is the principle ore of aluminum. As aluminum binds to other elements, extracting it is a complex process involving expensive electrolysis.

$71 million (£54 million)—the **highest price** ever **paid** for **a gemstone** (the **Pink Star diamond,** in 2017).

5,780 mineral species are recognized by the International **Mineral Association**. **59**

PRECIOUS AND SEMIPRECIOUS

Many minerals are attractive in appearance. They are often translucent and refract light so that they sparkle if cut to align with their natural crystal structure. Some are also extremely hard and durable and thus valued as jewels.

SAPPHIRE
Hardness: 9

Made of corundum, or aluminum oxide, this is the second-hardest natural mineral after diamond. Sapphire gets its blue color from traces of iron and titanium, but some gems are colorless.

RUBY
Hardness: 9

Also made of corundum, the color of ruby comes from traces of chromium. Both rubies and sapphires form in igneous rocks or through contact metamorphism.

AMETHYST
Hardness: 7

This form of quartz has a striking purple color, making it a popular semiprecious stone. The color comes from traces of iron or other metals. It can occur in large crystals, but the best color is often only in the outer layers. Most amethysts are mined in Brazil.

TOPAZ
Hardness: 8

Topaz is the hardest natural silicate. It is often pale yellow or brown, very rarely purple or blue—varieties so valuable that they are often created artificially by irradiating clear topaz.

TOURMALINE
Hardness: 7

The largest and most valuable tourmaline specimens grow in pockets in hydrothermal systems. A complex silicate of boron, it is often black but also comes in a range of colors.

ZIRCON
Hardness: 7

Zirconium silicate is one of the most widespread minerals. It is often overlooked, as most grains are tiny. Zircon is one of the oldest minerals on Earth.

EMERALD
Hardness: 7.5-8

Second to diamond in value, it is a form of beryl, colored green by chromium or vanadium—two elements not often found together, making it rare.

DIAMOND
Hardness: 10

The hardest of all minerals—and the most valued because it forms only at immense pressure deep in the mantle. It refracts light so sparkles in many colors.

MALACHITE
Hardness: 3.5-4

This ore is copper carbonate and is often found in cracks and caves in limestone. It has been mined for copper for at least 4,000 years but today is more often used in jewelry for its attractive, bright green, layered structure.

GALENA
Hardness: 7

With characteristic cubic crystals of dense lead sulfide, the principle ore of lead is easily recognizable. It can also contain traces of the more valuable metal, silver, and has been mined for both for 2,000 years.

CASSITERITE
Hardness: 6-7

This rare, dense, dark mineral is the main ore of tin. Its toughness and density mean that it can be concentrated in river gravels—the main commercial source today.

CINNABAR
Hardness: 5-6

This mineral is made of mercury sulfide, evaporated from solution in mineral veins. It is the only ore of mercury, which is extracted commercially with heat.

HEMATITE
Hardness: 6.5

This iron oxide mineral is the most important ore of iron and extracted in huge quantities. In pure form, it is also polished for jewelry due to its unusual texture and shine.

Weathering and erosion

Weathering dissolves or breaks down rocks on Earth's surface. Erosion moves rocks and soil to a new location. Some forces, such as the wind and water, can do both.

There are four main forces behind weathering and erosion—water, wind, ice, and gravity. Water in the form of rain, streams, rivers, waterfalls, and the sea can sculpt the rock. Wind moves small particles of rock and sand, which wear down any rocks they hit. A powerful force, ice can erode rock by forming crystals inside rocks that crack them or as huge glaciers that carve out valleys, carrying rocks with them. Gravity pulls rocks downward, shaping the landscape as they go.

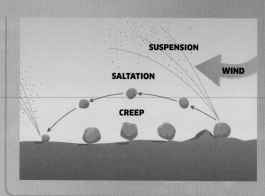

How wind moves sand
Clay dust, sand grains, and rocks move in different ways in the desert. Fine clay dust is suspended in the air in clouds. Sand is lifted in a series of short hops (saltation), usually just off the ground. Heavier rock particles creep along the surface.

Chilean Coastal Range
The Pacific Ocean lies west of these coastal mountains. Cold ocean currents cool the air here, so it does not hold much moisture.

Clay pillars and caverns
As well as sandstone and limestone, the desert has layers of clay, made of fined-grained minerals, too. The clay is easily eroded into pillars and underground caves.

The amphitheater
This huge rock form has been shaped by the wind coming down from the Andes. The edge furthest away from this stream of hot air is higher and less eroded.

Sandstone pillars
Swirling sands, and ice crystals that form in cracks in the rocks, have shaped these pillars.

Mysterious white dust
Scientists used to think this white crust was created by sea mist, but they now know it is from groundwater. The Atacama Plateau was once a lake and heat draws water and minerals to the surface.

Top heavy
Rocks in sandy deserts often have a wide top and narrow base. The wind lifts sand, whipping it against the rocks, but it cannot lift heavier sand grains very high.

Pyramid rocks
More resistant to sculpting by wind-blown sand than soft sedimentary rocks, even hard igneous rocks become pitted and polished over time.

The Atacama Desert
This desert in Chile, South America, is one of the oldest and driest deserts on Earth. Mountain ranges on either side stop rain from reaching the area, and its landscape is sculpted by the wind and by occasional intense rainstorms. Weathering of the volcanic mountains of the Andes brings new rocks down to the desert, where the wind breaks them down and whips them across this high plateau, eroding the rocks and forming dunes.

How dunes form
For moving sand to form a dune, it has to meet an obstacle, such as a pebble. The dune starts with a small bump, then more sand arrives. Eventually, the side facing the wind forms a crest and the smaller grains slip down the other side to create the dune. This process can take years.

CREST

MOVING SAND

WIND

SLIP FACE

Hot, dry air
The Atacama Desert is a rain-shadow desert (see page 131). Winds rise to cross the Andes, cooling as they rise, and the moisture in the air condenses and falls as rain on the eastern side of the range. The now dry wind warms as it descends into the desert, sucking out any moisture.

PREVAILING EASTERLY WIND

Volcanic mountains
The Chilean Andes are dominated by volcanoes, many of which are active. The sand in the Atacama Desert is mostly quartz, from igneous rocks produced by volcanic activity and then eroded.

Mountain erosion
Wind, melting snow, and occasional intense rains erode the higher mountain slopes, carrying rock particles down into the desert.

Dunes
Where dunes form, they can be very high, reaching heights of hundreds of feet (meters).

The Three Marias
Strangely shaped rocks in the desert are often named by local residents after people and objects they resemble.

Water-worn channels
It rarely rains here, but when it does, the water runs quickly down the slopes, forming deep channels in the soft rock.

Falling rubble
Broken rocks, or scree, at the foot of the cliff are a result of weathering by frost, which cracks the rock, and erosion by gravity.

Cracked earth
Plants cannot survive in parched areas of the desert. Without plant roots to hold the soil and sand in place, the ground is even more exposed to weathering and erosion.

Living geology

The processes that shape the Earth involve not only the creation of rocks, but also the transformation of rocky landscapes by weathering and erosion.

There are few places where this can be seen more clearly than the Grand Canyon, in Arizona. This spectacular gorge extends 1.1-mile (1.8-km) at its deepest point, where we can see how rocks were laid down layer by layer over hundreds of millions of years, before being lifted by tectonic forces and worn away by water.

The Grand Canyon

Around 65 million years ago, the Colorado River was gently meandering over a fairly flat plain. Then, tectonic forces began to lift the land. The river had to find a way through, so it carved a path through the rocks, revealing 1.7 billion years of Earth's history for geologists to analyze.

Blowing in the wind
By studying sand grains in different layers, geologists know what conditions were like at the time. This layer (the Coconino Sandstone) has smooth grains typical of wind erosion, so they know the land was a desert around 275 mya.

South rim
This side of the canyon receives less rain and snow and leans away from the gorge, so it is less eroded than the North rim.

Cushioned by water
In this layer (called the Hermit Formation), the sand grains are more angular, so geologists know that the area was covered by sea around 280 mya. Water smooths big pebbles, but it cushions tiny sand grains against abrasion.

Only a handful of caves in the canyon have been explored, but it is believed that there are **1,000 caves hidden there.**

Under pressure
More than 1.7 billion years ago, igneous rock (granite) came up from the mantle, changing the sedimentary layers into metamorphic schist.

278 miles (447 km)—**the length** of **the Grand Canyon**.

18 miles (29 km)—**the width** of **the canyon** at its widest point.

30°F (17°C)—how much **hotter** it is, on average, at the bottom of the canyon compared **to the rim**.

63

Flat top
Hard rock layers are not so easily eroded and leave flat-topped headlands (buttes).

Crumbling sides
Over millions of years, water has seeped into gaps in the rock. Water expands as it freezes, cracking the rock and breaking off chunks.

North rim
Almost 1,000 ft (300 m) higher than the South rim, it is colder here, and more exposed to rain and snow. The canyon on this side is therefore more eroded.

Wet and dry
Many of the layers in the canyon are sedimentary—either sandstone (from when the area was a sandy desert), or limestone (laid down under warm, shallow seas that covered the land).

Kaibab Limestone (270 mya)
This hard limestone cap was formed in a warm shallow sea.

Coconino Sandstone (275 mya)
The area was covered by desert.

Redwall Limestone (340 mya)
Another ocean-covered period

Bright Angel Shale (515–505 mya)
This silt and mudstone layer formed in a river delta or shallow seashore.

Vishnu Basement Rocks (1.68+ billion years old)
These igneous and metamorphic rocks were formed by intense heat and pressure.

Tilted and faulted
Around 1.4 billion years ago these ancient rocks were tilted, faulted (cracked), and uplifted, then eroded.

Missing chapter from the book
Some time between 1.5 billion years ago and 550 mya, the ground was tilted and eroded before new flat layers were laid on top. One billion years of rock layers are missing in between, and scientists are trying to figure out why.

The White Cliffs of Iturup

Not all rock is hard! These cliffs of soft, white pumice are freshly eroded into a network of gullies each time it rains.

Iturup is part of a volcanic island arc, the Kuril Islands, off the coast of Japan—a section of the Pacific Ring of Fire. The volcanoes are fed by dark, dense basalt, but as the lava quickly cools, gas bubbles get trapped and create a light, porous rock called pumice.

Fossils

Fossils are the preserved remains of plants and animals that were buried in sediments. By unearthing fossils, paleontologists (fossil experts) can explore past worlds.

Layers of sedimentary rock can read like the pages of a book. They show the story of life on Earth, from the first sponge through the greatest dinosaurs to humans. Hard body parts, such as bones, teeth, and shell, are more likely to be preserved as fossils. However, traces of soft parts, such as skin and feathers, are sometimes found.

Digging for dinosaurs

Some 125 million years ago (mya), volcanoes in Liaoning province in northeastern China produced thick clouds of ash and pyroclastic flows, suffocating animals and burying them. Today, the area reveals fantastic fossils, particularly of dinosaurs. This is a cross section of rock from the Early Cretaceous period (131–120 mya) exposed by a dig.

Baby mammoth

In 2007, an icy tomb in the Siberian permafrost thawed out, revealing a perfectly preserved baby mammoth. Although this animal died 42,000 years ago, scientists found her mother's milk in her stomach. More than a quarter of the woolly mammoth's DNA (the unique set of instructions found inside all life) has been recovered.

Psittacosaurus (120 MYA)

The name means "parrot lizard." Although this plant-eating dinosaur had a beak, it was not directly related to birds. One well-preserved fossil has clumps of long bristles on its tail.

Long hind legs
Psittacosaurus was up to 6 ft (2 m) long and walked on its back legs. Its large eyes suggest it may have been active at night.

Liaoningocladus boii
This fossilized leaf would have fallen from a conifer tree on a wooded lake shore.

Confuciusornis (122 MYA)

Named after the Chinese philosopher Confucius, this crow-sized bird is the first known to have a beak without teeth. Hundreds have been discovered in the rocks of Liaoning, including 40 in a single layer.

Tail feathers
Confuciusornis was covered in feathers. Some fossils show long tail streamers that were probably for display.

Fossilized footprint
We can tell how big a creature was by studying its footprints. These are from a *Jeholosaurus,* a three-toed ornithopod dinosaur with an estimated body length of 28 in (71 cm).

Clawed fingers
Confuciusornis had strong clawed fingers on its wings, used to perch on trees.

Dinosaur skull
The skull of a young dinosaur is still lodged in the rock face, along with many other fossils.

77 tons (70 metric tons)—the estimated **weight of *Argentinosaurus*,** one of the **heaviest dinosaurs** ever found.

2.5 ft (75 cm)—the wingspan of a **dragonfly fossil** from **275 million years ago.** That is roughly the **same size as a crow.**

67

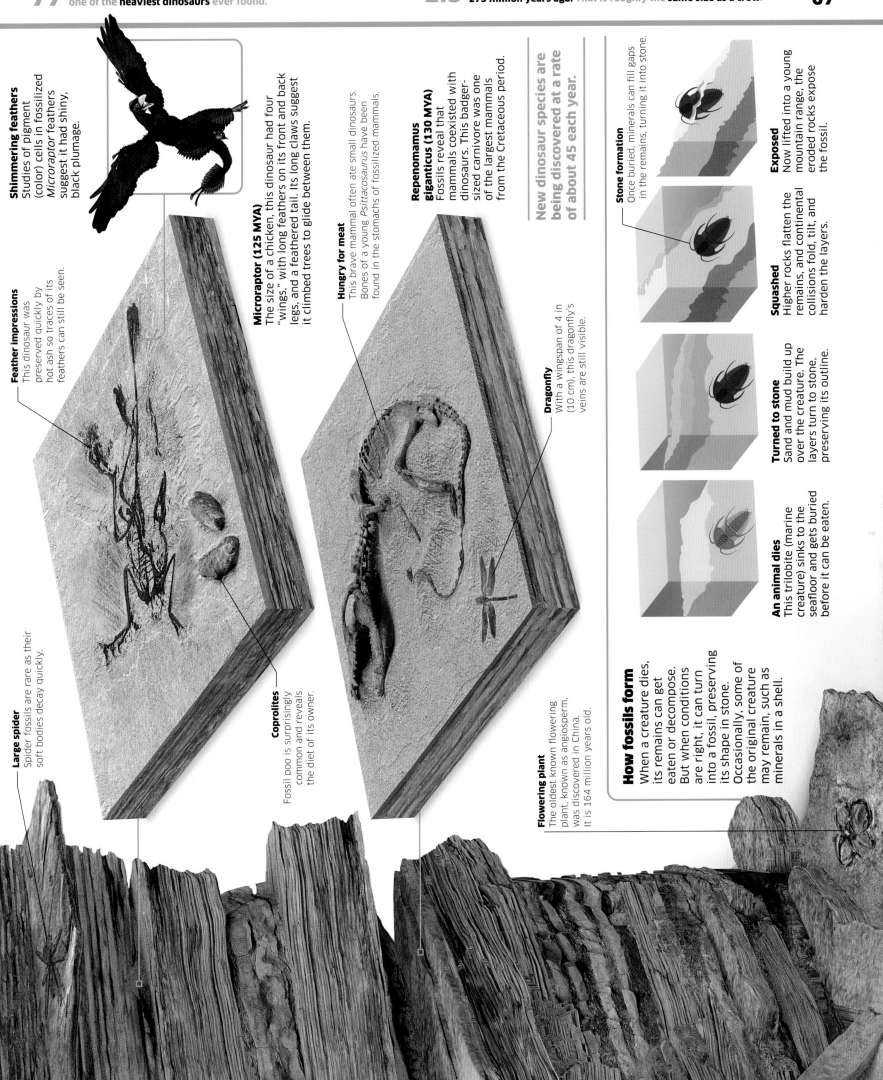

Shimmering feathers
Studies of pigment (color) cells in fossilized *Microraptor* feathers suggest it had shiny, black plumage.

Feather impressions
This dinosaur was preserved quickly by hot ash so traces of its feathers can still be seen.

Microraptor (125 MYA)
The size of a chicken, this dinosaur had four "wings," with long feathers on its front and back legs, and a feathered tail. Its long claws suggest it climbed trees to glide between them.

Hungry for meat
This brave mammal often ate small dinosaurs. Bones of a young *Psittacosaurus* have been found in the stomachs of fossilized mammals.

Repenomamus giganticus (130 MYA)
Fossils reveal that mammals coexisted with dinosaurs. This badger-sized carnivore was one of the largest mammals from the Cretaceous period.

New dinosaur species are being discovered at a rate of about 45 each year.

Large spider
Spider fossils are rare as their soft bodies decay quickly.

Coprolites
Fossil poo is surprisingly common and reveals the diet of its owner.

Dragonfly
With a wingspan of 4 in (10 cm), this dragonfly's veins are still visible.

Flowering plant
The oldest known flowering plant, known as angiosperm, was discovered in China. It is 164 million years old.

How fossils form
When a creature dies, its remains can get eaten or decompose. But when conditions are right, it can turn into a fossil, preserving its shape in stone. Occasionally, some of the original creature may remain, such as minerals in a shell.

An animal dies
This trilobite (marine creature) sinks to the seafloor and gets buried before it can be eaten.

Turned to stone
Sand and mud build up over the creature. The layers turn to stone, preserving its outline.

Squashed
Higher rocks flatten the remains, and continental collisions fold, tilt, and harden the layers.

Stone formation
Once buried, minerals can fill gaps in the remains, turning it into stone.

Exposed
Now lifted into a young mountain range, the eroded rocks expose the fossil.

BLUE PLANET

Rushing and flowing from small mountain streams all the way into vast oceans, the water on Earth is an ever-moving resource that supports all life. As it travels, it carves out dramatic features in the landscape–from icy mountain caves to large lakes that stretch across continents.

EARTH'S WATER

From rain droplets in the clouds to the deepest ocean trenches and from snow on mountain tops to rivers, lakes, and oceans, water makes its way through Earth, shaping the landscapes around it. Without water, there would be no life on Earth.

WHAT IS WATER?

While we tend to think of water as a tasteless, colorless liquid, it is one of the only substances that exists naturally in three states: solid, liquid, and gas. Water is a compound of two elements: hydrogen and oxygen. It exists as molecules. Each molecule is made up of two hydrogen atoms joined to one oxygen atom.

Solid, liquid, and gas

Water changes state depending on its temperature. It can be found as solid ice (below 32°F or 0°C), as liquid water, or as water vapor (above 212°F or 100°C).

Clouds
Tiny water droplets make up clouds in the atmosphere.

Water vapor
Water is found in the atmosphere in the form of water vapor.

Sea
Most of Earth's water is liquid water held in the oceans.

Ice
Water that is frozen solid on Earth's surface occurs as ice.

Changing states

Through the water cycle, water can freeze and turn to ice, and melting ice turns to water. Liquid water may also evaporate to form water vapor or condense back to water. Through deposition, water vapor can turn into ice without first melting and changing to a liquid. The reverse process is called sublimation.

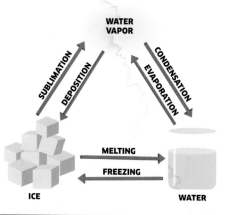

WATER VAPOR

SUBLIMATION
DEPOSITION
CONDENSATION
EVAPORATION

MELTING
FREEZING

ICE
WATER

WHERE IS EARTH'S WATER?

About 97 percent of Earth's water occurs as saltwater in the oceans. The remaining water is freshwater, including water locked in ice caps, snow and glaciers, groundwater, and in lakes, rivers, and streams. The atmosphere holds roughly 0.004 percent of Earth's water, with clouds carrying a tiny proportion (less than 0.001 percent).

Water distribution on Earth

It may seem as though there is plentiful water on Earth, but the majority is held in the oceans. Although some animals, such as gulls and sea lions, are able to consume seawater, it is undrinkable for most land mammals due to its high salinity.

Earth's total water
Compared to Earth's size, the total volume of liquid water is very small.

Earth's surface
About 71 percent of the Earth is covered by water. The remaining 29 percent is land.

Freshwater
Only 3 percent of Earth's water is freshwater. This includes water under the surface, called groundwater.

ALL WATER

Saltwater
The vast majority (97 percent) of water on Earth is salty water found in oceans.

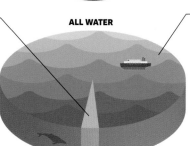

Ice caps and glaciers
Almost 70 percent of Earth's total freshwater is locked up in ice caps.

ALL FRESHWATER

Groundwater
About 30 percent of freshwater is found as groundwater in spaces under Earth's surface.

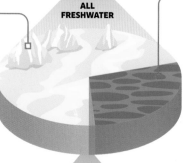

Ground ice and permafrost
Most surface freshwater is in ground ice and permafrost–soil that is frozen permanently.

SURFACE WATER AND OTHER FRESHWATER

Lakes
More than 20 percent of surface water is stored in depressions on Earth's surface called lakes.

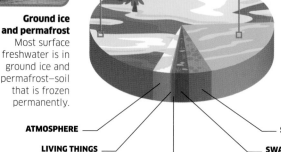

ATMOSPHERE

LIVING THINGS

RIVERS

SOIL MOISTURE

SWAMPS AND MARSHES

RIVER BASINS AND WATERSHEDS

Freshwater flows in rivers from their source down to the sea. A river basin is an area of land drained by a river and its tributaries and can vary greatly in shape, size, and complexity depending on its location. The boundary of a river basin is called a watershed.

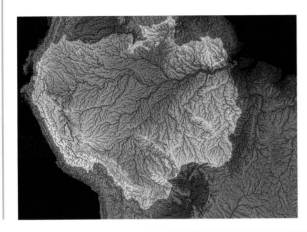

Amazon basin
The Amazon River and its tributaries drain a large area of land, from its headwaters in the Peruvian Andes to its delta in Brazil, where it joins the Atlantic Ocean. It is the largest drainage system in the world.

Ocean salinity

The average chemical composition of the ocean is approximately 4.5 oz (128 g) of salts per gallon (3.8 liters) of water. Sodium chloride makes up the bulk of salts in seawater, followed by magnesium, sulfate, and calcite.

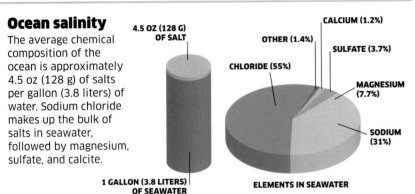

4.5 OZ (128 G) OF SALT

1 GALLON (3.8 LITERS) OF SEAWATER

CALCIUM (1.2%)
OTHER (1.4%)
SULFATE (3.7%)
CHLORIDE (55%)
MAGNESIUM (7.7%)
SODIUM (31%)

ELEMENTS IN SEAWATER

OCEAN WATER

The oceans of the world contain a vast quantity of seawater. This has a number of a properties that vary with depth, place, and the seasons. Among these, the concentration of salts changes along with temperature, driving currents that affect Earth's climate.

Ocean temperature

This cross section of the North Atlantic in summer shows how ocean temperature varies with depth. The surface layer, which is 100–1,000 ft (30–300 m) deep, is warmer than the underlying colder, saltier waters.

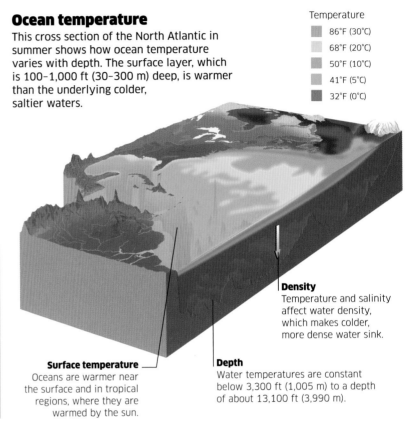

Temperature
86°F (30°C)
68°F (20°C)
50°F (10°C)
41°F (5°C)
32°F (0°C)

Density
Temperature and salinity affect water density, which makes colder, more dense water sink.

Surface temperature
Oceans are warmer near the surface and in tropical regions, where they are warmed by the sun.

Depth
Water temperatures are constant below 3,300 ft (1,005 m) to a depth of about 13,100 ft (3,990 m).

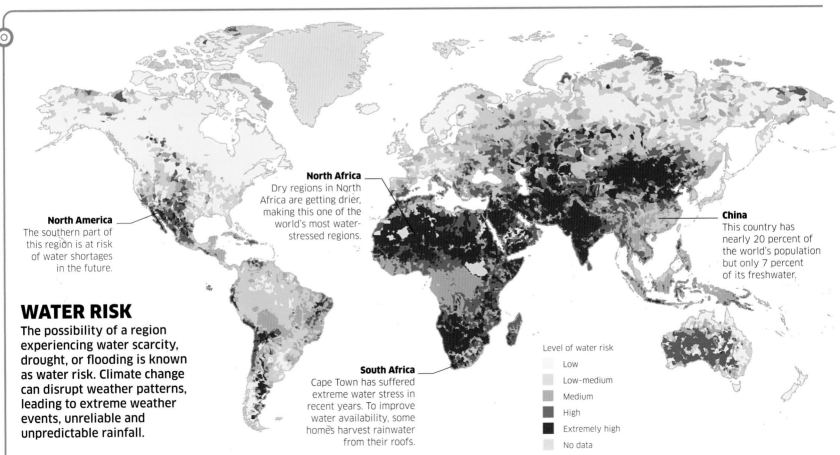

WATER RISK

The possibility of a region experiencing water scarcity, drought, or flooding is known as water risk. Climate change can disrupt weather patterns, leading to extreme weather events, unreliable and unpredictable rainfall.

North America
The southern part of this region is at risk of water shortages in the future.

North Africa
Dry regions in North Africa are getting drier, making this one of the world's most water-stressed regions.

China
This country has nearly 20 percent of the world's population but only 7 percent of its freshwater.

South Africa
Cape Town has suffered extreme water stress in recent years. To improve water availability, some homes harvest rainwater from their roofs.

Level of water risk
Low
Low-medium
Medium
High
Extremely high
No data

72 blue planet ○ **THE WATER CYCLE**

44 percent of **household wastewater** around the world was **not safely treated** before returning to the **water cycle in 2020.**

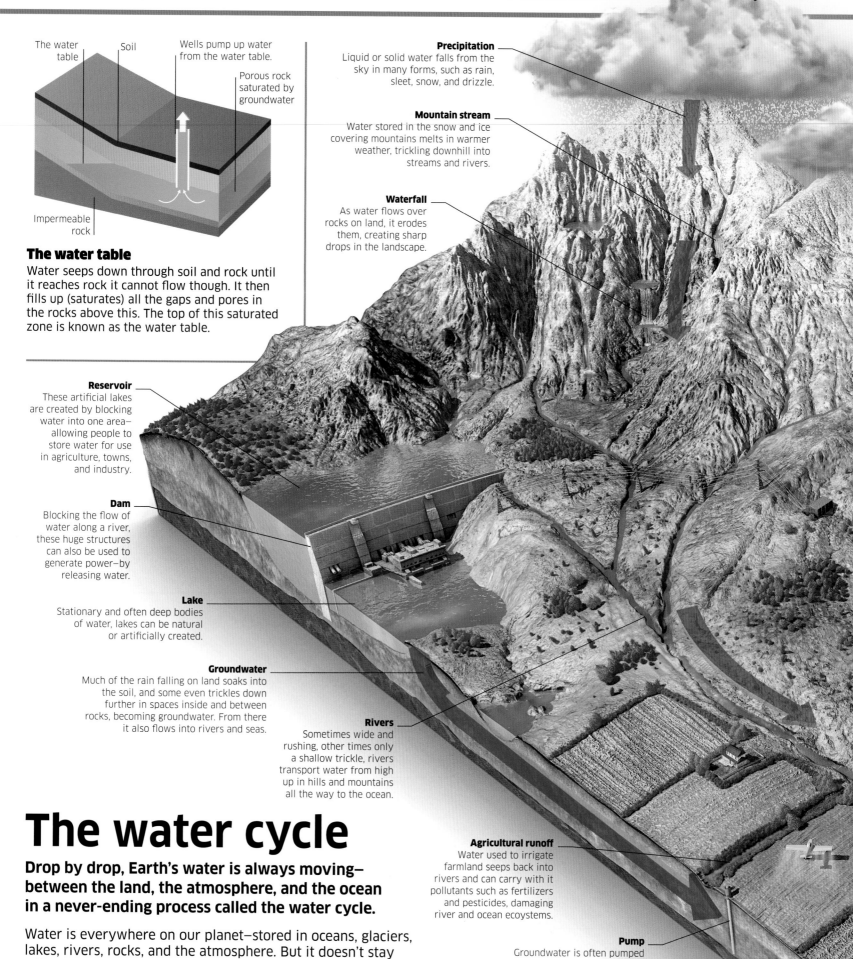

The water table | Soil | Wells pump up water from the water table. | Porous rock saturated by groundwater

Impermeable rock

The water table
Water seeps down through soil and rock until it reaches rock it cannot flow though. It then fills up (saturates) all the gaps and pores in the rocks above this. The top of this saturated zone is known as the water table.

Precipitation
Liquid or solid water falls from the sky in many forms, such as rain, sleet, snow, and drizzle.

Mountain stream
Water stored in the snow and ice covering mountains melts in warmer weather, trickling downhill into streams and rivers.

Waterfall
As water flows over rocks on land, it erodes them, creating sharp drops in the landscape.

Reservoir
These artificial lakes are created by blocking water into one area—allowing people to store water for use in agriculture, towns, and industry.

Dam
Blocking the flow of water along a river, these huge structures can also be used to generate power—by releasing water.

Lake
Stationary and often deep bodies of water, lakes can be natural or artificially created.

Groundwater
Much of the rain falling on land soaks into the soil, and some even trickles down further in spaces inside and between rocks, becoming groundwater. From there it also flows into rivers and seas.

Rivers
Sometimes wide and rushing, other times only a shallow trickle, rivers transport water from high up in hills and mountains all the way to the ocean.

The water cycle

Drop by drop, Earth's water is always moving— between the land, the atmosphere, and the ocean in a never-ending process called the water cycle.

Water is everywhere on our planet—stored in oceans, glaciers, lakes, rivers, rocks, and the atmosphere. But it doesn't stay still. Heat from the sun causes seawater to evaporate and turn into water vapor in the atmosphere. Here it cools, forming clouds, dew, or fog, and falls back to the land as rain or snow. There, rushing, flowing rivers carry it back to the ocean, where the cycle begins again.

Agricultural runoff
Water used to irrigate farmland seeps back into rivers and can carry with it pollutants such as fertilizers and pesticides, damaging river and ocean ecosystems.

Pump
Groundwater is often pumped up to the surface and used on farms or for other purposes.

Arable farm land
Crops need to be watered, or irrigated, which can require a large amount of water.

3000 BCE—the age of the **oldest known dam,** built in Jordan.

40,000 gallons (151,000 liters)—the amount of water a large oak tree can release into the atmosphere every year.

73

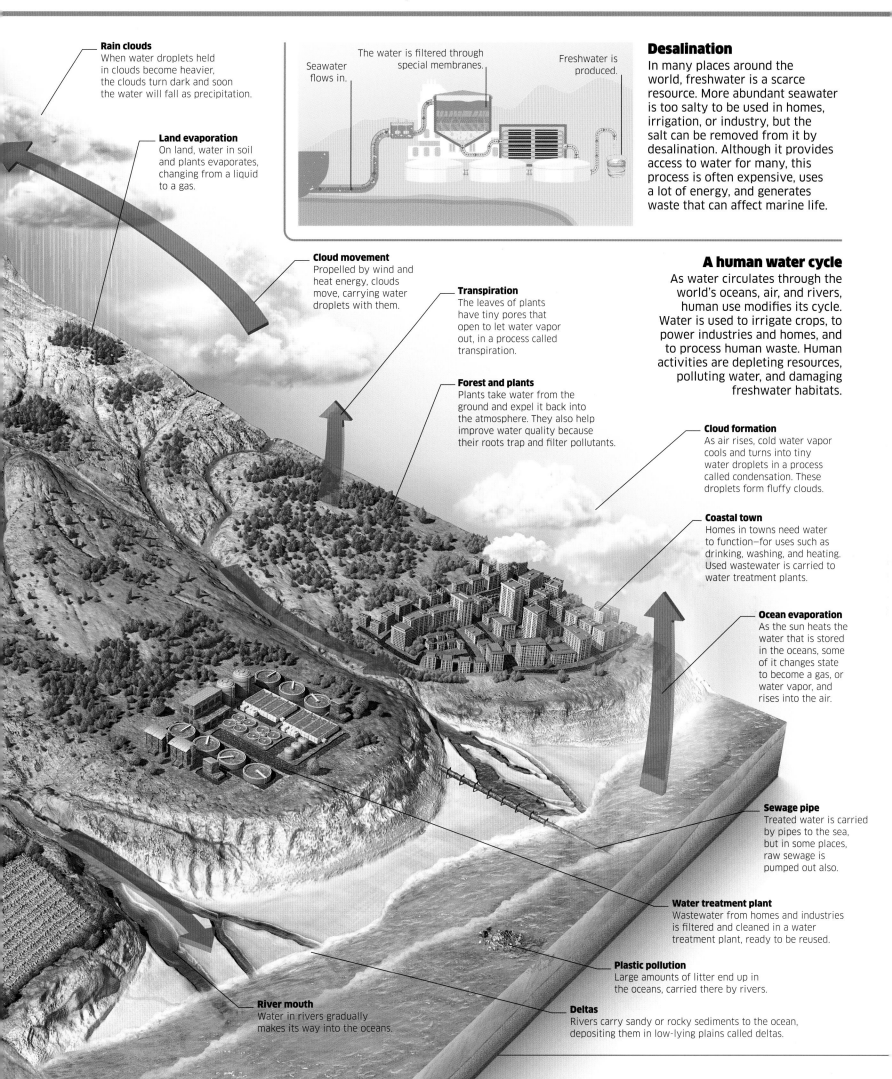

Rain clouds
When water droplets held in clouds become heavier, the clouds turn dark and soon the water will fall as precipitation.

Land evaporation
On land, water in soil and plants evaporates, changing from a liquid to a gas.

Seawater flows in.

The water is filtered through special membranes.

Freshwater is produced.

Desalination
In many places around the world, freshwater is a scarce resource. More abundant seawater is too salty to be used in homes, irrigation, or industry, but the salt can be removed from it by desalination. Although it provides access to water for many, this process is often expensive, uses a lot of energy, and generates waste that can affect marine life.

Cloud movement
Propelled by wind and heat energy, clouds move, carrying water droplets with them.

Transpiration
The leaves of plants have tiny pores that open to let water vapor out, in a process called transpiration.

Forest and plants
Plants take water from the ground and expel it back into the atmosphere. They also help improve water quality because their roots trap and filter pollutants.

A human water cycle
As water circulates through the world's oceans, air, and rivers, human use modifies its cycle. Water is used to irrigate crops, to power industries and homes, and to process human waste. Human activities are depleting resources, polluting water, and damaging freshwater habitats.

Cloud formation
As air rises, cold water vapor cools and turns into tiny water droplets in a process called condensation. These droplets form fluffy clouds.

Coastal town
Homes in towns need water to function—for uses such as drinking, washing, and heating. Used wastewater is carried to water treatment plants.

Ocean evaporation
As the sun heats the water that is stored in the oceans, some of it changes state to become a gas, or water vapor, and rises into the air.

Sewage pipe
Treated water is carried by pipes to the sea, but in some places, raw sewage is pumped out also.

Water treatment plant
Wastewater from homes and industries is filtered and cleaned in a water treatment plant, ready to be reused.

Plastic pollution
Large amounts of litter end up in the oceans, carried there by rivers.

River mouth
Water in rivers gradually makes its way into the oceans.

Deltas
Rivers carry sandy or rocky sediments to the ocean, depositing them in low-lying plains called deltas.

74 blue planet ○ **GLACIERS**

170 ft (50 m)—the usual **maximum height reached by drumlins,** which occur in **clusters of hundreds** or even **thousands**.

Glaciers

When snow falls and builds up on mountain slopes, glaciers start to form— huge flowing streams of ice that carve mighty paths down mountains.

Glaciers exist only in areas that are cold enough for winter snowfall to survive the summer thaw. Pushed downward by the force of gravity and their own weight, these huge icy masses carve out valleys as they flow and leave behind sediments and debris when they melt. Today, glaciers are retreating at alarming rates due to climate change.

Glaciated valleys

Glaciers can flow for hundreds of thousands of years—leaving behind a dramatically altered landscape when they melt. This valley glacier formed from the merging of two others high up in the mountains. Plowing through its surroundings while carrying rocky debris, it created many unique geographical features.

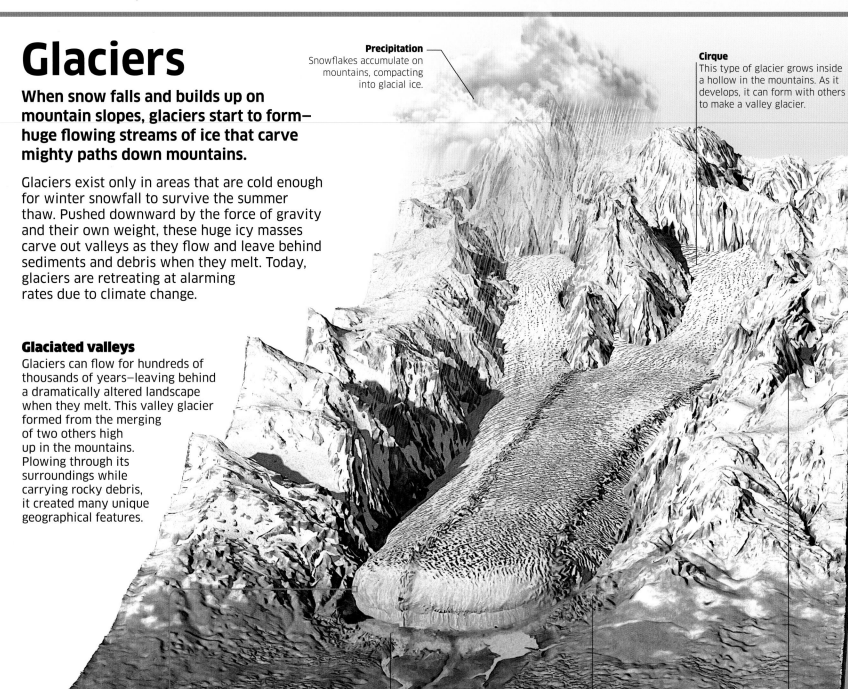

Precipitation
Snowflakes accumulate on mountains, compacting into glacial ice.

Cirque
This type of glacier grows inside a hollow in the mountains. As it develops, it can form with others to make a valley glacier.

Meltwater
A stream of meltwater flows out of the base of the glacier at its end, or terminus.

Terminal morraine
Semicircular deposits of rock debris form at the end of the glacier.

Rocky walls
A valley glacier is surrounded by peaks of rock on both sides.

Terminus
The glacier's clifflike edge or ending is called its terminus. This moves forward when the glacier advances and retreats when the glacier stops flowing and starts to melt. Huge chunks of ice can break off it and crash into the chilly lake below.

Fjords

When valley glaciers form next to coastlines, the glaciers melt, leaving behind deep, glacial-carved valleys that are filled by the sea. These long, narrow fjords are spectacular geological landforms and are popular tourist sites in many countries, such as Norway, where there are more than a thousand.

11,000 years ago—the **end of the last period of glaciation.**

2.1 ft (65 m)—the **estimated sea level rise if all the ice in the Thwaites Glacier, Antarctica**—nicknamed the Doomsday glacier—**were to melt.**

75

Pyramidal peak
The sharp sides of these peaks are formed when mountains are eroded by glacial ice.

Tarn lake
The hollow created by a cirque glacier is now filled by a lake.

Truncated spur
This rocky protrusion is a mountain ridge that has had its end cut off by a glacier.

Glacial striations
Rocks hold evidence of past glaciers. These striations or scratches were carved out by sharp debris carried by the ice as it moved over the rocks.

River valleys
Glaciers carve out U-shaped valleys in the landscape. When rivers flow through them, the valleys are reworked into V-shapes.

Floodplain
Away from the steep mountains, the land becomes flatter, and streams and rivers periodically flood an area called the floodplain.

Erratics
Blocks of rocks carried by the glacial ice dot the landscape.

Ribbon lake
A long, narrow lake fills a depression left behind by glacial erosion.

Kettle lake
As ice hidden under glacial deposits melts, a depression forms, later filling with water.

Drumlins
Clusters of low, oval-shaped mounds of glacial deposits are aligned with the direction of ice flow, giving scientists clues about past glacier movement.

Retreating glaciers

Scientists are tracking glaciers to reveal how global warming has affected them. The Muir Glacier, in Alaska, once covered the landscape. Since 1941, the ice has retreated incredibly rapidly, by more than 7 miles (12 km), and its thickness has reduced by more than 2,625 ft (800 m). Retreating glaciers can threaten nearby water supplies, and cause landslides and flooding.

1941

2004

Cool cavern

Meltwater running through or under glaciers can carve out cavities that grow into dramatic ice caves hidden between the ice and the rock or sediment below.

Deep inside Iceland's vast Vatnajökull Glacier, water flowing beneath the ice sculpts large caves. These ice-blue caves change all the time, as water melts and freezes again. Glacial melting can release sediments that were locked in the ice, giving the caves their distinctive crystal blue color in the light. As glaciers are melting at unprecedented rates due to climate change, ice caves are becoming rarer.

78 blue planet ○ **RIVERS**

The **Amazon River** is the **largest river** in the world **by volume**.

2 million—the estimated **number** of **streams** in the US.

Upland areas

Rivers usually start their course upstream, in higher areas of land. When rain falls on high ground, or snow and ice on mountains melt, water gathers and starts to flow in channels. Water may also come from springs, where it is held underground as groundwater and then flows to the surface through an opening.

Precipitation
Clouds release rain and snow, which add water to rivers.

River source
This is one of the sources of the river Ljubljanica in Slovenia. Here, groundwater reaching the surface is feeding the river.

Valleys, canyons, and gorges

As rivers flow over steep slopes, they wear away the rocks under them, gradually sculpting the landscape by creating valleys, depressions on Earth's surface. When valleys are sculpted by rivers, they are V-shaped. Canyons and gorges are narrow valleys with tall, rocky walls.

Taroko Gorge
A river flows through this very steep, narrow gorge in Taiwan.

From source to sea

A river runs down from snowcapped mountains to the sea, shaping landscapes along the way. A river's shape, energy, and size changes as it flows downstream.

Higher tributary
These often start off in uplands.

Lower tributary
Later, tributaries merge and flow into the main river.

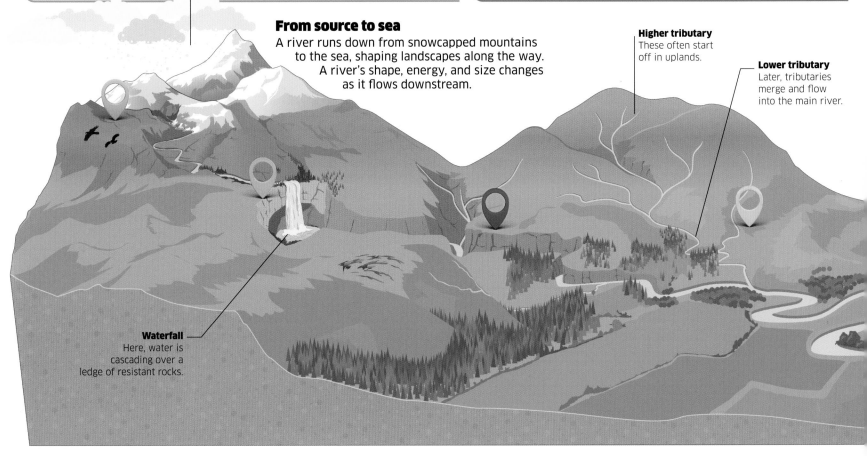

Waterfall
Here, water is cascading over a ledge of resistant rocks.

Rivers

Fresh water flowing from mountains and hills down to the sea along a clearly defined route, or channel, is called a river. Rivers can sculpt a landscape, eroding sediments, transporting them, and depositing them further downstream.

At the start of their life, rivers rush rapidly down steep slopes and valleys, creating waterfalls and rapids. Smaller streams join the main river channel and continue to flow downstream. As the landscape becomes flatter, rivers slow down and become curvier. Rivers eventually flow into the sea or another body of water, such as a lake.

Waterfalls

As rivers flow, they erode the rocks in the landscape under them, wearing them away. When rivers flow over a layer of hard rock overlying softer rocks, the water erodes the softer rocks. The harder rocks are left behind as a step in the landscape, creating a waterfall. Over time, the water erodes the more resistant rock too.

A steep fall of water
At Seljalandsfoss Waterfall in Iceland, water is cascading over a ledge of hard rocks.

741 ft (226 m)—the **height** of **Kaieteur Falls** in Guyana.

4,160 miles (6,695 km)—the **length** of **the Nile**, generally credited as the **longest river in the world**.

11 miles (19 km)—the **length** of **Taroko Gorge** in Taiwan.

79

Tributaries

Rivers are fed by smaller side streams called tributaries, which typically start in areas of high ground. These streams eventually merge with a larger river, which is flowing downstream toward the sea, transporting water and sediment. The total area that feeds water to a stream or river is called a drainage basin.

Small tributaries
Thousands of streams often feed very large rivers, like the Everglades "River of Grass" in Florida.

Meanders

In flat land, the water flow slows down and rivers form loops called meanders. These snakelike curves form when one bank of the river is eroded more than the other, due to the speed of the water being greater at the outside of the bends in a river. Eroded sediment is deposited on the inside of the next bend, where the river flows slowly. The shape of a meander changes over time, but they are often known as "S bends."

Outside of the river curve
Fast-flowing water erodes the sediment here.

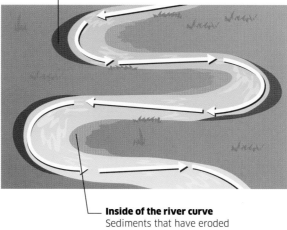

Inside of the river curve
Sediments that have eroded upstream are deposited here.

River mouth

The end of a river, where it flows into the sea or a lake, is called its mouth. This is where rivers release their water and sediment. Some rivers deposit sediment outward at the mouth, forming a buildup called a delta. The area at a river's mouth where sea water mixes with fresh water is called an estuary.

River meets the ocean
At the river's mouth, sediments such as sand are deposited.

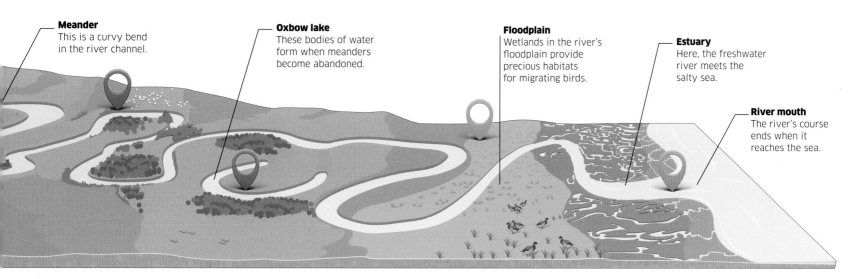

Meander
This is a curvy bend in the river channel.

Oxbow lake
These bodies of water form when meanders become abandoned.

Floodplain
Wetlands in the river's floodplain provide precious habitats for migrating birds.

Estuary
Here, the freshwater river meets the salty sea.

River mouth
The river's course ends when it reaches the sea.

Oxbow lakes

As sediment is eroded and deposited by meandering rivers (see above), their loops become more pronounced. After rain, a fast-flowing river may flood and carve out a more direct channel, cutting off a loop. This then forms a crescent-shaped lake.

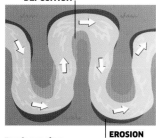

DEPOSITION

EROSION

Bank erosion
Meanders become more exaggerated as the land along the edge of a river is eroded.

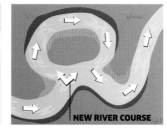

NEW RIVER COURSE

Flooding
If the river bursts its banks during a flood, it may cut a new, straighter course.

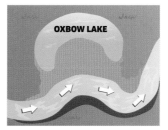

OXBOW LAKE

Oxbow lake
The meander is cut off from the main river course and forms an oxbow lake.

Floodplain

Rivers can flood periodically, bursting their banks. The flatland surrounding a river channel that becomes submerged in times of flood is called a floodplain.

Levees
These are ridges of sediment that build up at the boundaries between river channels and floodplains.

Waterfalls

Rivers carve out spectacular natural features, such as waterfalls. These bodies of water fall over a steep ledge, often flowing over different types of rocks.

When a river flows down a slope, it speeds up and may cascade downhill as turbulent rapids. This fast-flowing water erodes the soft rock below, making the riverbed steeper. However, if there is harder rock on top, a waterfall may form.

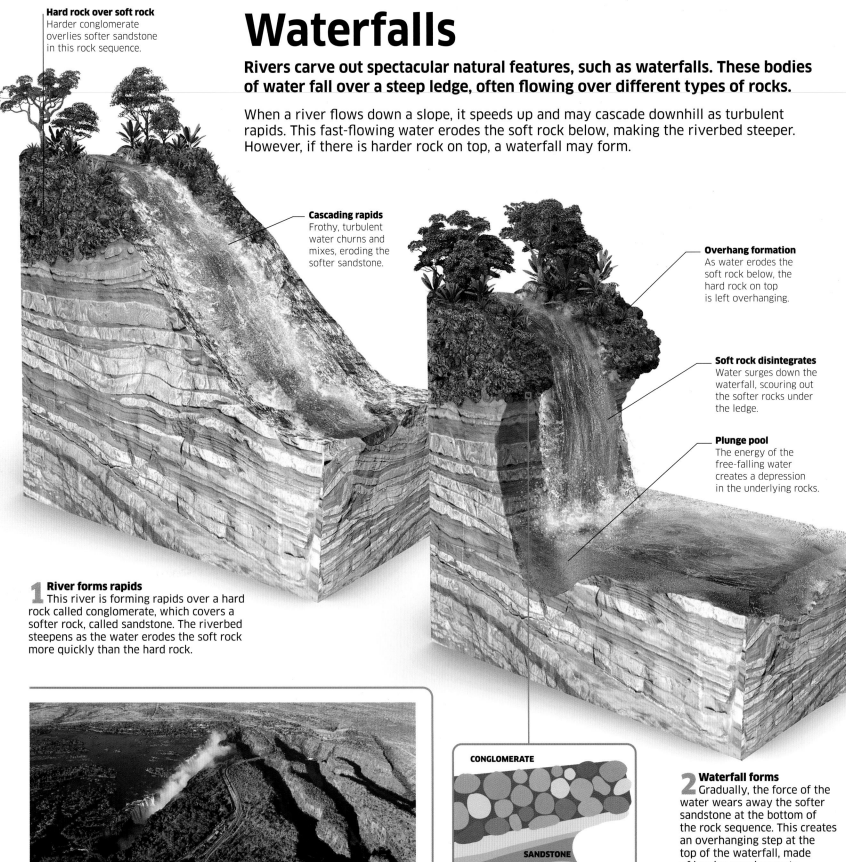

Hard rock over soft rock
Harder conglomerate overlies softer sandstone in this rock sequence.

Cascading rapids
Frothy, turbulent water churns and mixes, eroding the softer sandstone.

Overhang formation
As water erodes the soft rock below, the hard rock on top is left overhanging.

Soft rock disintegrates
Water surges down the waterfall, scouring out the softer rocks under the ledge.

Plunge pool
The energy of the free-falling water creates a depression in the underlying rocks.

1 River forms rapids
This river is forming rapids over a hard rock called conglomerate, which covers a softer rock, called sandstone. The riverbed steepens as the water erodes the soft rock more quickly than the hard rock.

CONGLOMERATE

SANDSTONE

2 Waterfall forms
Gradually, the force of the water wears away the softer sandstone at the bottom of the rock sequence. This creates an overhanging step at the top of the waterfall, made of harder conglomerate.

Victoria Falls

Between Zambia and Zimbabwe, the Zambezi River flows over gorges made of basalt and sandstone, creating Victoria Falls. The gorges formed 180 million years ago, when cooling lava made cracks in the ground. Later, when the river changed direction, water wore away the fractures. Over time, the waterfall has retreated from crack to crack.

Layers of rock
Here, a layer of sandstone was deposited first by an ancient river. It is older than the overlying conglomerate, a sedimentary rock containing large pebbles called clasts, deposited by a later river.

Billions of gallons
(liters) of water cascade over Niagara Falls, which retreats by 1 ft (0.3 m) yearly.

The energy of water at waterfalls can be **converted to electricity**. This is known as **hydroelectric power**.

355 ft (108 m)—the height of **Victoria Falls**, the world's largest continuous sheet of falling water.

81

Canyon formation

As they flow, streams and rivers erode their channels downward toward the base level, the lowest level to which they can erode. Streams can carve deep trenches in a landscape. They are called valleys if they have gently sloping walls or canyons if their walls slope steeply.

Steep-sided canyon
Massive sandstone cliffs rise up on either side of this narrow slot canyon in the Zion National Park in Utah.

Slot canyons
If a stream erodes downward faster than the canyon walls can collapse, a slot canyon forms.

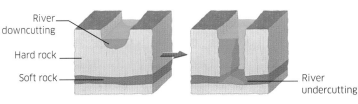

River downcutting
Hard rock
Soft rock
River undercutting

Stair-step canyons
When water cuts through alternating hard and soft layers of rock, a stair-step shape develops.

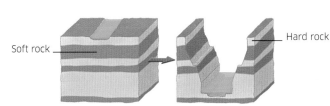

Soft rock
Hard rock

V-shaped valley
If the walls collapse as fast as the stream erodes downward, landslides create a V-shaped valley.

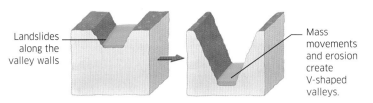

Landslides along the valley walls
Mass movements and erosion create V-shaped valleys.

How waterfalls form

When water flows over soft rock, erosion begins. When it flows over a layer of hard rock, an overhanging step in the riverbed is created. The water cascades down the step in a waterfall. As the water erodes the harder rock, the overhang falls into the pool below. This cycle of erosion continues, eventually wearing away the step and flattening the landscape.

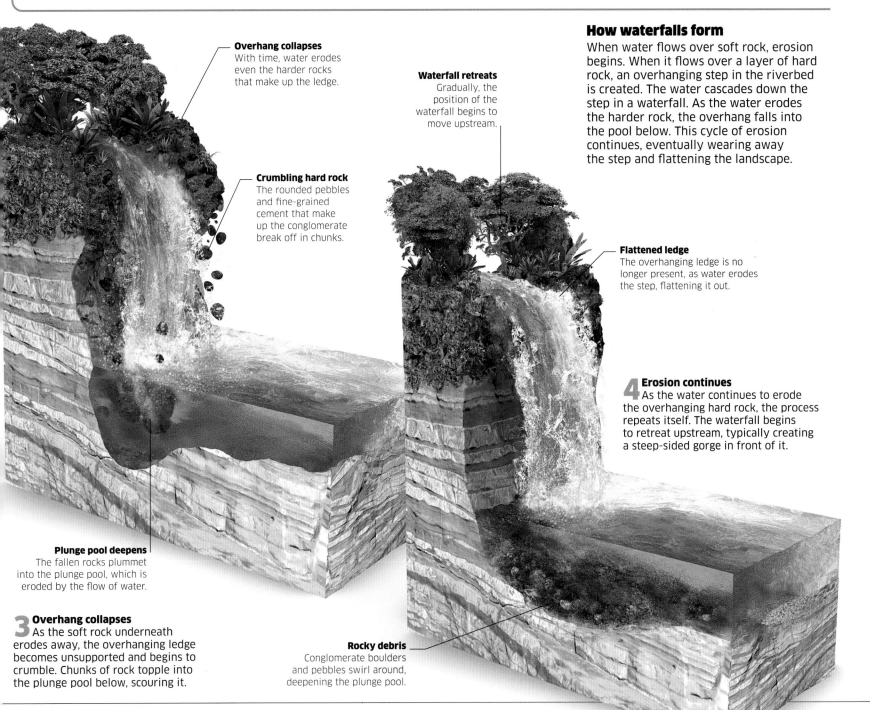

Overhang collapses
With time, water erodes even the harder rocks that make up the ledge.

Crumbling hard rock
The rounded pebbles and fine-grained cement that make up the conglomerate break off in chunks.

Waterfall retreats
Gradually, the position of the waterfall begins to move upstream.

Flattened ledge
The overhanging ledge is no longer present, as water erodes the step, flattening it out.

4 Erosion continues
As the water continues to erode the overhanging hard rock, the process repeats itself. The waterfall begins to retreat upstream, typically creating a steep-sided gorge in front of it.

Plunge pool deepens
The fallen rocks plummet into the plunge pool, which is eroded by the flow of water.

3 Overhang collapses
As the soft rock underneath erodes away, the overhanging ledge becomes unsupported and begins to crumble. Chunks of rock topple into the plunge pool below, scouring it.

Rocky debris
Conglomerate boulders and pebbles swirl around, deepening the plunge pool.

82 blue planet ○ **LAKES**

Tiny lakes, measuring only a few
square yards are called ponds.

Lakes

Lakes are bodies of water surrounded by land. The water can come from rivers, rain, melting snow and ice, or groundwater.

Lakes are usually fed by a river, but they can also form when water held underground seeps to the surface or when rainwater collects in a depression. Lake water is relatively still compared to that of rivers, but not completely motionless. Lake currents are driven by wind currents, temperature changes, and slow movements of water in and out of the lake.

⊚ LAKE TYPES

Lakes are so diverse that some scientists recognize more than 70 different types. There are many ways of classifying lakes. One way is to look at how they formed. The most common lakes were formed by retreating glaciers during the last glacial period, but lakes can be formed in other ways too, such as landslides. Some lakes are even made by humans.

Tectonic basins

Movements of the Earth's crust that cause faults can create depressions, which may fill with water to form tectonic lakes. The depressions in which lakes form are called basins. Lake Baikal, in Russia, formed around 25 million years ago when Earth's crust thinned and sank down along faults that border it.

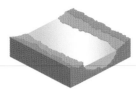

Lake Baikal, Russia
Daily fluctuations in air temperature cause ice to expand during the day and contract at night, leading to the formation of cracks in the ice.

Volcanic lakes

Lakes often form inside inactive volcanoes or craters where the magma is still cooling. If magma chambers empty during a volcanic eruption, the roof of the chamber can collapse, leaving a depression later filled by a lake.

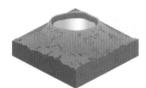

Lake Quilotoa, Ecuador
This lake lies inside a caldera, a volcano whose magma chamber roof has collapsed on itself.

Glacial lakes

When glaciers retreated at the end of the last glacial period, about 10,000 years ago, they left behind many lakes. These lakes formed inside basins scoured by the ice as it slowly eroded and left behind sediments.

Rila Lakes, Bulgaria
A string of seven lakes in this mountain range was formed from the action of ice gradually retreating.

Landslide lakes

If loose debris on a slope suddenly moves and blocks a river, a lake can form. These lakes can range in size, from a few cubic yards to bodies of water several cubic miles and so high they block an entire mountain valley.

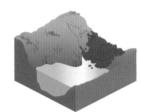

Attabad Lake, Pakistan
On January 4, 2010, a huge landslide blocked the Hunza River, forming this lake.

Solution lakes

When rain or stream water slowly dissolves soluble rocks, basins can form. Over time, these basins can collapse to form sinkholes, which are another cavity in which lakes can form.

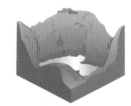

Red Lake, Croatia
A sinkhole formed when the ceiling of a large cave hall collapsed. It later filled with water, becoming a lake.

Fossils can be found in **dry lake beds,** such as **dinosaur footprints** in crater-lake sediments in **Angola**.

5,439 cu miles (22,670 cu km)—the **volume of water** held by the **Great American Lakes**.

83

EXTREME LAKES

Some lakes form on mountain tops, while others form below sea level. The largest lakes in the world contain vast amounts of water or span thousands of miles. The five American Great Lakes (pictured) are large interconnected freshwater lakes that contain one-fifth of the world's fresh water. Lake Superior has the largest surface area of any freshwater lake, but Lake Baikal (also pictured) holds more water than all of the Great Lakes put together.

12,500 ft (3,810 m) above sea level between Peru and Bolivia, Lake Titicaca, is the world's highest navigable lake.
With an area of more than 143,000 sq miles (370,000 sq km), the Caspian Sea is the world's largest inland body of water and biggest salt lake.

Lake Huron
This is the second-largest Great Lake, at 23,000 sq miles (59,000 sq km).

Lake Erie
The shallowest of all the Great Lakes is also the warmest.

Lake Michigan
This is the only Great Lake situated entirely within the US.

Lake Ontario
This lake is smallest of all the Great Lakes in surface area.

Lake Superior
This is the largest lake out of the five, with 2,900 cubic miles (12,100 cubic km) of water.

Lake Baikal
In southeast Siberia in Russia, Lake Baikal is 5,387 ft (1,642 m) deep, making it the world's deepest lake.

BEAVER DAM LAKE

When beavers build dams made of plant material, mud, stones, and other debris, lakes are formed on one side. The dams protect beavers from predators, help to trap nutrients, and also create wetland habitats for many other species. Over time, beavers can create elaborate structures, with several tunnels underneath.

Beaver lodges
These clever herbivores build and maintain small protective domes in the deep pools of water created by their dams, made from sticks, mud, and rocks. The lodges function as a dry living area and as their food store.

SALT LAKES

Most lakes contain fresh water, but some are salty. When lakes are open, which means they have an outlet, their water is generally fresh. When lakes are closed, with no outlet, the only way water can leave is through evaporation. As water evaporates, it leaves behind salts, leading to the formation of salty lakes.

Spotted Lake
This Canadian lake is made up of briny pools. In the fall, it is covered by groundwater, rainwater, and snowmelt, but during the summer, the water evaporates and the pools are exposed. Spotted Lake is also rich in many minerals, including calcium and silver.

Lake Natron
Pink lakes form when particular algae or bacteria release red pigments in salty waters. Lake Natron in Tanzania gets its color from blooms of salt-loving microorganisms known as cyanobacteria.

Dead Sea
Located between Israel, the West Bank, and Jordan, this is one of the world's saltiest lakes. It has been slowly shrinking over the last 50 years, due to irrigation projects that have diverted its source, the Jordan River. This has made the lake's water even saltier.

84 blue planet ○ **CAVES**

400 miles (640 km)—the estimated **length of the world's largest cave system, Mammoth Cave**, **US**.

Limestone pavement
The limestone rock above the cave is riddled with cracks—called grykes—making it look like a human-made pavement.

Rivers
Surface water from rivers can penetrate cracks in the limestone layers, causing them to dissolve and widen over time.

Columns
Over time, stalagmites and stalactites can grow to join each other in single speleothems called columns.

Stalactites
These long pointy mineral formations that hang from the cave's ceiling form over time, as water drips downward.

Soda straws
Translucent and very fragile, smaller, delicate, hollow stalactites are called soda straws.

Flowstone
Over time, groundwater flowing down the surface of cave walls can create clothlike sheets of rock called flowstone.

Drip curtain
Curtainlike layers of calcium carbonate rock deposits form when water flows along the floor and walls of the cave.

Underground stream
Streams and rivers underground flow through passages, carving out channels. They often reemerge from cave entrances further downstream.

Drip-by-drip
Each karst cave is an underground cavity naturally formed as limestone rock dissolves. When mineral-rich groundwater drips into caves, it leaves behind solid mineral deposits. From thin, icicle-like rocks hanging from the cave ceiling, to mounds on the cave floor, the rocks that form inside caves can take many dynamic shapes and are called speleothems.

Cave pool
A stream from above cascades down into the cave, joining a pool of deep water.

Stalagmite
When drips of groundwater hit the cave floor, they build upward-pointing cones called stalagmites.

230 ft (70 m)–the **height of the world's largest stalagmite**, in Cueva San Infierno, Cuba.

6,000 The **number of caves in the Kras plateau**, covering around **27 percent of Slovenia's territory**.

85

Karst landscapes cover around
20 percent
of the world's land surface.

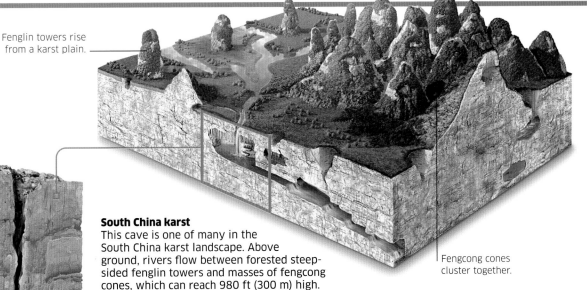

Fenglin towers rise from a karst plain.

Fengcong cones cluster together.

South China karst
This cave is one of many in the South China karst landscape. Above ground, rivers flow between forested steep-sided fenglin towers and masses of fengcong cones, which can reach 980 ft (300 m) high.

Dry cave
As the water table moves, caves that once were full of water can become dry. Some can still grow as groundwater slowly widens the cracks around them.

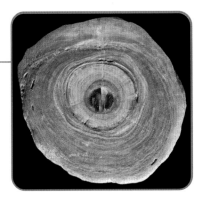

Stalactites
Stalactites are made of thin layers of calcite that have built up over time. By dating these layers and studying their chemistry, scientists can uncover clues about the climates of the past, which helps them study climate change.

Caves

Few landscapes illustrate the dynamic nature of the Earth better than karst landscapes, formed when rocks dissolve. Over time, small cracks can develop into vast underground caves..

Water is the rock sculptor of karst landscapes. Because the groundwater in rocks and soil is slightly acidic, it slowly dissolves types of sedimentary rock such as limestone or dolomite. In regions where the rock is of these types, the water erodes huge sections–creating complex systems of caves and streams deep underground. But these rocky formations do not stay the same for long. Eventually, when the water table (see pages 72–73) drops, the caves dry out and sometimes collapse to form deep sinkholes.

How a karst landscape forms

In order to form, karst needs a thick section of limestone. This rock type forms in ancient oceans and rises to the surface over time. When water reaches and dissolves the rock, the landscape changes dramatically.

Sinkholes and caves form.

1 Sinkholes
Circular depressions on the surface of the terrain start to form where water dissolves the limestone.

Cave network

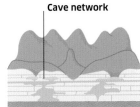

2 Dissolution
A cave network forms as water fills cracks in the rock and dissolves it. New caves form when the water level sinks.

Spires dot the landscape.

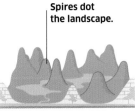

3 Mature landscape
Old caves collapse and the ridges and walls between adjacent sinkholes are eroded, leaving towering spires.

86 blue planet ○ **OCEAN WATERS**

321 million cu miles (1.34 billion cu km)—**how much water** the oceans are estimated to contain.

WORLD CURRENTS

There are two types of ocean currents that flow around the globe: surface currents and deep ocean currents. Whereas surface currents are driven by winds, deepwater currents are affected by a variety of factors, including temperature and salinity. Cold dense water sinks down and travels thousands of miles, before warming and rising up again in a slow global conveyor belt.

Rising up
In the Indian Ocean, cold, deep waters warm up and become less salty, rising up to flow near the surface as they continue their journey.

Gulf Stream
This warm, surface current is responsible for Europe's mild climate.

Gyres
Circular patterns of surface currents are called gyres. These flow counterclockwise in the southern hemisphere and clockwise in the northern hemisphere.

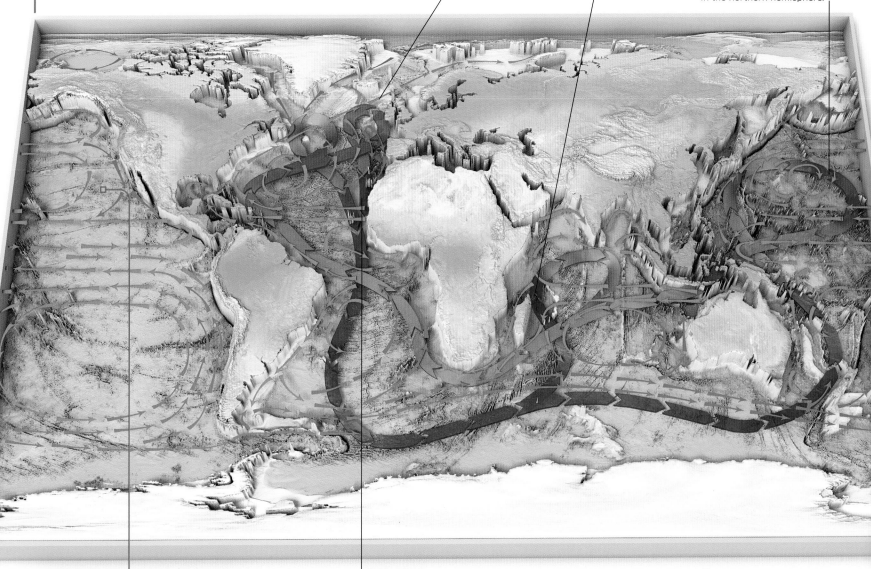

Sinking down
In the North Atlantic, water cools and sinks before traveling south.

Key

→ Cold surface currents

→ Warm surface currents

⫸⫸ Global ocean conveyor

Great Pacific Garbage Patch
Two giant masses of tiny plastic particles and other trash swirl around the North Pacific Ocean, propelled by the surface currents of a gyre. They contain just a small amount of the many plastics that end up in our oceans and enter the marine food chain.

Ocean waters

Full of crashing waves, ebbing and flowing tides, and powerful currents, the oceans and seas around the globe are in constant motion. They contain most of the planet's water.

The vast blue expanses of the world's oceans are visible from space, giving Earth the nickname the blue planet, but it is how the water within them moves that makes these swirling masses so important. As water circulates on the surface or deep down, energy, nutrients, and oxygen are spread around the globe. Ocean water also warms and cools the atmosphere, affecting the weather and climate both at sea and on land.

112 ft (34 m)—the height of the **largest officially recorded wave**, observed in the Pacific Ocean in 1933.

5 trillion—the estimated **number of pieces of plastic** in the oceans, **weighing 250,000 tons** (227,000 metric tons).

87

TIDES

Every day, ocean waters advance and retreat along coastlines due to the rise and fall of tides. But these rapid movements of water are caused by the interaction of the moon, Earth, and the sun—far out in space. The moon is pulled into orbit around Earth by Earth's gravity, but its gravity pulls on Earth, too—affecting the huge amount of water on its surface.

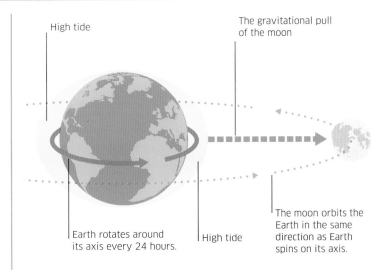

High tide

The gravitational pull of the moon

Earth rotates around its axis every 24 hours.

High tide

The moon orbits the Earth in the same direction as Earth spins on its axis.

Lunar tides

As the Earth rotates on its axis, the moon's gravity pulls a bulge of water toward it, creating a high tide. At the same time, another bulge, or high tide, forms on the opposite side of Earth, flung out by Earth's spin. In between the two bulges, tides are low. There are approximately two tides every 24 hours.

The sun and tides

Twice a month, when the sun, moon, and Earth align, extreme high and low tides occur. This is due to the combined gravitational pull of both the moon and sun. Tides are less extreme when the sun and moon are at right angles to Earth.

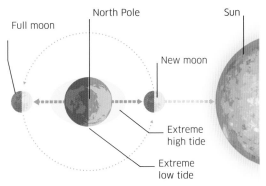

Full moon

North Pole

Sun

New moon

Extreme high tide

Extreme low tide

Spring tides
When Earth is aligned with both the moon and the sun, during a full or a new moon, the biggest tides take place, due to the combined pull of their gravity.

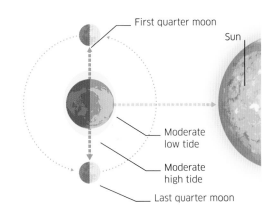

First quarter moon

Sun

Moderate low tide

Moderate high tide

Last quarter moon

Neap tides
The smallest tides occur when the Moon and Sun are at a right angle to Earth, as they each partially cancel out each other's gravitational pull.

Coastal effects

While tides are barely noticeable in the deep ocean, their effects are obvious on coastlines. Most coasts experience two high tides and two low tides every day. The difference in water level between high and low tide is called tidal range, and this can have a huge effect on coastal communities and ecosystems.

High tide
At high tide, rocky shores are covered by water, and organisms such as crabs and fish move around in search of food.

Low tide
Tide pools teeming with organisms are left behind at low tide. Predators look for newly exposed prey.

WAVES

When wind blows across the ocean's surface, it creates tiny ripples that can grow into much larger waves that crash and break on shorelines. Waves are influenced by the wind's duration, speed, and fetch (the distance over which the wind is blowing).

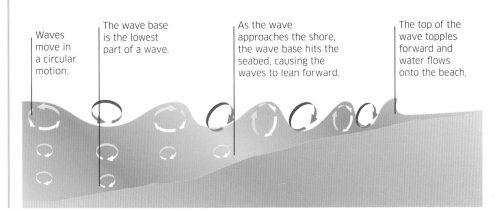

Waves move in a circular motion.

The wave base is the lowest part of a wave.

As the wave approaches the shore, the wave base hits the seabed, causing the waves to lean forward.

The top of the wave topples forward and water flows onto the beach.

Ripples
Winds blowing on the ocean's surface create small, gentle ripples that are close together.

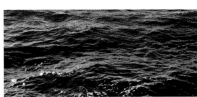

Chop
Further wind turns ripples into small waves about 3.3 ft (1 m) in height, called chop.

Swell
When waves have enough energy to travel beyond the fetch, they form big, regular, unbroken waves called swell.

WEATHER AND CLIMATE

Weather describes the conditions on any given day, such as hot or windy. Climate highlights the average weather over time. Climate has changed naturally over millions of years, but an increase in greenhouse gases in our atmosphere caused by human activity is warming our planet faster than ever before.

WEATHER OR CLIMATE?

A short-term event, such as a rainy or sunny day, is known as the weather. Climate is the average weather calculated over a period of time, often years. Put simply, the climate can be represented by the variety of clothes in your cupboard, but the weather determines what you choose to wear on a specific day.

WEATHER TYPES

There are five main types of weather. They can combine in different ways to determine how weather feels on a given day. For example, a cloudy, windy day may feel colder than a calm, sunny day, yet the actual temperature measured on a thermometer may be the same on both of those days.

Precipitation
This is water in clouds that falls in different forms, such as rain, hail, sleet, or snow.

Wind
Moving air generates wind. Its speed can be measured using tools such as an anemometer.

Cloudiness
This relates to the level of cloud cover in the sky. There are 10 types of clouds (see pages 102–103).

Temperature
This is a measure of the amount of heat in the air. It is recorded on a thermometer.

Visibility
Fog, mist, smog, and dust in the air can all reduce the visibility in any given location.

CLIMATE ZONES

The location of a place is the main factor to understanding its climate. Places near the equator—an imaginary line around the center of the planet—receive more direct heat from the sun so have an overall warmer climate than places near the poles. There are four main climate zones, as shown on this map. In each of these zones, there will also be variations due to other factors, including elevation, wind, and proximity to the sea.

Chicago, Illinois, US
In this temperate city, there are warm summers, cool winters, and a range of seasons. The amount of rain depends on factors such as closeness to the ocean.

Murmansk, Russia
This port city is located near the poles, where summers are often short and can be quite warm, but winters are long and always very cold. Precipitation in this zone often falls as snow.

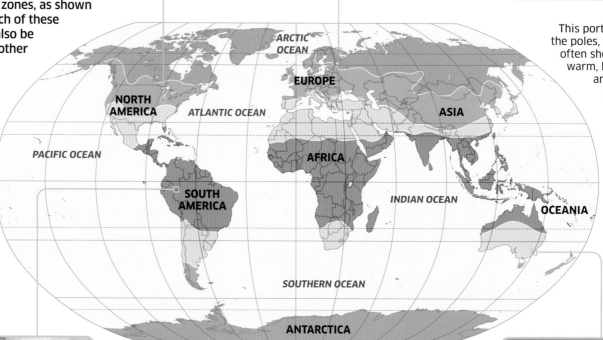

ARCTIC OCEAN
EUROPE
ASIA
NORTH AMERICA
ATLANTIC OCEAN
AFRICA
PACIFIC OCEAN
SOUTH AMERICA
INDIAN OCEAN
OCEANIA
SOUTHERN OCEAN
ANTARCTICA

Zones
- Polar
- Temperate
- Subtropical
- Tropical

Leticia, Colombia
This city next to the Amazon River is in a tropical climate and is characterized by high temperatures and warm, moist air. Places here often have a very rainy wet season and a dry season, with very little or no rain.

Sydney, Australia
Further away from the equator, this large beachside city has a summer climate that can be very hot and dry as there are fewer clouds here than in the tropics. However, temperatures drop during winter.

SEASONS

Throughout the year, everywhere on Earth experiences a cycle of weather conditions, from warm to cold or from wet to dry. This cycle has the largest changes in polar regions and the smallest changes near the equator. These changes are called the seasons and are caused by the way that the Earth orbits around the sun.

Around the sun

The Earth spins on an axis. Its axis is at an angle to its orbit around the sun. As it travels around the sun, the tilt of its axis remains fixed. At different times of the year certain regions of the Earth are tilted toward or away from the sun. This leads to the variation of the seasons through the year.

March
Both hemispheres receive equal amounts of sunlight. Days are growing longer in the north, leading to spring. In the south, shorter days of fall have arrived.

December
The southern hemisphere tilts toward the sun, making it summer. The northern hemisphere tilts away, making it winter.

Orbit
It takes 365 days for Earth to travel around the sun.

Sun
The sun remains fixed in space as the Earth orbits around it.

June
The northern hemisphere tilts toward the sun, making it summer there. The southern hemisphere is tilted away from the sun, so it is winter.

September
As in March, both hemispheres get the same amount of sunlight. It is fall in the northern hemisphere and spring in the southern one.

Axis
Earth rotates around an imaginary line called the axis.

WINTER   SPRING   SUMMER   FALL

Four seasons

In temperate regions, the year has four distinct seasons with different weather. It is the amount of daylight and the intensity of the sunlight that affects the weather of each one. In winter, the days are short, dark, and cold. The days grow longer and warmer in spring and new life begins. The longest, lightest, and warmest days are in summer, becoming shorter and cooler again in fall.

WET SEASON AT ETOSHA NATIONAL PARK

DRY SEASON AT ETOSHA NATIONAL PARK

Two seasons

Tropical and subtropical regions have two distinct seasons: wet and dry. The temperature doesn't change much, but the seasons are determined by whether it is raining heavily or not. At Etosha National Park in Namibia, the lush and green wet season changes to the dry season, when water sources become scarce.

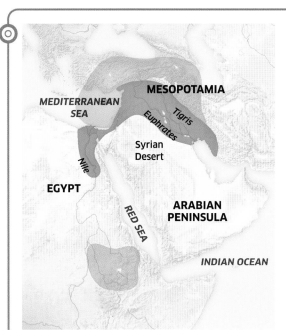

MESOPOTAMIA
MEDITERRANEAN SEA
Tigris
Euphrates
Nile
Syrian Desert
EGYPT
ARABIAN PENINSULA
RED SEA
INDIAN OCEAN

Key
- Fertile Crescent, fed by the Tigris, Nile, and Euphrates rivers.
- Prevailing rainfall near river sources

CLIMATE AND FARMING

More than 10,000 years ago, humans started farming for the first time around the world. They grew crops and kept animals. One of these places was the Fertile Crescent located in parts of modern-day Turkey, Iran, Iraq, Syria, Israel, Jordan, and Egypt. Farming was only possible because of the warm climate and reliable water supply from rainfall that fed the river sources in the region.

EXTREME WEATHER

In Chicago, Illinois, blizzards see hundreds of drivers stranded in their cars overnight. Extreme weather like this can strike anywhere, from heavy snow in polar regions, torrential rain in the tropics, drought in the subtropics, or any of these conditions in the temperate zone depending on the season. Scientists predict that extreme weather will get worse due to climate change.

Atmospheric circulation

Air in the atmosphere is always moving. The pattern of winds around the globe—both near Earth's surface and higher up in the atmosphere—is known as atmospheric circulation.

The winds here are caused by the heating of Earth by the sun. The tropical region around the equator—an invisible line circling the middle of the planet—is heated more strongly than the polar regions. The winds move heat from the equator toward the poles in both hemispheres, while also moving cooler air toward the equator.

Global winds

On a global scale, the winds form a series of "cells"—known as the Hadley, Ferrel, and Polar cells—which transport warm air toward the poles and cooler air toward the equator. Without these cells, the equator would become hotter and hotter, while the poles would keep getting colder.

Why the wind blows

The sun warms some places more than others. Where the air is warm, it is lighter, so it rises. Colder air moves in to replace this rising air, creating winds near the Earth's surface. At higher levels, the rising air cools and may eventually sink back toward the surface.

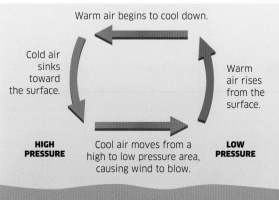

Warm air begins to cool down.

Cold air sinks toward the surface.

Warm air rises from the surface.

HIGH PRESSURE

Cool air moves from a high to low pressure area, causing wind to blow.

LOW PRESSURE

Polar cell
Over the poles in both hemispheres, cold, dense air sinks toward the surface and flows away from the poles, warming up as it goes. The cold air is replaced by warm air flowing toward the poles high in the atmosphere.

North Pole

Ferrel cell
In the middle latitudes of both hemispheres, warm air moves toward the poles and cool air moves toward the equator, in a series of wavelike motions. These waves can grow or decay and move around from day to day.

Hadley cell
Near the equator, hot air rises and then flows away from the equator, both northward and southward. As it cools, it sinks back down. Cooler air flows in near the surface to replace the hot air.

Southern polar jet

Prevailing winds
Wind speed and direction are variable near the Earth's surface within the Ferrel cell. However, they typically blow from the southwest in the northern hemisphere and from the northwest in the southern hemisphere.

South Pole

The **polar jet stream** helped power the **fastest subsonic flight** from **New York to London**, in **4 hours and 56 minutes**, in 2020.

262 mph (442 km/h)—the **wind** in **jet streams** can often reach **speeds in excess** of this.

93

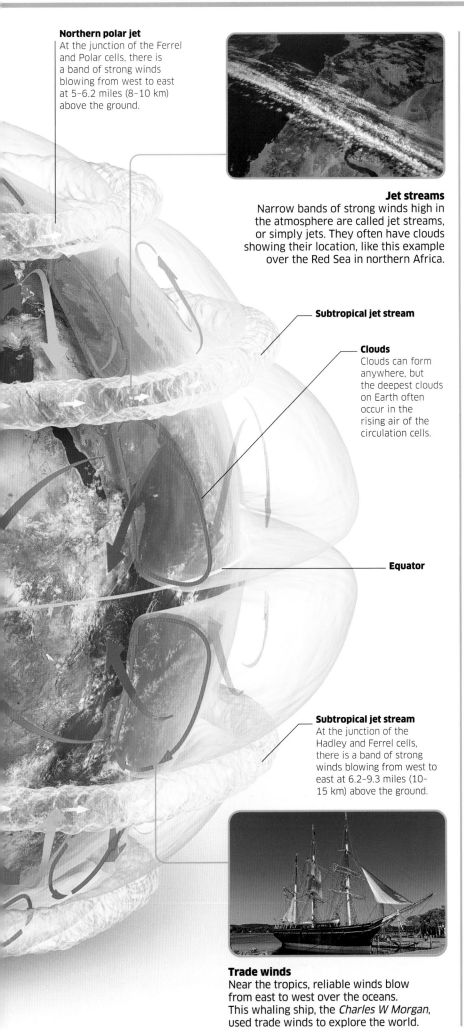

Northern polar jet
At the junction of the Ferrel and Polar cells, there is a band of strong winds blowing from west to east at 5–6.2 miles (8–10 km) above the ground.

Jet streams
Narrow bands of strong winds high in the atmosphere are called jet streams, or simply jets. They often have clouds showing their location, like this example over the Red Sea in northern Africa.

Subtropical jet stream

Clouds
Clouds can form anywhere, but the deepest clouds on Earth often occur in the rising air of the circulation cells.

Equator

Subtropical jet stream
At the junction of the Hadley and Ferrel cells, there is a band of strong winds blowing from west to east at 6.2–9.3 miles (10–15 km) above the ground.

Trade winds
Near the tropics, reliable winds blow from east to west over the oceans. This whaling ship, the *Charles W Morgan*, used trade winds to explore the world.

El Niño and La Niña
El Niño and La Niña are changes to the normal weather patterns across the Pacific Ocean and can affect the weather right around the world. These events happen once every three to seven years and often last for about a year. Both El Niño and La Niña cause increased rainfall in some world regions and drought in others.

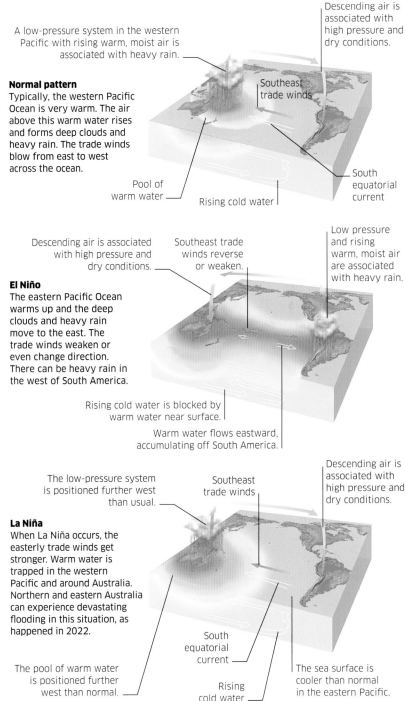

A low-pressure system in the western Pacific with rising warm, moist air is associated with heavy rain.

Descending air is associated with high pressure and dry conditions.

Normal pattern
Typically, the western Pacific Ocean is very warm. The air above this warm water rises and forms deep clouds and heavy rain. The trade winds blow from east to west across the ocean.

Southeast trade winds

Pool of warm water

Rising cold water

South equatorial current

Descending air is associated with high pressure and dry conditions.

Southeast trade winds reverse or weaken.

Low pressure and rising warm, moist air are associated with heavy rain.

El Niño
The eastern Pacific Ocean warms up and the deep clouds and heavy rain move to the east. The trade winds weaken or even change direction. There can be heavy rain in the west of South America.

Rising cold water is blocked by warm water near surface.

Warm water flows eastward, accumulating off South America.

The low-pressure system is positioned further west than usual.

Southeast trade winds

Descending air is associated with high pressure and dry conditions.

La Niña
When La Niña occurs, the easterly trade winds get stronger. Warm water is trapped in the western Pacific and around Australia. Northern and eastern Australia can experience devastating flooding in this situation, as happened in 2022.

The pool of warm water is positioned further west than normal.

South equatorial current

Rising cold water

The sea surface is cooler than normal in the eastern Pacific.

El Niño surfing
During El Niño conditions, there are often more tropical storms in the center of the Pacific Ocean. Around the islands of Hawaii, these storms can generate massive waves that are ridden by some of the world's best surfers.

The causes of climate change

Earth's climate has always varied, but there is evidence that it has been warming faster than before over recent years.

Two main factors control Earth's climate—the amount of energy coming from the sun, and how much of that energy is trapped in the atmosphere. Both natural processes and human activities influence the climate, but how have these processes changed in the past, and how are they changing now?

NATURAL CLIMATE CHANGE

Climate has always varied naturally due to changes in Earth's orbit or the effects of volcanic eruptions. Scientists know about these changes from geological evidence, studying tree rings, and drilling and analyzing ice cores. Large changes in the climate, such as ice ages and interglacial periods, usually happen over thousands of years. Massive volcanic eruptions can cause rapid changes in climate, but these are short-lived.

Milankovitch cycles

The Earth's orbit around the sun changes slowly over thousands of years. This causes warmer and colder periods and also leads to more or less distinct variations between the seasons. There are three factors behind these changes, known as Milankovitch cycles.

Change in orbit
At present, the planet's orbit around the sun is more circular.

Sun

Orbital eccentricity
Earth's orbit varies between a more circular or elliptical shape over a 100,000-year period. This changes the intensity and duration of the seasons.

Earth's axis of rotation

Earth's orbit around the sun

Obliquity
Varying over a 42,000-year period, obliquity is the angle Earth's axis of rotation is tilted as it travels around the sun. When the tilt is large, the difference between summer and winter becomes more extreme.

Polar shift
The polar region that points toward the sun changes as the axis wobbles.

Precession
The tilt of the axis "wobbles" on a 26,000-year period. This makes seasonal contrasts in one hemisphere larger, while reducing them in the other hemisphere.

GREENHOUSE EFFECT

Energy from the sun heats Earth's surface. If all of this heat then escaped through the atmosphere back to space, Earth would be very cold, with an average temperature below freezing. Greenhouse gases in the atmosphere stop some of the heat from escaping, keeping the Earth at a temperature that can support life.

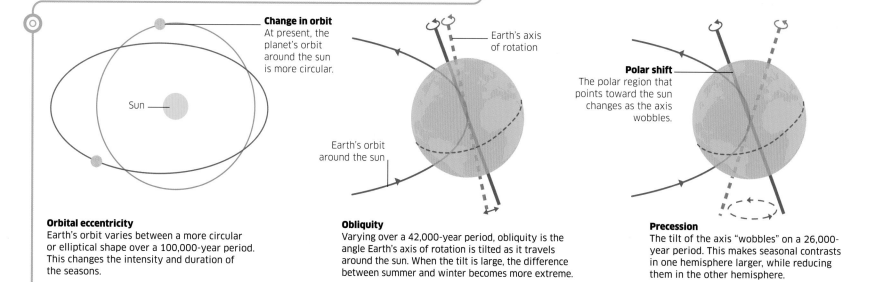

1 Energy from the sun—solar energy—passes through the atmosphere and heats up the surface of the Earth.

2 Some solar energy is reflected back to space by clouds, snow, and ice sheets. Some bounces off them and back to Earth, warming the surface.

3 The warm surface of the Earth emits an invisible form of radiation called infrared energy up into the atmosphere.

4 Some of this infrared energy escapes into space, but most is absorbed by greenhouse gases in the atmosphere.

5 Some of this trapped infrared energy is radiated back to the surface, keeping it warmer than it would be without the greenhouse effect.

Atmosphere

0.04 percent—the **proportion of the Earth's atmosphere** made up of **carbon dioxide**, the **main greenhouse gas**, in 2022.

1.8°F (1°C)—the **increase in global average temperature** since the second half of the 19th century **caused by human activity**.

95

HUMAN-MADE CLIMATE CHANGE

In the 18th and 19th centuries, humans first started burning coal to drive factories and fuel trains and later to generate electricity. Since then, other fossil fuels such as oil and gas has also been used. Burning fossil fuels creates carbon dioxide, which has been adding to the natural amounts of greenhouse gases in the atmosphere. As a result, Earth's surface and atmosphere have started to warm up.

Industrial Revolution

Built in 1779 over the Severn River in the UK, the Iron Bridge—and the village named after it—was the birthplace of the Industrial Revolution. This region had abundant natural resources, including coal and iron ore. This led to the production of iron cylinders for steam engines, iron rails, and iron barges.

Increasing carbon dioxide

At the start of the Industrial Revolution, the increase of carbon dioxide in the atmosphere due to burning fossil fuels was relatively low and confined mainly to Europe. Since the middle of the 20th century, emissions have been increasing rapidly, driven by economic growth in countries such as the USA and, more recently, China.

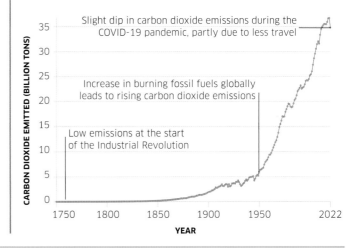

Slight dip in carbon dioxide emissions during the COVID-19 pandemic, partly due to less travel

Increase in burning fossil fuels globally leads to rising carbon dioxide emissions

Low emissions at the start of the Industrial Revolution

CARBON DIOXIDE EMITTED (BILLION TONS)

YEAR

HUMAN IMPACTS

Many human activities emit greenhouse gases. As the scale and intensity of these activities has increased over the past century, so has their effect on the climate, causing global warming. The choices we make about these activities now will affect climate change over the next century and beyond.

Burning fossils fuels
The single biggest factor in the increase of greenhouse gases in the atmosphere is the burning of fossil fuels to generate energy for homes and industry.

Deforestation
Trees remove carbon dioxide from the atmosphere. Cutting them down—for agriculture and development—leads to the build up of greenhouse gases.

Travel
Planes and buses and cars with gasoline or diesel engines all emit greenhouse gases, and cause air pollution. Traffic on roads in cities is a serious environmental problem.

Population growth
As the world's population increases, so too does global consumption. This includes food and goods, and the energy used to produce them.

Farming
Trees are cleared to make space for farms. Animals, especially cows, emit a greenhouse gas called methane. Farm machinery, such as tractors, emits carbon dioxide.

Transporting goods
Commercial ships, cargo aircraft, and freight trucks that transport all the goods we consume around the world contribute to greenhouse gas emissions.

Fast fashion
The fashion industry produces a vast amount of greenhouse gases in the manufacture and transport of clothes around the world.

WAYS TO TRAVEL

Different forms of transportation increase our greenhouse gas emissions by different amounts. This graphic shows the estimated amount of carbon dioxide emitted per person traveling from Paris to Toulouse in France—a journey of 420 miles (676 km)—in various ways. Flying produces very high emissions. Sharing transportation with others helps reduce emissions—a single driver generates three times as much carbon dioxide per person as they would if sharing with three others.

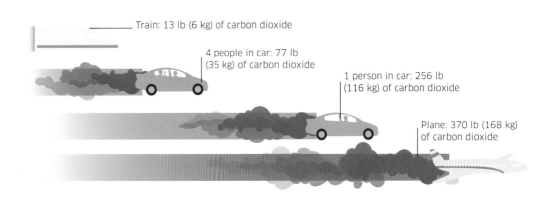

Train: 13 lb (6 kg) of carbon dioxide

4 people in car: 77 lb (35 kg) of carbon dioxide

1 person in car: 256 lb (116 kg) of carbon dioxide

Plane: 370 lb (168 kg) of carbon dioxide

96 **weather and climate** ○ **GREENHOUSE GASES**

220 lb (100 kg)—the amount of **methane** typically belched by a **single cow** in one year.

Greenhouse gases

A natural layer of gases in the atmosphere traps the sun's energy to keep Earth warm. Acting like a greenhouse, they are known as greenhouse gases.

Without this layer, Earth's average surface temperature would be well below freezing. However, human activity around the world is causing the emission of increasing levels of greenhouse gases. This is trapping more warmth and causing global temperatures to rise.

Water vapor
Water vapor is a naturally occurring greenhouse gas. As the atmosphere warms up, it is able to hold more water vapor. This increases its effect, and so makes global warming even worse.

Tipping the balance
Most of the greenhouse gases in the atmosphere have occurred through natural processes and help maintain a stable climate. However, increases in greenhouse gases due to human activity are adding to the natural amounts and are warming the planet.

Key

- Carbon dioxide produced naturally
- Carbon dioxide produced by human activity
- Methane produced by human activity
- Methane produced naturally
- Nitrous oxide produced by human activity

Carbon dioxide
Carbon dioxide is the most common naturally occurring greenhouse gas. It is also the one that is produced in largest amounts by human activity, especially when burning fossil fuels. The amount of carbon dioxide in the atmosphere in 2022 was about 50 percent higher than in 1800—and amounts are still rising.

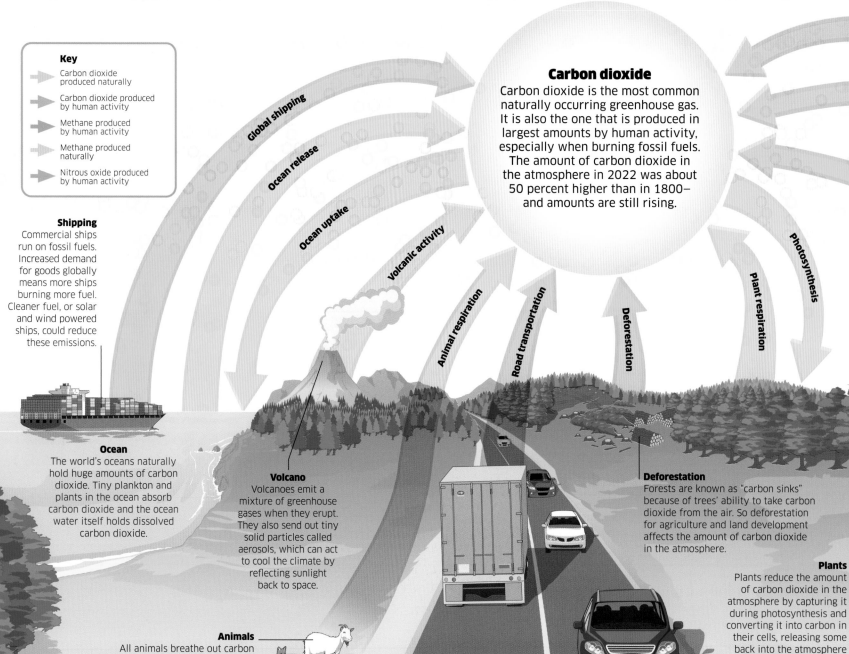

Global shipping

Ocean release

Ocean uptake

Volcanic activity

Animal respiration

Road transportation

Deforestation

Plant respiration

Photosynthesis

Shipping
Commercial ships run on fossil fuels. Increased demand for goods globally means more ships burning more fuel. Cleaner fuel, or solar and wind powered ships, could reduce these emissions.

Ocean
The world's oceans naturally hold huge amounts of carbon dioxide. Tiny plankton and plants in the ocean absorb carbon dioxide and the ocean water itself holds dissolved carbon dioxide.

Volcano
Volcanoes emit a mixture of greenhouse gases when they erupt. They also send out tiny solid particles called aerosols, which can act to cool the climate by reflecting sunlight back to space.

Animals
All animals breathe out carbon dioxide. This is part of the natural cycle of carbon dioxide, with animals and people breathing it out and trees and plants taking it in.

Deforestation
Forests are known as "carbon sinks" because of trees' ability to take carbon dioxide from the air. So deforestation for agriculture and land development affects the amount of carbon dioxide in the atmosphere.

Plants
Plants reduce the amount of carbon dioxide in the atmosphere by capturing it during photosynthesis and converting it into carbon in their cells, releasing some back into the atmosphere through respiration. Plants act as a natural control on the greenhouse effect.

Road transportation
Most road vehicles are powered by fossil fuels, such as gas or diesel. As more electric vehicles appear on the roads, the greenhouse gas emissions of road transportation will reduce, especially if the electricity used to charge them comes from renewable energy.

5.1 tons (4.6 metric tons)—the amount of **carbon dioxide** emitted by a typical **family car** running on gasoline over **one** year.

16 percent—the amount of **carbon dioxide emissions** that forests in the US absorb per year.

97

Ozone layer

A gas found mainly in the stratosphere, ozone absorbs harmful ultraviolet rays from the sun. In the 1980s, scientists found that some chemicals were destroying the ozone, especially near the South Pole (pictured in blue). An international treaty banned these chemicals and now ozone amounts are recovering.

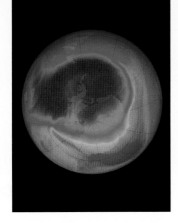

Biggest threats

There are many human-made sources of greenhouse gases. This chart shows which ones are the biggest.

Energy in industry (24%)
Energy used in producing goods and materials such as steel and chemicals

Energy in transportation (16%)
Road transportation, rail, aviation, and shipping

Energy in buildings (18%)
Heating and lighting, running domestic electrical appliances, and cooking

Other energy (15%)
Greenhouse gas leaks during extraction and transportation of fossil fuels

Industry (5%)
Carbon dioxide emissions from chemical and cement manufacture

Waste (3%)
Trash in landfill sites emitting methane as it rots

Agriculture (19%)
Agricultural practices that emit or generate greenhouse gases

Aviation

Aviation
All aircraft burn fossil fuel to power their engines, releasing carbon dioxide into the atmosphere.

Nitrous oxide

Nitrous oxide is a greenhouse gas that occurs in tiny quantities but can have an enormous effect. It has a global warming potential 300 times stronger than carbon dioxide. Most human-made emissions of nitrous oxide come from fertilizer in farm soils.

Methane

Methane occurs in tiny amounts in the atmosphere, but it is a powerful greenhouse gas. Just 1 kg (2.2 lb) of methane has the same warming effect as 25 kg (55 lb) of carbon dioxide. Farming activities are the largest human-made source of methane.

Wetlands
Covering 6 percent of the world, wetlands are one of the biggest natural sources of methane.

Glaciers
The bright white ice of glaciers reflects sunlight back out to space, cooling the planet. If glaciers melt, this natural cooling effect is reduced. This is known as ice-albedo feedback.

Power plants

Homes

Farming machines

Nitrous oxide

Wetland emission

Farming animals

Permafrost

Power plants
To supply power for homes, businesses, and industry, coal, oil, and natural gas are burned in power plants, emitting carbon dioxide. Moving to renewable power is important for reducing greenhouse gas emissions.

Fossil fuels
Fossil fuels like oil, gas, and coal are made of carbon that has been stored underground for millions of years. Burning these fuels puts carbon into the atmosphere as carbon dioxide.

Homes
Heating homes, cooking, and using electricity generated by fossil fuels all contribute to greenhouse gas emissions.

Farm machines
Most farm machines like tractors are powered by diesel fuel, and emit carbon dioxide into the atmosphere as they work.

Farm animals
The digestive systems of farm animals, especially cattle, generate methane, which is released into the atmosphere. More cattle farming means higher methane emissions.

Melting permafrost
In some cold parts of the world, such as near the poles, the ground is permanently frozen. As the planet warms, some of this permafrost melts, releasing methane into the atmosphere.

The effects of climate change

Climate change is already altering our world radically, as animals lose habitats, ice caps melt, and wildfires spread. There are many things, however, that we can do as individuals to reduce the impacts of climate change.

Earth's climate has changed in the last 150 years, largely because of human activity that increases greenhouse gases in the atmosphere. This increase is causing the average temperature of the Earth to rise, but the weather and climate are changing in other ways, with a range of different consequences.

MELTING ICE CAPS

As the temperature of Earth rises, the Arctic ice cap has started to melt, and mountain glaciers are shrinking. Snow and ice are white, which means they reflect sunlight back out to space, helping keep the Earth's surface cool. As they melt, less sunlight is reflected and so the Earth warms up more. The image below shows how much the area of the Arctic ice cap has reduced since 1980.

Key
■ 1980
■ 2000
■ 2019

PREDICTING THE FUTURE

Scientists use their knowledge of the Earth's atmosphere to predict how the climate might change. They look at different estimates of future global greenhouse gas emissions to assess potential temperature changes.

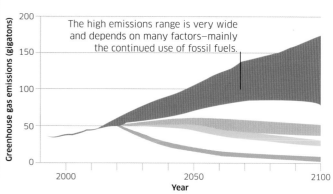

The high emissions range is very wide and depends on many factors—mainly the continued use of fossil fuels.

High emissions
In this scenario, global greenhouse gas emissions continue increasing through the 21st century. This will lead to very significant heating.

Current path
Here the current greenhouse emissions are assumed to stay constant through the century. This also leads to significant warming by 2100.

Meeting targets
Governments have set targets for reducing greenhouse gas emissions. If the targets are met, then the world will still warm, but less significantly.

Low emissions
Only in a scenario where emissions are cut drastically and greenhouse gases removed from the atmosphere can global warming be reversed.

IMPACTS OF CLIMATE CHANGE

Global warming has had an impact on all parts of the globe. Weather patterns are changing and extreme weather events, such as droughts and flooding, are increasing in number and becoming more extreme. Some parts of the world are becoming less hospitable places to live as growing crops or finding sufficient amounts of drinking water get harder.

Changing weather
The number of heavy rainfall events has grown in frequency and intensity in many parts of the world since the 1950s. This increases the chances of flooding, which damages homes, infrastructure, and crops.

Heating Earth
Almost every continent on Earth is seeing rising average temperatures. The frequency and intensity of heat waves are increasing, and in some regions this is accompanied by more frequent wildfires.

Warming seas
Warm water is less dense than cold water. So as the oceans heat up they expand, causing rises in sea level. As a result, low-lying coastal regions are experiencing more flooding, including large cities around the world.

Melting ice
Some glaciers are receding and, in some cases, disappearing completely. In places where people rely on water released from glaciers, it can lead to shortages in the summer months.

Habitat loss
Changing climate can alter wildlife habitats. From 2014 to 2016, strong ocean warming off a 200-mile Californian coast killed 90 percent of bull kelp forests, which are home to sea otters and other marine species.

Climate migration
As the climate changes, people in some areas are forced to leave their homes, to escape floods, droughts, and other extreme conditions.

10 plastic bottles recycled saves enough energy to **power a laptop** for more than **25 hours**.

The **greenhouse gas emissions** of global textile manufacture per year are **more than** international **flights and global shipping** combined.

99

CARBON FOOTPRINT

A carbon footprint is a way to measure the greenhouse gases released by a country, a business sector, or individuals. In general, people living in wealthier nations have lifestyles that contribute the most emissions and so have the largest carbon footprints. This graphic shows the carbon footprint of Australia in 2020, by sector.

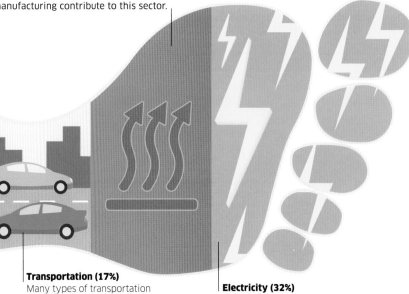

Stationary energy (19%)
The fossil fuels involved in generating electricity and for mining and manufacturing contribute to this sector.

Waste (3%)
Decomposing trash, especially food waste, generates methane, a powerful greenhouse gas. Improved food supply chains and planning by consumers could reduce this.

Industrial processes (5%)
The manufacture of cement and some chemical products generates carbon dioxide as a by-product.

Leaks (10%)
As gas is extracted from the ground and transported, some of it leaks and escapes into the atmosphere. This increases greenhouse gas emissions.

Agriculture (14%)
Farm machinery burning diesel fuel, livestock generating methane, and the use of fertilizers all add greenhouse gases to the atmosphere.

Transportation (17%)
Many types of transportation burn fossil fuels, releasing carbon dioxide. Changing to electric vehicles can help reduce our carbon footprint.

Electricity (32%)
Generating electricity is a major source of greenhouse gas emissions. Renewable energy, such as solar, wind, and hydropower can make a big difference here.

CHANGING HOW WE LIVE

As individuals, we cannot change government policy by ourselves. There are several things we can do, however, to reduce our individual carbon footprints and help combat climate change. Some of these are quite simple and do not involve big changes to our lifestyle. Here are some of them.

Recycling
Taking cans and other packaging to be recycled saves energy and resources. Recycling processes use less energy than making new containers from raw materials.

Environmentally friendly fashion
Choosing clothes that will last and will be used many times reduces our greenhouse gas emissions— every garment we buy has its own carbon footprint.

Less meat
Meat production generates a lot of greenhouse gas emissions. Moving to a diet with less—or no—meat is one way to reduce our carbon footprint.

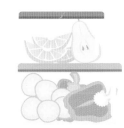

Reducing food waste
Planning meals so that we throw away less food is another effective way to reduce the greenhouse gas emissions we are responsible for.

TAKING ACTION

To combat climate change, everyone must take action—from international bodies and governments down to communities and individuals. Government commitment is key, as they control policy in areas such as power generation and green transport. Community groups and individuals can use their voice to influence climate policies.

Paris agreement
In December 2015, at a conference in Paris, 196 countries signed a treaty to limit the effects of climate change. Governments committed to producing plans to reduce their greenhouse gas emissions. The aim was to stop global temperatures from rising by more than 3.6°F (2°C), and ideally by less than 2.7°F (1.5°C).

School strikes
School students cannot directly influence government policies. With demonstrations and school strikes, however, they can let their governments know how much they care about climate change. Started by Swedish climate activist Greta Thunberg in 2018, this is now a global movement.

100 weather and climate ∘ **WEATHER**

467 in (11,862 mm)—the **amount of rain** in **Mawsynram, India**, in one year, making it the **rainiest place** on Earth.

HOW WEATHER WORKS

Rising air will cool and eventually the water vapor—which can be up to 4 percent of the atmosphere, depending on the temperature—will start to condense, forming clouds and rain. Sinking air warms up and so any clouds will start to evaporate. If we know where air is rising or sinking, then we can start to understand the weather.

Weather fronts

Weather fronts occur at the boundary between warm and cold masses of air. They are regions where air is likely to be rising, leading to the formation of bands of clouds and rain.

Cold front

Where a cold air mass is moving toward a warm air mass, the lighter warm air will be pushed up and over the denser cold air. As the air rises, it cools and starts to form clouds and rain.

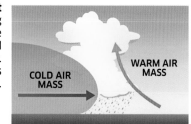

Warm front

At a warm front, warm air is moving toward cold air. The lighter warm air rises at an angle over the top of the cold air. The rising warm air cools and forms cloud and rain.

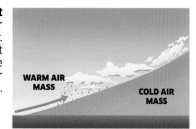

Occluded front

At an occluded front, a warm air mass is squeezed upward by two colder air masses on either side. Clouds form in the warm air as it rises, and rain falls from the clouds.

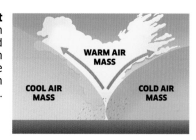

Pressure systems

The pressure of the atmosphere is a good guide to the weather over a wide region. High and low pressure areas have typical weather types associated with them.

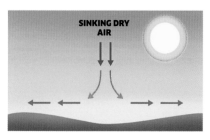

High pressure

In an area of high pressure, the air in the atmosphere will be sinking, as shown by the arrows. As the air sinks, it becomes warmer and drier, which stops clouds and rain from forming. This usually leads to fine and settled weather.

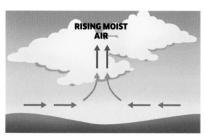

Low pressure

In an area of low pressure, the air is rising. As it rises, it cools, and eventually clouds and rain form. Low pressure often marks a region of unsettled weather. Cyclones and hurricanes are extreme examples of low-pressure zones.

Weather

When we talk about the weather, we mean the state of the atmosphere on any day. Is it warm or cold, wet or dry, windy or calm? These things make a difference to what we do, how we dress, and how we travel around.

The way that the weather feels depends mainly on whether or not it is cloudy or raining. As well as causing rain, clouds also block the sun, affecting the temperature. Weather forecasters can predict how the weather will change from day to day, partly by understanding the processes that cause clouds to form or disappear.

Reading a weather map

Weather maps, such as this one showing a large part of Europe, have lines of constant pressure, called isobars, which highlight areas of high and low pressure. Where the isobars are close together, it is likely that the wind will be very strong. Weather fronts also show the locations of bands of cloud and rain.

Low-pressure zone
Rings of isobars with the lowest pressure at the center mark a low-pressure zone. This may cause unsettled weather over the English Channel.

Occluded front
A cold front has caught up with a warm front, lifting warm air off the ground. This may generate a band of cloud and rain over southeast England.

Isobars
These are lines on a weather map that link places of equal atmospheric pressure.

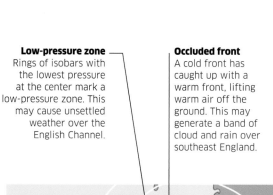

Cold front
Marked with blue triangles, a cold front here suggests possible heavy and thundery rain across northern Spain and parts of western France.

Warm front
Identified by red semicircles, this warm front may lead to clouds and light rain across Belgium and eastern France.

High-pressure zone
Rings of isobars with the highest pressure at the center mark a high-pressure zone. Sunny weather is likely over the Mediterranean Sea.

−128.6°F (−89.2°C)—the **coldest ground temperature** ever recorded, at **Vostok Station, Antarctica,** in 1983.

2,000 The approximate **number of weather balloons** launched **around the world** every day.

101

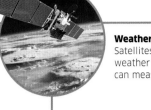

MEASURING THE WEATHER

In order to make an accurate forecast of the weather, meteorologists—scientists who observe and study the weather—use lots of different instruments. This includes everything from satellites in space to weather buoys on the seas.

Weather satellite
Satellites in space have a great view of the weather systems on Earth. Instruments on board can measure temperature, humidity, and winds.

Ship
The crew on many commercial ships record the weather and radio their readings back to weather centers on land.

Weather balloon
Weather balloons carry a package of instruments up through the atmosphere, recording the weather and transmitting the data back to the ground.

Weather buoy
To record the weather at sea, automated weather stations are mounted on floating buoys. They transmit readings via satellites.

Aircraft
Commercial airliners measure the temperature and wind speed as they fly. They radio the measurements back to weather centers on the ground.

Stevenson's screen
This is a box painted white, with slats to allow air to flow past the thermometers inside without them being exposed to direct sunshine.

Automated station
In remote areas, there are no people to read instruments, so automated stations are set up to record and transmit weather readings.

WET WEATHER

When rising air cools, it can form clouds and sometimes rain, leading to all types of wet weather. To predict where rain—or any type of precipitation—might fall, it's important to understand the reasons that cause air to rise. However, in some areas, clouds stay close to the ground, resulting in fog.

How clouds form

If air is forced to rise, it will always cool. If it cools down enough, then the water vapor in the air condenses, forming tiny water drops—this is called its dew point. A cloud begins to form immediately after this.

Warm air rises
During the day, the sun heats the ground and so air near the ground warms up. Warm air is less dense than cold air so the air rises until it cools to its dew point, forming cumulus, or puffy, type clouds.

Air cools to dew point and clouds form

Warm air near the ground

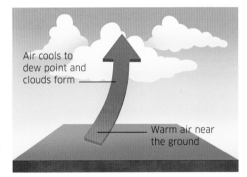

Wind moves up and over the hill

Mountain effects
If the wind is blowing toward a hill or mountain, air will be forced to rise up and over it. In the process, it cools and may form clouds. As a result, rain over hills or mountains is usually heavier than above flat regions.

What is fog?

Fog forms when air just above the ground becomes saturated. This happens if the air is cooled to its dew point without rising. Fog is made up of very tiny water drops that usually do not get big enough to form rain. There are two main ways that fog can form.

Advection fog
Warm moist air that blows across a cold surface can be cooled to its dew point. The fog here sits over the bay at Golden Gate Bridge in San Francisco, California.

Radiation fog
At night, the ground cools down by radiating heat, cooling the air above it to its dew point. This is common in valleys, seen here in the Peak District in the UK.

Types of precipitation

Precipitation can take many different forms depending on the temperature of the air and what caused the precipitation to form. The main types are shown here.

Rain
Large drops of water

Drizzle
Drops less than 0.01 in (0.5 mm)

Snow
Crystals of frozen water

Sleet
A mixture of snow and rain

Frost
Ice formed on a cold surface

Hail
Solid, often large, lumps of ice

Dew
Drops condensing onto the ground

102 weather and climate ○ **CLOUDS**

67 percent—the **area** of the Earth's atmosphere that is cloudy on an average day.

Clouds

Clouds are the atmosphere's weather makers. All the rain, snow, hail, and sleet—collectively known as precipitation—that falls on Earth starts off in a cloud as tiny water drops or ice crystals.

The sky is full of invisible water in the form of water vapor. Clouds usually form where air is rising. As the air rises it cools. Water vapor in the air condenses to form water drops, or ice crystals if the temperature is cold enough. There are 10 main types of clouds and their names describe how they look, often combining Latin words such as *cirrus* (wispy), *cumulus* (heaped), and *stratus* (layered). The different shapes and sizes of clouds are due to how fast the air is rising and whether the cloud is made from water or ice.

CIRROCUMULUS

Height of base: 20,000–33,000 ft (6,000–10,000 m)
Composition: Ice

This is one of the rarest clouds to spot. Turbulent air high up creates the lumpy or rippled pattern in the cloud. It does not produce precipitation but can be a sign of bad weather on the way.

NIMBOSTRATUS

Height of base: 4,900–9,800 ft (1,500–3,000 m)
Composition: Water and ice

This wide, gray cloud often produces rain. It sometimes strays into the low cloud region. As the rain gets heavier, the base of the cloud gets lower, bringing persistent rain or snow.

ALTOCUMULUS

Height of base: 6,500–20,000 ft (2,000–6,000 m)
Composition: Water and ice

This cloud is white or pale gray with a lumpy texture. It may contain super-cooled water drops—these are drops that are at temperatures below 32°F (0°C) but are liquid rather than frozen. This cloud rarely produces rain, and even if rain does fall, it evaporates before it reaches the ground.

STRATUS

Height of base: 0–1,300 ft (0–400 m)
Composition: Water

This cloud is usually a gray shapeless mass. It is the lowest-lying type of cloud, often seen covering the tops of hills or even buildings in the form of mist or fog. It never produces heavy rain unless occurring together with other clouds, but it is often responsible for very light rain or drizzle.

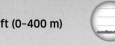

CUMULUS

Height of base: 1,000–6,500 ft (300–2,000 m)
Composition: Water

This lumpy cloud that can look a bit like a head of cauliflower is created by rising currents of warm air called thermals. It often appears on warm days as the sun heats the ground up. If this cloud starts to grow taller and darker, then rain showers may be on the way.

5,500 tons (5,000 metric tons)—the **weight of water** in a typical **cumulonimbus** cloud.

500 million—the number of **tiny water drops** in 35 sq ft (1 sq m) of a **small cumulus** cloud.

103

CIRROSTRATUS

Height of base: 20,000–33,000 ft
(6,000–10,000 m)
Composition: Ice

This almost transparent cloud can span large areas of the sky. When it appears on a night with a full moon, the ice in the clouds creates a ring of light, or halo, around the moon. This cloud does not produce any precipitation.

CIRRUS

Height of base: 20,000–33,000 ft
(6,000–10,000 m)
Composition: Ice

Moving high up in the atmosphere, this cloud is made of ice crystals and looks like strands of hair or feathers. The direction of the streaks shows the wind direction at that level. This cloud produces snow that never reaches the ground.

Passenger plane
The cruising altitude of a passenger plane is around 36,000 ft (11,000 m).

High clouds
Above 20,000 ft
(6,000 m)

ALTOSTRATUS

Height of base: 6,500–20,000 ft
(2,000–6,000 m)
Composition: Water and ice

Usually gray or blue in color, this rather wide and featureless cloud is so thin that the sun's rays can be seen shining right through it. But if it gets thicker and darker, this indicates that precipitation may be on the way soon. Like altocumulus, altostratus can be made of super-cooled water drops.

Medium clouds
6,500–20,000 ft
(2,000–6,000 m)

STRATOCUMULUS

Height of base: 1,000–6,500 ft
(300–2,000 m)
Composition: Water

As its name suggests, this white or gray mass looks like a mix of stratus and cumulus clouds. Appearing in all kinds of weather conditions, this is the most common cloud type around the world. It rarely produces anything more than the lightest drizzle.

CUMULONIMBUS

Height of base: 650–6,500 ft
(200–2,000 m)
Composition: Water and ice

This cloud starts life as a cumulus cloud, but if there is enough energy in the atmosphere, it can grow quickly, towering up to several miles in height. Producing heavy rain, thunder, and lightning, this cloud causes some of the most dramatic weather, from hail storms to tornadoes.

Low clouds
Below 6,500 ft
(2,000 m)

104 weather and climate · **STORMS**

15 The **largest number of hurricanes** in the **Atlantic Ocean** in a single year, in 2005.

Storms

Powerful disturbances in the atmosphere are known as storms. They can produce the most exciting—and sometimes scariest—weather imaginable, often leaving a trail of destruction in their wake.

Storms come in many shapes and sizes. While most types of storms involve heavy rain and strong winds, some of them feature ice or even dust. From hurricanes and cyclones in the tropics to wind storms and ice storms in the far northern reaches of Earth, most parts of the world experience some sort of stormy weather throughout the year.

TYPES OF STORMS

Although there are many different types of storms, they fall into three broad groups. Convective storms are the smallest in size and are driven by heat from the sun. In the tropics, hurricanes, cyclones, and typhoons are all types of tropical storms. Outside of the tropics, extratropical storms can generate heavy rain, strong winds, and during the winter, snow and ice.

Convective storms

From 0.6 miles (1 km) to 62 miles (100 km) across and lasting from an hour to a day, convective storms are driven by heat from the sun. Warm air rises rapidly and forms deep cumulonimbus clouds. Formed in most places around the world, convective storms can produce heavy rain and hail, lightning, gusty winds, and in extreme cases, tornadoes.

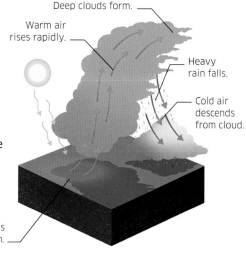

Deep clouds form.

Warm air rises rapidly.

Heavy rain falls.

Cold air descends from cloud.

Surface of land is heated by the sun.

Tropical storms

Spanning up to 310 miles (500 km) across, tropical storms are fueled by heat and water vapor from warm tropical oceans. As warm air in the center of the storm starts to rise, the winds around the storm start to increase, often reaching damaging speeds and generating huge waves.

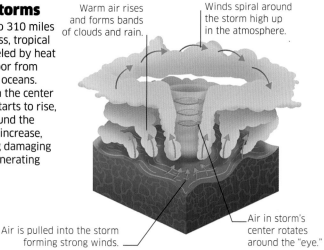

Warm air rises and forms bands of clouds and rain.

Winds spiral around the storm high up in the atmosphere.

Air is pulled into the storm forming strong winds.

Air in storm's center rotates around the "eye."

Extratropical storm

Occurring outside the tropics, these storms are big, sometimes more than 620 miles (1,000 km) across. Flows of warm and cold air combine in these storms to generate big masses of cloud, strong winds, heavy rain, and in the winter, snow and ice.

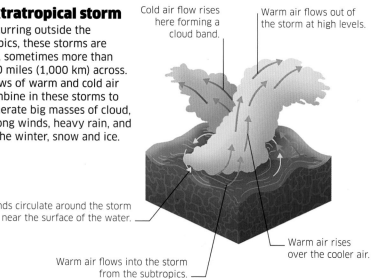

Cold air flow rises here forming a cloud band.

Warm air flows out of the storm at high levels.

Winds circulate around the storm near the surface of the water.

Warm air rises over the cooler air.

Warm air flows into the storm from the subtropics.

LIGHTNING STRIKES

Lightning is nature's firework display. Few weather events can be as exciting to watch, but it is important to stay safe—lightning can be dangerous. It involves massive currents of electricity passing through the air at incredible speeds, up to 270,000 mph (430,000 km/h)!

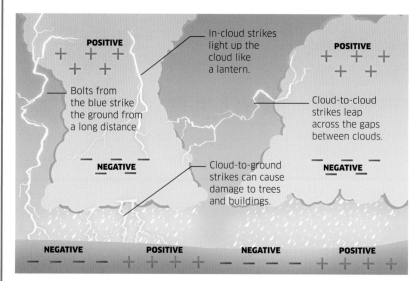

POSITIVE

In-cloud strikes light up the cloud like a lantern.

POSITIVE

Bolts from the blue strike the ground from a long distance.

Cloud-to-cloud strikes leap across the gaps between clouds.

NEGATIVE

Cloud-to-ground strikes can cause damage to trees and buildings.

NEGATIVE

NEGATIVE POSITIVE NEGATIVE POSITIVE

How lightning works
The air currents in convective storms move electrical charges, which are positive or negative, around inside clouds. When there are big differences in charges, a lightning strike occurs to even out the differences.

Catatumbo lightning
Some areas experience a lot of lightning. The Catatumbo River, where it flows into Lake Maracaibo in Venezuela, is one such place. This region experiences 602 lightning strikes per square mile (233/sq km) each year.

300 The **number of days with lightning** per year in **Lake Maracaibo** in Venezuela.

15 billion—the **cost of the damage**, in euros, of **Wind Storm Lothar**, in 1999.

105

MEASURING STORMS

Scientists need to measure the strength of storms to understand how they work. This helps to make better weather forecasts, which means that people are warned and prepared when a storm is about to hit.

Hurricane wind scale

The strength of all the hurricanes, tropical cyclones, and typhoons around the world is measured on the same scale based on five levels of wind speed.

Some damage to homes and tree branches may snap

Category 1:
74-95 mph (119-154 km/h)

Major damage to homes and trees, and intermittent power loss

Severe damage, with some uprooted trees blocking roads

Category 2:
96-110 mph (155-177 km/h)

Category 3:
111-129 mph (178-208 km/h)

Extreme damage to homes and trees, as well as major power outages

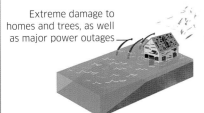

Catastrophic damage and flooding makes region uninhabitable for months

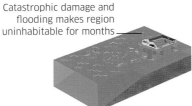

Category 4:
130-156 mph (209-251 km/h)

Category 5:
157 mph (252 km/h) or higher

Hurricane hunter

Some scientists deliberately fly airplanes into the heart of hurricanes to measure their power. This can be the only way to understand how the air flows around the storm and how the clouds build up. The aircraft release instruments called dropsondes (pictured) into the clouds, and these float down to the ground on parachutes taking measurements as they fall.

Close to the action

For convective storms like the ones that produce tornadoes, it can be too dangerous to take weather instruments into the storm. Scientists drive near the storm and then use a radar mounted on a truck to measure the flow of air in the cloud from a safe distance. They need to leave quickly if the storm moves toward them.

STORMS AROUND THE WORLD

Some types of storms can occur anywhere around the world, but others happen only in particular places. Convective storms with hail and lightning can happen almost anywhere from the tropics to the polar regions. Dust storms happen only in or close to deserts or places with very dry soil. Only a few places on Earth have the right conditions to produce damaging tornadoes.

North American ice storm
In 1998, heavy rain falling onto subzero surfaces coated everything with ice. This brought down trees and power lines and damaged buildings.

Hurricane Eta
This Caribbean hurricane in 2020 brought devastating winds and flooding to coastal parts of Nicaragua and Honduras. Another hurricane hit two weeks later.

Australian dust storm
An intense storm over the central Australian desert in 1998 blew a thick cloud of orange dust over several cities on the west coast, including Sydney.

Wind Storm Lothar
Boxing Day 1999 saw an extratropical storm cross France and Germany. Trees and power lines fell and 3.4 million people had no electricity.

Daulatpur-Saturia tornado
in 1989, Bangladesh experienced a destructive tornado, the worst in the nation's history. This one made 80,000 people homeless.

Tropical cyclone Idai
Idai was only a category 2 storm when it hit Mozambique in 2019, but heavy rain and a massive storm surge caused extensive coastal flooding.

106 weather and climate ∘ **TORNADOES**

300 mph (483 km/h)—the **highest estimated wind speed** in a tornado, at **Bridge Creek, Oklahoma**, in 1999.

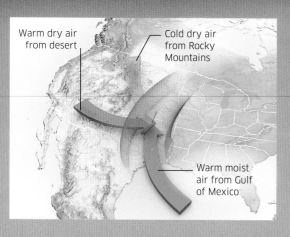

Warm dry air from desert

Cold dry air from Rocky Mountains

Warm moist air from Gulf of Mexico

Buildup
Tornadoes form in specific conditions. Warm, humid air near the ground contains lots of energy, which interacts with layers of air above. This is exactly what happens over the central plains of the US—a region known as Tornado Alley.

Tornadoes

A tornado is a narrow, twisting column of air that reaches from a thunderstorm to the ground.

Tornadoes contain some of the most destructive weather on Earth. Wind speeds in a tornado can exceed 250 mph (400 km/h), which can lift and move whole houses. Those are rare events. Most tornadoes last for minutes. Only a few last longer than an hour and cause the extensive damage that makes the news headlines.

Inside the twister
Debris is picked up by the wind. Lighter objects, such as doors and branches, are carried high up into the air. Heavier objects, such as cars and cows, can also be lifted off the ground.

Stages of a storm
In the hours before a tornado forms, the atmosphere goes through several stages that can lead to the formation of a supercell thunderstorm. These storms bring heavy rain and hail, thunder, and strong winds, and sometimes generate a tornado.

Updraft
Inside the cloud, the updraft rotates more intensely as the air rises.

Wind from northwest
At higher levels, air is blowing from the northwest.

Wind from west
The wind from this direction blows along the rotating tube.

Rotating tube of air
Winds are not yet very strong, so the tube rotates slowly.

Wind from south
The wind near the ground comes from the south.

Rotating tube tilts to vertical
Air rising at different speeds causes the tube to tilt upward.

Cloud forming
As the rising air cools to its dew point clouds form.

Rising hot air
The warm air above the ground becomes buoyant.

Downdraft
Cold air caused by rain evaporating descends outside the cloud.

Heavy rain
A deep cloud can produce heavy rain and lightning.

1 Wind shear
If the wind suddenly changes direction, speed, or both, this is called wind shear. It creates a rotating tube of air, invisible to the eye. It can last for several hours before a cloud starts to form.

2 Updraft
During the day, the sun heats the ground. Rapidly rising currents of air, called updrafts, start to form. These updrafts tilt the rotating tube of air up and a cloud starts to form.

3 Supercell thunderstorm
Once clouds start to form, they can grow quickly into deep cumulonimbus. The storm starts to rotate and heavy rain and hail fall. A downdraft of cold air from the cloud hits the ground and spreads out, causing gusty winds.

$28 billion (£21.5 billion)—the **cost of property damage caused by the 2011 US tornado season**, the **largest amount** on record for a single year.

2.6 miles (4 km)—the **width of the largest tornado** ever recorded, in **El Reno, Oklahoma**, in 2013.

107

Funnel cloud
The funnel is made of water droplets, dust, and debris.

Wreckage
The tornado cuts a swathe of damage, flattening crops and damaging buildings.

4 Tornado
The rotation in the storm becomes focused into a narrow column of air that starts to spin faster. If this column emerges from the base of the storm, it is called a funnel cloud. If it reaches down to the ground, it becomes a tornado.

Winter tornadoes
The main tornado season in the US is spring and early summer, but in December 2021, there were 202 tornadoes, compared to an average for that month of just 24. Scientists believe that climate change may make winter tornadoes more likely.

Dust storm

Rolling across the desert at high speed, dust storms such as this one in Arizona combine strong winds and a dry surface to create an awesome but hazardous weather event.

Also known as haboobs, these breathtaking spectacles originate from a downburst of cold air from a thunderstorm in a dry area, which may be many miles (kilometers) away. Cold air is dense so it hugs the ground, picking up dust as it travels across the desert at up to 60 mph (96 km/h). Haboobs are seen across the dusty desert regions of the world.

Storm Bernd
The devastating storm that caused the floods stayed over the region for three days. The German Weather Service named it Bernd.

Heavy rain
The storm produced more than 3.9 in (100 mm) of rain in three days. This is more than the normal total for the whole month of July.

Steep-sided region
The Ahr Valley has very steep sides, mostly covered in forest. In some places, the trees have been cleared for vineyards.

Ahr River
This is a small river, flowing into the much larger Rhine River. In summer, the Ahr River is usually quite shallow.

1 Storms and heavy rain
A slow-moving rainstorm lingers over the region for several days. At this stage, there is no flooding, but the soil is becoming saturated and small streams are starting to fill and run down the valley sides. The river is rising slowly.

Wet soil
Not all the flooding is due to the river overflowing. In areas around the river, such as valley slopes and forests, heavy rain infiltrates the soil pore spaces until they can hold no more water. If this continues, the area will flood.

Rain falls to the ground.

Vegetation traps some rain.

Air gaps (pore spaces) in the soil fill up.

Solid rock

2 Flooding begins
With streams full to overflowing and the soil completely saturated, the fields in the valley start to flood. The river is running faster and bursting its banks, spilling onto roads and into houses. Fallen trees, cars, and other debris are washed down the river.

Floods

From coastal cities to riverside villages, floods have the potential to severely damage buildings and roads and to destroy crops and the natural landscape, even uprooting trees.

In July 2021, parts of Europe were hit by devastating floods, including the German Ahr Valley. Flooding in inland areas, such as this valley, can be caused by heavy rain that falls in a few minutes or hours—known as flash flooding. But this flood was caused by rain falling over three days, filling the river until it overflowed—known as fluvial flooding. Climate change is expected to worsen intense rainfall events.

Valley underwater
This is the town of Altenahr, Germany, before, during, and after the floods. Nestled between steep hills, this town was affected by an overflowing river and water from heavy rain rushing down the steep slopes and into populated areas, destroying everything in its path. Clearing the debris after the event took many weeks. In fact, six months after the flood, many people were still living in temporary homes.

6 hours– the **time it took,** in February 2022, for **12 in (300 mm) of rain** to fall in **Queensland, Australia,** causing **flash flooding** and **mass evacuations.**

24 in (61 cm)–the **depth of flowing floodwater** that can **float a car** and **carry it away.**

111

Hurricane Ida

Flooding along coastlines can be caused by a storm surge–a raised sea level generated by strong winds at sea. In August 2021, Hurricane Ida led to devastating floods in Louisiana, with a catastrophic storm surge 9.8–13 ft (3–4 m) above normal high-tide levels.

Thames Barrier

The Thames Barrier protects the city of London, UK, from storm surges in the North Sea, which could flow up the river estuary and flood the city. When a storm surge happens at the same time as high tide and very heavy rainfall, the barrier is closed.

Hydraulic system

Lifting mechanism

SURGE TIDE

RIVER FLOW

Riverbed

Gate closed

Open
Water flows freely when the gate is open.

Closed
The gate blocks the surging water.

Overflowing river
The river is full and starts to overflow onto the flat valley floor. Flood defenses designed to protect buildings cannot cope with so much water.

Water runs down
Rainwater runs quickly down the steep valley sides, and small streams grow rapidly, carrying water into the river, which is now flooding.

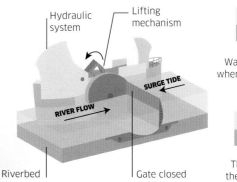

Mass wreckage
In Altenahr, most buildings were flooded and some were completely destroyed. Roads and bridges were also badly damaged, with mud and debris covering a wide area.

Lucky escape
Buildings on higher ground escape the flooding. This chapel was just above the flood level.

Roads
Most roads in the valley are flooded and cars are washed away, some with people inside.

Saturated soil

Like a sponge, the soil can hold only a certain amount of water before it starts to overflow. After heavy rain, puddles form on the surface, which can build up to flood the area.

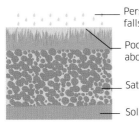

Persistent, heavy rain falls to the ground.

Pool of water rises above vegetation.

Saturated soil

Solid rock

Debris buildup
Branches or whole trees, building materials, trailers, and cars pile up against bridges and block the river, making the flooding worse.

3 The aftermath
After the rain stops, the water gradually recedes. This reveals how flood debris has piled up against bridges, acting like a dam and causing more water to spill out of the river. Damage to homes and businesses is extensive and some buildings are destroyed completely.

Fire triangle

Wherever they occur, all fires need three key ingredients to start—oxygen, fuel, and heat. In a forest, there is always plenty of oxygen in the air. The fuel comes from the trees, with dead leaves and branches more likely to burn following dry weather. Heat is provided by hot weather.

OXYGEN

HEAT

FUEL

3 Cloud forms

If the atmosphere is unstable, the cloud will extend and deepen above the fire. Clouds like this have their own special name—pyrocumulus—which means a cumulus cloud that is caused by a fire.

Fire whirl

The extreme heat generates rapidly rising currents of air. These may start to spin and can suck up a tongue of whirling flames.

Plume cools **2**

As the air in the plume rises, it cools and water vapor in the plume starts to condense. The natural process of cloud formation is made stronger and faster by the heat from the fire.

Aerial firefighting

Firefighters use specially adapted helicopters to drop water on the fire. They can scoop up water from lakes and reservoirs.

Smoke rises **1**

The fire generates smoke and heats the air, which starts to rise in a plume above the fire. Strong winds blow in toward the fire to replace the rising air.

Spreading fire

Strong winds and dry vegetation cause the fire to spread. Fires also spread more rapidly uphill because hot air rises.

Damaged homes

Buildings in forested areas are at risk in a fire. People should evacuate immediately when advised and drive away from the fire.

Fighting fire

Dressed in protective clothing, firefighters risk their lives to tackle flames often in temperatures exceeding 104°F (40°C).

Forest fires

Forest fires—sometimes called bushfires or wildfires—are a dramatic example of what can happen when extreme heat and drought combine with devastating results.

Fires are a natural occurrence in many forested areas but have become more frequent and widespread in recent years. They can destroy natural habitats and, as human settlements expand into forest areas, impact human lives too. Sadly, people often cause fires with careless behavior, sometimes intentionally. In fact, nearly 85 percent of forest fires in the United States are thought to be started by people.

Fire and weather

Weather conditions can be a factor in the starting of forest fires. But sometimes forest fires—such as this one in Australia—can create their own weather systems that can sustain the flames and cause it to spread. The huge amounts of heat from the fire act to drive rising air and strong winds, and can even generate thunderstorms.

2019 The **driest year on record in Australia**, which includes the **highest average temperature** and **lowest rainfall**.

121.3°F (49.6°C)—the **Canadian record high temperature**, in Lytton on June 29, 2021. Days later, the **town was destroyed** by a **forest fire**. **113**

4 Thunderstorm brews
Once the cloud is large enough, perhaps several miles (kilometers) deep, it can generate rain and even thunder. The fire now has its own weather system, with deep cloud, rain, and strong winds near the ground.

5 Rain pours
Heavy rain falls from the thunderstorm, which evaporates before reaching the ground due to intense heat in the air. This can also generate a downward current of air that causes strong wind gusts near the ground.

Facing the heat

Heat waves and drought are weather conditions that often occur together. Scientists have shown that climate change has already made heat waves more likely across most of the globe, and droughts have also become commonplace in some regions, including North America and the Mediterranean. Climate change will make such events even more likely.

North American drought
In June 2021, large parts of the western United States and Canada were affected by a period of hot dry weather, which led to many forest fires.

European heat wave
The summer of 2021 was the warmest to date in Europe, and people cooled off wherever they could. Forest fires affected many countries around the Mediterranean.

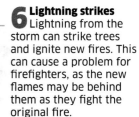

6 Lightning strikes
Lightning from the storm can strike trees and ignite new fires. This can cause a problem for firefighters, as the new flames may be behind them as they fight the original fire.

Flying from danger
Birds, such as this galah, escape the fast-spreading fires. They will need to find a new home in a safer forested region.

Wind gust
Downbursts from the thunderstorm can cause strong wind gusts that topple trees and fan the flames even further.

Fire break
This is a line through the forest where the trees have been cleared to stop the flames from spreading past the break.

Helping native animals
After devastating forest fires in the southern hemisphere summer of 2019–2020, many animals, such as this koala, were rescued and treated by local volunteers.

LIFE ON EARTH

Different climate conditions around the world shape its landscapes to create unique conditions for life. From lush forests to dry deserts, each of these biomes teems with cleverly adapted plants and animals. Many face threats from human activity and climate change.

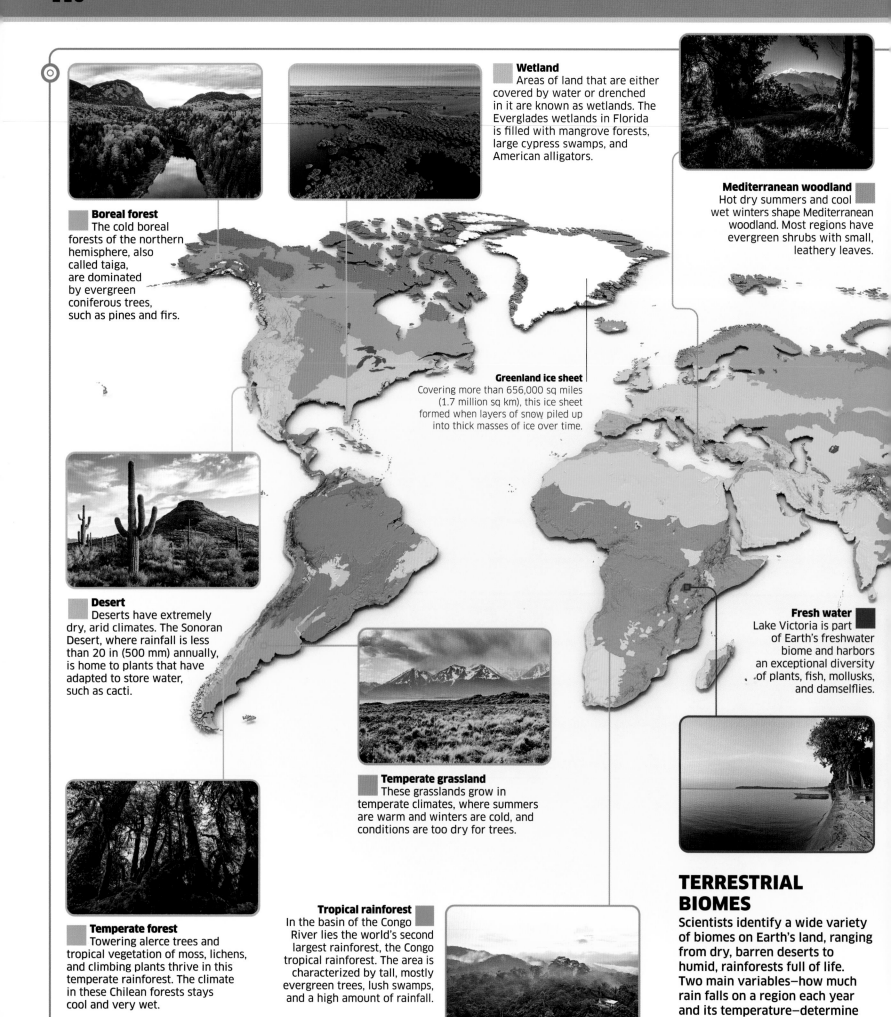

Wetland
Areas of land that are either covered by water or drenched in it are known as wetlands. The Everglades wetlands in Florida is filled with mangrove forests, large cypress swamps, and American alligators.

Boreal forest
The cold boreal forests of the northern hemisphere, also called taiga, are dominated by evergreen coniferous trees, such as pines and firs.

Mediterranean woodland
Hot dry summers and cool wet winters shape Mediterranean woodland. Most regions have evergreen shrubs with small, leathery leaves.

Greenland ice sheet
Covering more than 656,000 sq miles (1.7 million sq km), this ice sheet formed when layers of snow piled up into thick masses of ice over time.

Desert
Deserts have extremely dry, arid climates. The Sonoran Desert, where rainfall is less than 20 in (500 mm) annually, is home to plants that have adapted to store water, such as cacti.

Fresh water
Lake Victoria is part of Earth's freshwater biome and harbors an exceptional diversity of plants, fish, mollusks, and damselflies.

Temperate grassland
These grasslands grow in temperate climates, where summers are warm and winters are cold, and conditions are too dry for trees.

Temperate forest
Towering alerce trees and tropical vegetation of moss, lichens, and climbing plants thrive in this temperate rainforest. The climate in these Chilean forests stays cool and very wet.

Tropical rainforest
In the basin of the Congo River lies the world's second largest rainforest, the Congo tropical rainforest. The area is characterized by tall, mostly evergreen trees, lush swamps, and a high amount of rainfall.

TERRESTRIAL BIOMES

Scientists identify a wide variety of biomes on Earth's land, ranging from dry, barren deserts to humid, rainforests full of life. Two main variables—how much rain falls on a region each year and its temperature—determine which biome will develop.

Arctic tundra
At cool latitudes in the Arctic, tundra has low-growing plants, such as grasses and mosses. Underground ice, called permafrost, prevents deep-rooted trees from growing.

Alpine tundra
This treeless habitat with low-lying vegetation is found on mountains at high altitudes all over the world. Temperatures at night are typically below freezing.

EARTH'S BIOMES

Biomes are Earth's major habitats, such as tropical rainforests or oceans. They cover large areas where plants and animals are adapted to live under certain conditions. In different parts of the world, biomes of the same type—such as savannas in Africa and Australia—can look very similar but can vary a lot in their species.

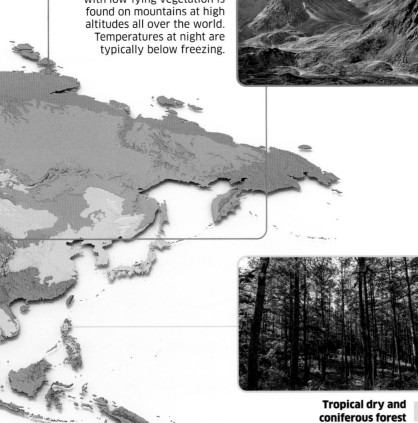

Tropical dry and coniferous forest
Some kinds of tropical forests are dominated by conifers, or—in places with a pronounced dry season—have deciduous trees that lose their leaves when rainfall levels drop.

Tropical grassland
This tropical grassland has two seasons—wet and dry. Its vegetation includes scattered trees.

Ocean
Oceans accommodate a variety of marine species, from tiny plankton to golden butterfly fish in vibrant coral reefs.

ECOREGIONS

Biomes can be further divided into smaller areas called ecoregions—areas of land or water with a distinct mixture of environmental conditions, plants, and animals. Large biomes, such as forests, grasslands, and deserts, can be subdivided into 867 terrestrial ecoregions.

Amazonian ecoregions

Diverse ecoregions exist within the Amazon rainforest, with different communities of animals that have evolved in separate geographical regions. For instance, ecoregions separated by rivers have their own species of spider monkeys.

Napo ecoregion
White-bellied spider monkeys live in riverside and marshy rainforests.

Guianan ecoregion
Red-faced black spider monkeys live in the high rainforests of the interior.

Southwest Amazon ecoregion
Black spider monkeys live in rainforest-savanna borders.

Tapajós-Xingu ecoregion
White-whiskered spider monkeys live in drier semideciduous rainforests.

Microhabitats

Little patches of habitat, such as rock pools on a seashore or treetop plants in a rainforest, are called microhabitats. They provide homes for animals small enough to live there.

Treetop pool
Bromeliad plants high up in the rainforest canopy collect water in their leaves. These provide a small treetop pool for insect larvae and frogs.

118 life on earth ∘ **ARCTIC TUNDRA**

164 ft (50 m)—the **depth of a sinkhole discovered in the Yamal Peninsula** in northwest Siberia in 2020.

Arctic tundra

High in the northern hemisphere lie vast, cold, treeless landscapes where long winters give way to short summers.

Life in the Arctic tundra is well adapted to the dramatic seasonal changes that take place above and below ground. Some animals, such as caribou, migrate to warmer grounds in winter, while others stay and endure the inhospitable, icy conditions. Due to climate change, this vital habitat is warming rapidly and the permafrost below is breaking up, causing dramatic changes in the landscape.

Polygonal ground
Patterns of polygons up to 100 ft (30 m) across form on the surface of the tundra around icy wedges and troughs in the ground. In the warmer months, they are flooded by meltwater.

Caribou
These animals' wide hooves help them migrate long distances across the uneven surfaces of the tundra.

Wolf
Fierce predators of the tundra, packs of wolves hunt animals such as caribou and muskox.

Ptarmigan
Ptarmigans like to forage on rocks covered in lichens and eat vegetation such as purple saxifrage.

Summer

When the snow melts, rocky ground and wet, marshy habitats open up to the animals of the tundra. Lichens, mosses, and shrubs grow around colorful flowers, such as the Arctic poppy and purple saxifrage, all making the most of the weak sunlight.

Snowy owl
Predatory snowy owls often swoop down and pounce on lemmings using their large, sharp talons, or claws.

Brown lemming
These small rodents have big appetites, feeding on grasses and other vegetation.

Active layer
A compact layer of soil above the permafrost thaws in summer and remains frozen throughout the winter.

Permafrost
Below the tundra's surface lies a thick frozen layer called permafrost. In warmer months, it is thawing due to climate change.

Melted ice
As winter ice melts in the soil, pools of water form above it.

Ice wedge
When snow melts in spring, water fills cracks in the soil, where it freezes to form wedges of ice.

Arctic hare
Buds, berries, mosses, leaves, roots, and twigs are the main diet of Arctic hares.

Mosquito
Rising temperatures have allowed mosquitoes to thrive. They harass caribou, biting their skin and contributing to their decline.

1,970 ft (600 m)—the **thickness of the permafrost in the northern regions** of the Arctic.

−29°F (−34°C)—the average **temperature of the Arctic tundra** in winter.

1,200 years. The **age reached by some pingos** in Canada.

119

Pingo
These dome-shaped hills are made when the ground is pushed up due to the force of frozen water beneath.

Polar bear
With short ears to minimize heat loss, polar bears are well adapted to roam through the tundra.

Arctic fox
Thick, white winter coats and long, fluffy tails that act like blankets keep arctic foxes warm in winter.

Muskox
These large animals have both an outer, long-haired coat and an inner, woolly coat.

Common raven
Distinguished by its deep croaking call, this large and remarkably intelligent bird is very vocal.

A 2021 report estimated that the Arctic could lose **89 percent** of its permafrost by 2100.

Mystery sinkholes

For millennia, the frozen permafrost has been Earth's largest store of carbon on land. Today, rising temperatures are thawing the permafrost and releasing carbon dioxide into the atmosphere. In the Siberian Arctic, deep craters created by violent explosions puzzle scientists. Some believe that they are caused by methane trapped in the permafrost being released as it thaws.

Winter

Fierce, icy winds and snow drifts are among the challenges faced by tundra animals in winter, as plants die or go dormant. Some of them, such as Arctic hares, have adapted to change the color of their coats, turning white to blend in with the surroundings.

Permafrost
A mixture of ice, sand, soil, and rock makes up this underground layer of frozen permafrost—a hugely important carbon sink.

Arctic hare
Camouflaged by their winter snowy coat, the hares' large hind feet help them to move around and dig into the snow.

Ptarmigan
The ptarmigan's feathered feet keep it warm and act like snowshoes that prevent it from sinking into soft snow.

Ice wedge
These wedge-shaped masses of ice grow annually as water infiltrating cracks expands when it freezes.

Lemming burrow
Lemmings carve a network of burrows in the snow and nest there for the winter, feeding on moss and grassy tufts.

Chilly climes

The coldest habitats on our planet are found either at extreme northern or southern latitudes or at high altitudes, where temperatures are cold enough to turn snowfall to ice.

These biomes include the icy polar expanses at the top and bottom of the Earth and the alpine tundra. Despite the harsh conditions, animals and plants manage to survive in these places, although many migrate to warmer climates in winter to avoid the freezing temperatures. These cold but vital habitats are particularly threatened by climate change, which is causing ice sheets and permafrost to melt, with devastating consequences for the planet.

Krummholz trees
Between the tree line and the more open alpine vegetation appear strange looking trees with a bent appearance. These have been shaped and deformed by the strong icy winds. Stems grow only on the downwind side of their trunks, causing the trees to become more and more bent and to have flag-shaped branches.

Mountain weta
This giant insect can live at altitudes of up to 5,900 ft (1,800 m) and can withstand below-freezing temperatures.

⊙ ALPINE ZONATION

Traveling up a mountain, such as the Southern Alps in New Zealand, reveals a wide range of ecosystems that change with the elevation. From lush lowland forests to treeless tundra and snowy mountain tops, all are inhabited by wildlife well adapted to their high-altitude homes. Above the tree line, the height at which trees no longer grow, the alpine tundra begins and habitats get progressively harsher.

Nival
Permanent snow and ice cover the steep mountain tops of the nival zone. This cold level is an oxygen-starved environment, with only lichens, mosses, and very few flowering plants.

Alpine
Few plants survive on the rocky scree and fell-fields of the alpine zone. Cushion plants form in low mounds, with their shoots and leaves packed tightly in, so they can survive the harsh open environment.

Rock wren
The rock wren gets its name because it forages on rocks. It makes warm nests on the ground, but these leave it vulnerable to predators such as stoats.

Subalpine
These grasslands are dominated by slow-growing tussock grasses that are resistant to frost and retain water well. They shelter lizards, insects, and birds.

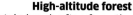

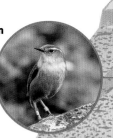

Mountain buttercup
The world's largest buttercup, this plant with its big, white flowers has long roots to reach liquid water when the surface is frozen.

High-altitude forest
Mountain beech often form the tree line and are mixed with silver and red beech in forests below it. Beech trees can grow in very poor soil.

Kea
These endangered mountain birds have striking orange patches on their wings and are thought to be very intelligent.

Lower-altitude forest
At the foothills of mountains, large forests filled with broad-leaved and coniferous trees spread across the landscape.

At the North Pole, **the sun does not rise for six months in winter** or set for six months in summer.

6–9 ft (2–3 m)—the typical **thickness** of Arctic sea ice.

The **Arctic is warming twice as fast** as anywhere else in the world.

121

POLAR BIOMES

The polar habitats, around Earth's North and South poles, are cold and dry, with ice covering most of the land and sea. Bitterly cold winds and near-freezing waters are some of the challenges that life here has to contend with. On land, there are fewer trees or shrubs, and lichens, mosses, and algae are found at the base of the food chain. As well as climate change, overfishing and resource extraction threaten this biome.

Arctic vs. Antarctic

While both poles are covered in ice, most Antarctic ice is on land and most Arctic ice lies over sea. Polar ice is essential in regulating Earth's temperature. As sea ice melts, the ocean absorbs more sunlight and becomes warmer.

Key

- ■ Ice shelf
- Summer average sea ice extent 1990–2010
- Winter average sea ice extent 1990–2010

Antarctic ice
The continent of Antarctica is permanently covered by a thick ice cap and encircled by a thin layer of sea ice in the Southern Ocean.

Arctic ice
A large layer of sea ice covers the Arctic Ocean, which undergoes seasonal changes. There is also some land ice across Greenland and other small islands.

Life on ice

Survival is tough for animals in the polar regions. Seals, different species of which live at both poles, make use of the icy land, masses of floating ice that cover the oceans, and freezing seas to live, feed, and breed. They have thick fat or fur to keep them warm.

Breeding
Many seal species, such as harp seals, breed and care for their young on land, or on floating sea ice. The seal pups use the ice as a base from which to make their first trips into the water.

Feeding
The icy waters of the most northerly and southerly oceans are ideal hunting grounds. Seals' streamlined bodies allow them to dive deep to catch fish.

Drifting
Huge chunks of ice float in both seas and can be ideal resting spots for harbor seals. The animals can also carve breathing holes into the ice, where they can pop up for air.

SHIFTING TREE LINES

As temperatures warm due to climate change, trees can expand onto mountains. This causes the tree line to move to higher altitudes (or closer to the poles). But this warming and the presence of trees further up the mountainside changes the soil and causes usually permanently frozen ground to melt. As the permafrost melts, more greenhouse gases are released.

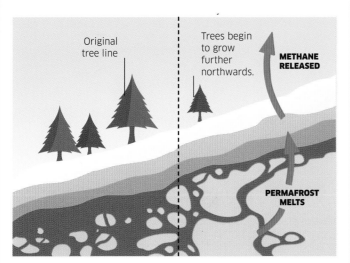

Original tree line

Trees begin to grow further northwards.

METHANE RELEASED

PERMAFROST MELTS

Trees move higher
As the tree line shifts, microbe activity decomposes plant material in the soil, releasing methane, a greenhouse gas 85 times more powerful than carbon dioxide.

ICY ADAPTATIONS

Many organisms have adapted to cold habitats in remarkable ways. Walruses developed tusks to use as ice picks, whereas some animals such as icefish can create a chemical that works as an antifreeze inside their bodies. This stops ice crystals from forming, which would otherwise kill off their body cells. Lichens can survive in temperatures as low as −4°F (−20°C) and still photosynthesize. They are sensitive to air pollution and are also used as indicators of environmental change.

Walrus
A walrus's thick layer of blubber acts as insulation in ice-cold waters.

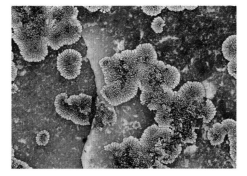

Lichens
A mix of an algae and a fungus, these unique organisms can grow even under snow cover.

Icefish
In the Southern Ocean, icefish make antifreeze chemicals that stop them from freezing.

122 life on earth ○ **FORESTS**

100 ft (30 m)—the estimated height of trees in the very first forests on Earth, formed during the Carboniferous period **360–300 million years ago**.

Forests

Providing shelter, shade, and food for many animals, forests spread across the planet in various forms. Each type has its own climate, mix of tree species, and diverse range of plants and animals.

The most widely found habitat on Earth, forests provide important environmental benefits. The abundance of trees they contain can help prevent floods by anchoring the soil with their roots, filter out pollutants before they enter the water, and provide clean air. They also absorb huge amounts of the greenhouse gas carbon dioxide.

WHAT ARE FORESTS?

Trees dominate forest habitats. Even though their masses of leaves often block out much of the light, many other plants and animals interact with them to form complex ecosystems. From the heights of the canopy down to the dead leaves on the forest floor, each part of the forest serves a function.

From forest to grassland

Many places around the world have trees, but not all are forests. In some areas, trees are more sparsely scattered across the landscape.

Forest
The thickest tree density is found here. The trees grow so close together that their leaves form a canopy.

Woodland
Plenty of trees grow in woodlands, but they are further apart, meaning the soil is less shaded.

Shrubland
Low-growing plants such as shrubs and bushes grow here, as the area is too arid for many trees.

Grassland
Trees are found on some grasslands but are not very tightly packed. Most animals feed on grasses instead.

Types of forests

Forests around the world vary in their climate, altitude, and the species of trees that grow there—from broad-leaved trees to tall snow-covered pines. The three main types of forests that occupy the most land on Earth are temperate forests, tropical forests, and boreal forests, but there are also other important subcategories.

Tropical dry and coniferous forest
Tropical regions with long dry seasons often contain lots of evergreen conifers or other trees that drop their leaves in times of drought.

Mediterranean woodland
Lush forests of Mediterranean woodland occur in places with hot, dry summers and cold, wet winters. Some of their trees have evolved a thick, fire-resistant bark.

Photosynthesis

Trees make their food using sunlight. They absorb carbon dioxide from the atmosphere and water from the ground and use the energy in sunlight to convert these into food. This process releases oxygen back into the atmosphere, an essential resource for humans and other life.

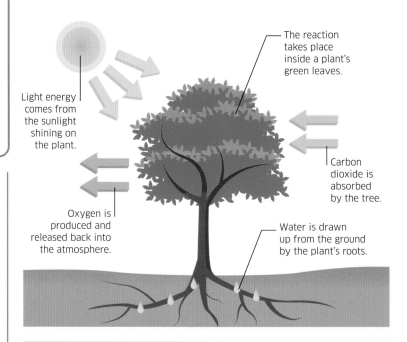

The reaction takes place inside a plant's green leaves.

Light energy comes from the sunlight shining on the plant.

Carbon dioxide is absorbed by the tree.

Oxygen is produced and released back into the atmosphere.

Water is drawn up from the ground by the plant's roots.

The forest floor

When dead leaves, bits of bark, stems, and tree branches fall to the forest floor, they start to decompose, adding nutrients to the soil. Within this damp leaf litter live organisms, including lizards, earthworms, fungi, algae, bacteria, and soil mites.

Life cycle of a tree

Trees can live for many years, and reproduce using tiny packages called seeds. These are carried far from the original tree by animals, wind, or water. The seeds of pine trees are held inside scale-covered cones, which protect them from ice, snow, and predators until they are ready to be spread.

Closed pine cones
Brown, ridged pine cones carry the seeds of pine trees. They grow on the tree branches and stay anchored there until the seeds are fully developed inside them.

Spreading seeds
When conditions are warm and the best for a seed to thrive in, the scales on pine cones open and release the seeds. These have wings that the wind catches.

Sprouting seed
Carried by the wind, the seeds land on the forest floor away from their parent tree so they will not have to compete with it for nutrients.

400 billion tons (363 billion metric tons) of **carbon are stored in the soils of boreal peatlands** worldwide.

3,600 miles (5,800 km)—the **length of the world's largest stretch of taiga, extending across Russia** from the Pacific Ocean to the Ural Mountains.

123

BOREAL FORESTS

Boreal forests, also known by the Russian word "taiga," are the Earth's largest biome on land. Named after Boreas, the Greek god of the north wind, these chilly forests are found across Siberia, Scandinavia, the US state of Alaska, and Canada. Winters in boreal forests are long and very cold and dark.

Conifers
A common tree type, conifers, such as spruce, pine, and fir, are typically evergreen. They have seed cones and long, needle-shaped leaves that reduce the water lost from the tree.

Berry bushes
Fruiting bushes, such as crowberries, carpet forest floors. These evergreen shrubs produce blueberry-like, edible berries clustered around the stalk that provide food for many animals.

Bogs
Many boreal forests contain moist patches of ground called bogs and peatlands. This squishy land is often made up of many dead plants. Trapped in the wet bog, they decompose much slower than they usually would, forming peat and releasing less carbon dioxide into the air. Bogs are important carbon sinks—environments that trap carbon.

Forest plants
Although they exist in colder, harsher climes than other forests, boreal forests are still home to a diverse range of plants. The northernmost boreal forests are dominated by evergreen trees, but southern parts also contain deciduous trees that shed their leaves, such as birch, poplar, and aspen. Shrubs of different heights, such as briars and berries, grow below tree height, while mosses carpet the forest floor and tree bark.

Mosses
On the boggy forest ground lie a variety of spongy mosses. These small plants do not have roots but use hairlike structures to anchor themselves.

Taiga survival
The trees of the taiga make ideal habitats for birds such as crossbills and owls, but many migrate during winter to avoid its harsh temperatures. Other animals, such as brown bears, hibernate during the cold months, hiding inside cozy dens and slowing their body systems down so that they do not need to eat.

Evergreen and deciduous

Trees use their leaves to make food from the sun. Evergreen trees—such as most needle-leaved conifers, like spruce—keep their leaves year-round. But deciduous trees lose all their leaves during the winter, which helps them save energy.

SPRUCE SPRIG

Needle-shaped leaves

MAPLE LEAF

Birch
Fast-growing trees with distinctive whitish bark, birches prefer damp, slightly acidic soils.

Mistletoe
This plant takes the form of ball-shaped growths—parasites that grow on trees, extracting nutrients from them.

Spruce
The needles of these evergreen trees have a waxy coating that helps them conserve water during the winter.

Oak
Often called the king of the woods, this deciduous tree has distinctive leaves with rounded lobes.

Crested tit
This little bird, known for its black-and-white head crest, is looking for insects and seeds to give it winter energy.

Lynx
These predators survive the harsh winter by hunting hares and other forest-dwelling creatures.

Snowdrops
Clumps of these hardy, white flowers bloom during winter.

Hedgehog
These small, spiny mammals hibernate to preserve energy when food is scarce in winter, sleeping in nests of leaves.

Brambling
Flocks of bramblings that have migrated south feed on conifer seeds and the nuts of beech trees.

Brown hare
Unlike hares from colder habitats, brown hares don't change their coat to white in winter, relying on speed and stamina to escape predators.

Primroses
One of the earliest flowers to emerge from winter, primroses provide butterflies with an important source of nectar.

Bluebells
Bell-shaped, sweet-smelling, violet-blue flowers bloom in the spring, carpeting the forest floor.

Orchids
A colorful family of flowers, rare orchids bloom in purple, white, and pink in forest glades.

Red deer
These social animals live in herds. In spring, the females leave the herd to give birth to young.

Wood anemones
With delicate white flowers tinged with pink in spring, this plant is a hallmark of ancient woodlands.

Great spotted woodpecker
These birds' strong beaks help them communicate with their mates by a repetitive motion known as drumming.

Through the seasons

More than 10,000 years ago, much of Europe was covered by temperate forests. One of the last remaining pockets of these ancient forests is Białowieża Forest, on the border between Poland and Belarus. As its trees change color with the passing of the seasons, the creatures that frolic on the forest floor find ways to adapt and survive.

55°F (12.5°C)—the **average annual temperature** of Bialowieza Forest, which **ranges from 23°F (–5°C) to 68°F (20°C)** during the year.

1,000 years old—the **age reached by some chestnut trees**, which can **grow up to 115 ft (35 m) tall.**

125

European honey buzzard
This bird of prey hunts insects, catching them in mid-air among the treetops.

Temperate forests

Experiencing both chilly, snow-covered winters and warm, balmy summers, these diverse forests are shaped by the seasons—changing dramatically throughout the year.

The trees and plants of temperate forests are attuned to their constantly changing temperatures—with many flowering in the spring and shedding their leaves in the fall. This seasonal leaf fall forms a decaying litter on the ground that helps fertilize the soil, allowing it to support the many kinds of life that flourish on the forest floor.

Chestnut
In fall, the female flowers of the chestnut tree develop spiny capsules containing three to seven brown nuts.

Pine marten
Depositing scats (droppings) in prominent places around the forest allows these agile, solitary mammals to mark their territory.

Fox
These shy, intelligent mammals are solitary hunters. Their thick tails help them balance and keep warm in the cold.

Raspberries
These sweet, red berries are a welcome meal for animals such as pine martens.

Hyphae   Cap

Eurasian jay
Fall nuts and seeds such as acorns are the favorite foods of these colorful birds, which bury some to save them for winter.

Foxgloves
An important source of nectar for pollinating bees, this bell-shaped pink flower also has medicinal uses.

Bison
Europe's largest land mammal, the European bison was once extinct in the wild. Herds have been successfully reintroduced to temperate forests.

Badgers
These nocturnal animals spend time in underground tunnels called setts. Here they raise their cubs who first emerge in early summer.

Lady's slippers
These summer-flowering orchids, which prefer shaded mixed and deciduous forests, are threatened with extinction due to habitat fragmentation.

Fly agaric
Below its bright red cap, this toxic fungus spreads a network of fine threads called hyphae through the soil, exchanging nutrients with trees and breaking down fall leaf litter.

Białowieża Forest in Poland is home to around 12,000 species of plants and animals.

Tropical rainforests

Home to as much as 50 percent of all species in the world, tropical rainforests are the most biodiverse places on Earth.

These wet, leafy forests are found close to the equator, where a warm, moist climate allows life to thrive. They experience the most rainfall of any biome—causing the densely packed trees to flourish and form lush green canopies that are also crucial stores of carbon dioxide. Despite their huge importance, only scattered pockets of these rich habitats remain, and their rapid destruction is contributing to climate change and species extinction.

Swarming bats
Swarms of fruit bats disperse around the rainforest, through the trees and above the canopy.

Emergent trees
There is little shelter in these very tall trees that rise high above the canopy layer. Here, birds fly among the isolated treetops.

Orangutan
The only great apes found in Asia, orangutans live solitary lives high in the trees. They feed primarily on fruit, plucking durian fruits with their long arms and ripping them open with their bare hands. All three species are critically endangered.

Rhinoceros hornbill
These large birds spend their life in the treetops, flying between trees to find food. They find cavities to nest in large trees.

Canopy layer
Light penetrates through a dense network of trees and branches called the canopy. Most animals in the rainforest live in this layer, which forms a leafy roof over the lower parts of the forest.

Towering trees
Tall trees called dipterocarps dominate the rainforest in Borneo's lowlands and can grow up to 66 ft (20 m) tall.

Under canopy layer
A dark, humid layer of shade-tolerant, mossy trees, covered in climbers and epiphytes trying to reach the light, dominates the under canopy layer.

Durian fruit
Juicy durian fruits are a sweet treat for the animals who eat them, but to humans they have a strong pong.

Flying lizard
The colorful five-banded gliding lizard sails between the trees using wing-shaped flaps of skin supported by elongated ribs. When not gliding, it clings to tree trunks and feeds on ants and other insects.

Red leaf monkeys
Bands of up to 13 red leaf monkeys spend nearly all their time in trees, eating seeds, flowers, and fruits.

6 percent of **Earth's land surface** is covered by **tropical rainforests**.

2,000 or more **tropical forest plants** have been identified by scientists as **useful for helping treat cancer**.

15,000 different plant species are found in Borneo.

127

Ferns

A type of plant called an epiphyte, ferns grow on a host such as a tree, spreading their roots into compost on tree branches.

Sunda cloud leopard

This wild cat found only in Southeast Asia is a carnivore, sometimes hunting monkeys.

Mountain tree shrew

Tree shrews forage close to the forest floor, looking for fruit, leaves, and seeds, and hunting for insects.

Pitcher plant

With a protective lid and a deep cup, this carnivorous plant digests the unwilling insects that become trapped inside it.

Giant forest ants

These oversized insects, which live in colonies of thousands, trail the forest floor, foraging for insects, honeydew, and leaves.

Sunda pangolin

Covered in masses of tough scales, these ant-eating animals are the most trafficked mammals in the world.

The forest floor

The bottom layer of a rainforest sees fungi and shade-tolerant plants grow among the giant roots of trees and a litter of decaying dead leaves.

Rafflesia arnoldii

Known as a corpse lily because of its rotting meat smell, this parasite on vines produces the world's largest flower, around 3.3 ft (1 m) wide.

Strangler fig

This tree-killer starts life as a seed on a branch high in the canopy, extending its roots down the host tree's trunk until it engulfs the entire tree.

Colugo

Using a kite-shaped membrane, this furry mammal can leap off a tree and glide more than 330 ft (100 m) to the next one.

Shrubs

Smaller trees and shrubs lie between the forest floor and understory layer.

Ironwood

Slow-growing, evergreen trees, known as ironwood trees, can reach up to 164 ft (50 m) in height.

Borneo rainforest

The rainforests on the island of Borneo are some of the oldest in the world—home to thousands of species, many of which are only found there. In the trees, there are four layers, where creatures make their home. Not much light filters down through them, meaning life in the treetops can be very different to that on the forest floor.

Cauliflory

Some flowers and fruits, such as those of the kalumpang tree, develop directly on the trunks, branches, and limbs of trees, instead of growing on a separate leafy shoot. This makes them closer to pollinators and animals who can spread their seeds far and wide.

Medicinal plants

More than 25 percent of all medicines used today are derived from rainforest plants. The rosy periwinkle, found in Madagascar's rainforest, is the source of two drugs, vincristine and vinblastine, that help treat childhood leukemia and Hodgkin's disease.

Mongolian Steppe

The largest temperate grassland in the world, the Eurasian Steppe extends from Hungary in central Europe all the way to China. It contains many diverse areas of grassland, such as this region in Mongolia—a type of meadow steppe dominated by long grasses and wildflowers that bloom in the summer months. Small mammals such as rodents feed on the grass, while lizards use dry open patches to bask in the sunshine, and birds swoop down to pick off insects.

Great bustard
Colorful and regal, the great bustard is the world's heaviest flying bird. Females weigh five times less than the males— the biggest difference between sexes of any bird.

Grasshopper
Feeding on and laying eggs on the long grasses in the steppe, these flying insects are abundant in the grasslands.

Mongolian marmot
Also called Tarbagan marmots, these furry rodents live in large colonies and construct elaborate underground burrows with nests for their young.

Grasses
Grasslands can contain a mix of long and short grasses. Bunch grasses such as this one grow into tall clumps with tufts at the ends.

Oriental plover
This elegant, long-legged bird changes its brown plumage when breeding to an orange-buff breast and a creamy eyebrow.

Brandt's vole
This small rodent feeds on the leaves of grasses in summer, their bulbs and roots in spring, and stores food underground for winter.

Fertile soil
The top layers of the dark-colored soil are packed with nutrients from decaying grass roots, making this the richest soil of any biome.

Viviparous lizard
Unique among lizards, the common Eurasian lizard incubates its eggs inside its body, then gives birth to live young.

Long roots
Some steppe grasses have long, many-branched roots that help hold the soil together. The roots of this Stipa grass penetrate up to 4.9–6.5 feet (150–200 cm) deep.

Earthworm
These wriggling invertebrates eat decomposing plants, recycling their nutrients. Their tiny burrows introduce more air into the soil.

9.8 ft (3 m)—the height grasses can reach in the wettest parts of temperate grasslands.

Almost **50 percent of all grasslands have already been degraded** and just **5 percent are protected** globally.

20 individuals—the size of the **largest Mongolian marmot families.**

129

Pollination

Insects such as bees visit flowers to get a food called nectar. While there, they pick up powdery grains called pollen by rubbing against a flower's anthers (the male part) and carry it to the stigma, the female part of another flower of the same species. This is called pollination—a flower must be pollinated to make seeds.

Anther with pollen

Temperate grasslands

Large, rolling landscapes of endless grass without trees or scrub, grasslands can appear devoid of life. But, when seen from close up, it becomes clear that the rich soil of this biome supports many plants and small animals.

Temperate grasslands have different names around the world—from the velds of South Africa to the Pampas of Argentina and Uruguay, the prairies of North America, and the steppes of Eurasia. Their hardy grasses, which feed many animals, can regrow quickly and are resilient to changing weather conditions.

Lady's bedstraw

This plant grows into tall clusters of yellow flowers. The blossoms emit a sweet honeylike scent, attracting insects.

Grasslands and grazing

Temperate grasslands are important regions for livestock grazing, historically used by nomadic groups that moved across the steppe with cattle, sheep, and other animals. Although grazing can increase biodiversity, some grasslands are at risk from overgrazing, which can threaten rare species and change the balance of vegetation types.

Formica ants

Complex ant communities make burrows in the soils, where their white larvae grow. They feed on whatever they find, working as a team to support the needs of their colony.

Adder

This venomous snake is an adept hunter, feeding on insects, small mammals, worms, and lizards.

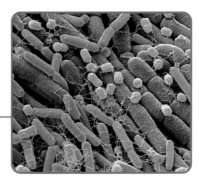

Soil bacteria

Simple life forms so small that they can only be seen under a microscope, masses of tiny bacteria live in the grassland soil. They play a critical role—decomposing dead matter and releasing minerals that are taken up by plants.

Tropical grasslands

Open habitats scattered with trees are found in warm, tropical regions around the world, where grasses and scrub flourish.

In these tropical grasslands, also known as savannas, weather conditions vary between a short wet season of heavy rainfall and a longer dry season. Life on the savanna is adapted to deal with this seasonal variability between flood and periods of barely any rainfall at all. For animals in some places, this means traveling long distances in search of watering holes.

Savannas around the world

Hot areas across Africa, South America, and Australia all have widely spaced trees and open grasslands where animals roam. In addition to these vast expanses of grass, some have larger wooded areas, while others may be partially flooded for some or all of the year, or exist at higher altitudes. Each has its own distinct plant and animal life.

African savanna
The largest savanna and perhaps the most well known, the African savanna is dominated by short grasses and bare ground, dotted with acacia trees. These provide shade for wildebeest and other animals and food for browsers such as the African savanna elephants above.

Australian savanna
Dense grass, scattered trees, and shrubs grow on the sandy soil of the Australian savanna, which stretches across the country's tropical north. Plants here are adapted to survive dry-season fires. Red kangaroos can cover vast distances by hopping fast, in search of food and water.

Mass migration
The seasonal rains dictate much of life in tropical grasslands. The savanna in East Africa sees an annual migration during the dry season, when the lands become too arid. Millions of wildebeest, zebra, and gazelles migrate 500 miles (800 km) from the Serengeti to the Maasai Mara in search of greener lands to graze upon.

Grazers and browsers

Savanna herbivores get their food by feeding on the vegetation. Animals that eat bushes and trees are known as browsers, whereas those that feed on large mouthfuls of grass are called grazers. Some animals are able to adapt to what is available and eat both.

Giraffe browsing
Their long necks allow giraffes to reach the leaves of tall acacia trees, but they also feed on flowers, fruits, and shoots.

Buffalo grazing
Large cattle such as buffalo keep the grass length short by their grazing, reducing the risk of fire.

Termite towers

Termites are an important part of the ecosystem in savannas around the world, including the Brazilian Cerrado, the largest savanna region in South America. These social insects break down and recycle dead grass, as well as build tall, nestlike structures called mounds to shelter in. Each mound is cleverly designed to keep the termites inside cool.

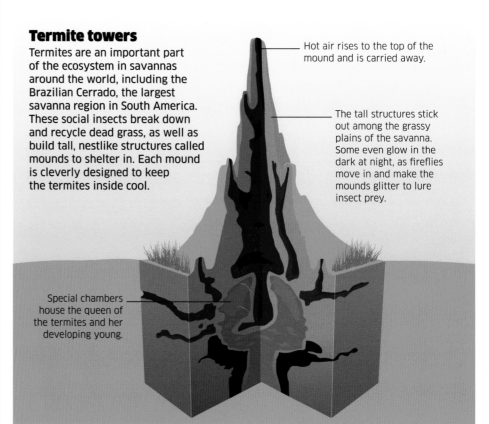

Hot air rises to the top of the mound and is carried away.

The tall structures stick out among the grassy plains of the savanna. Some even glow in the dark at night, as fireflies move in and make the mounds glitter to lure insect prey.

Special chambers house the queen of the termites and her developing young.

5 percent of the planet's **animals and plant species live in the Cerrado tropical grassland in Brazil**, the world's most biodiverse savanna.

3 in (76 mm)—the **average annual rainfall in the Sahara Desert**, one of the world's driest regions.

131

Desert conditions

The driest environments on Earth, deserts can be extremely hot or cold. With little plant life, the animals that live there must work hard to find food and water.

Although deserts are found in all climate zones, the majority are located just north and south of the equator. These areas get little rainfall, which is quickly evaporated by the blistering heat of the sun. There are many different types of deserts—some with towering dunes and others that are flat and cold.

Desert survival

Animals and plants living in deserts have adapted to survive the temperature extremes and drought in remarkable ways, with features that allow them to conserve water and stay cool.

Fennec fox
These North African mammals have very large ears in proportion to their bodies. These radiate heat to help keep the fox cool.

Saguaro cactus
This cactus, which grows in the Sonoran Desert in Arizona, stores water in its succulent stems. Animals such as these horned owls make their homes in the cactus.

Desert at night

Some deserts face dramatic temperature changes between day and night. In the Sahara Desert, temperatures in the day average over 100°F (38°C) but can fall to about 25°F (-3.9°C) at night. Many animals, such as desert jerboas, come out only at night, burrowing into the cool sand during the day.

Cold deserts

Not all deserts are hot. Antarctica gets very little rain or snow, making it a cold desert. The snow that falls has built up into thick ice sheets over a long time. Other cold deserts are found in flat, high-altitude parts of the world, such as the so-called Cold Desert in Indian-administered Ladakh.

How deserts form

Shaped by the wind, air currents, and moisture levels, deserts form in a variety of ways. Some are coastal, whereas others form in the heart of a continent.

Rain-shadow deserts
When moist air rising over a mountain cools and loses its capacity to hold water, rain falls on the windward side. This leaves dry air on the far side, forming a desert. Death Valley in the US is in the rain shadow of the Sierra Nevada.

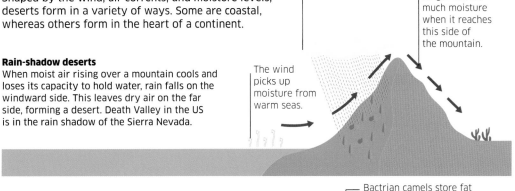

Air cools, releasing water as rain.

The wind no longer carries much moisture when it reaches this side of the mountain.

The wind picks up moisture from warm seas.

Midcontinent deserts
Some regions in continents, such as the Gobi Desert in Mongolia and China, become deserts because they are far from any ocean. The air that reaches them has already lost all its moisture.

Bactrian camels store fat in their two humps.

High-pressure deserts
At either side of the equator, hot, moist air rises and travels north or south. As it cools over the tropics, it loses most of its moisture as rain. The cool, dry air then sinks, creating areas of high pressure with dry climates, such as the Sahara Desert in northern Africa.

SAHARA DESERT

EQUATOR

Winds blow north from the equator.

Coastal deserts
In coastal areas close to cold ocean currents, cold air from the ocean moves over the land. The cooled air cannot hold enough water for precipitation.

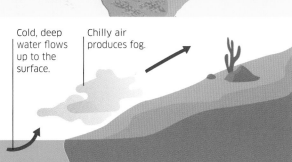

Cold, deep water flows up to the surface.

Chilly air produces fog.

Deserts

With strong winds, extreme temperature variations, and unpredictable rainfall that can fall in torrential downpours, deserts are extreme environments.

About one-third of the Earth's surface is desert, a dry landscape that receives less than 10 in (250 mm) of rainfall a year. The sun's energy could evaporate more water from a desert than falls as rainfall. Deserts have an arid climate—they are so dry that the few plants and animals that make their home there must be well adapted to the lack of moisture.

Deadvlei

Meaning "dead marsh," this unique area of the Namib Desert was previously flooded by a river, creating a striking white clay pan. Although the river was eventually cut off, the blackened skeletons of the dead trees that used to thrive there are still preserved today by the sunshine and dry climate.

Dipcadi
Using its curly leaves that spiral in many directions, this plant captures the water from fog and dew, storing it underground in small bulbs protected from the hot sun.

Rolling dunes
Some dunes in the Namib Desert can reach 985 ft (300 m) high and stretch across an area of up to 20 miles (32 km).

Fairy rings
Researchers are still unsure what creates these intriguing circles of grass on the desert floor. One theory suggests they may have been made by termites harvesting water.

Elephants
Herds of elephants migrate toward water sources, taking advantage of seasonal rivers.

Weaver nest
Sociable weaver birds nest in acacia trees that grow near rivers in the desert, making the largest bird nests in the world.

Giraffes
Traveling groups of giraffes, called journeys, feed on leaves, shoots, and other vegetation.

Bushman's grass
Found on gravel plains and at the base of dunes, this grass harvests water from fog and provides shade for small animals.

Meerkats
Living in colonies, meerkats are social animals that cooperate to find food and look out for predators.

Nara melon
This spiny, leafless shrub has round, melonlike fruits full of watery, orange-yellow pulp.

Namib Desert

This vast desert stretching down the coast of southwestern Africa includes a range of habitats. Its southern part is home to massive dunes where plants and animals must work hard to leech moisture from the environment. In the north, gravelly terrain allows more animals to thrive, drinking from ephemeral (temporary) rivers that flow only after heavy rainfall.

Namaqua chameleon
The adaptations of this clever chameleon allow it to change color to reflect light in the hot sun and absorb it when it is cool.

Golden mole
Using a system of tunnels, these small, blind rodents swim through the soft sand of the dunes in search of insects.

Tenebrionid beetle
To harvest water from fog, these beetles tilt their body forward, allowing water to run down into their mouths.

Web-footed gecko
This pale, almost translucent gecko uses webbed feet to burrow in the sand and large eyes to detect prey at night.

White lady spider
Large and leggy, these spiders signal to each other by drumming, or dancing, on the sand.

Peringuey's adder
Preying on geckos and lizards, Peringuey's adder can perfectly camouflage itself in the sand before it strikes.

Gemsbok
These antelopes do not sweat until their body temperature exceeds 113°F (45°C), allowing them to conserve water.

Fog
Fog rolling in from the southern Atlantic Ocean is a critical source of water in the Namib Desert.

Gravel plains
Huge areas of gravel lie in the north of the desert, mixed with sand and some grass.

Salt pans
When water evaporates, deposits of white, glimmering salt crystals accumulate on desert plains.

Ostrich
These flightless birds roam the desert in small herds, getting most of their water from plants.

Rhinos
When dry riverbeds flood, thirsty black rhinos flock to the water. These animals are critically endangered.

Welwitschia
This plant has just two leaves that grow continuously, split by the wind and curling along the ground.

Wetlands

Salty oceans are not the only watery environments on Earth. Rivers, lakes, ponds, and large waterlogged areas known as wetlands are all crucial freshwater habitats–home to more than 100,000 species of plants and animals.

Marshes, swamps, bogs, and fens are examples of wetlands–flooded areas covered in water plants that are incredibly biodiverse inland habitats. They typically form close to rivers that periodically flood, or at the edges of lakes and oceans. The Pantanal in South America is the world's largest freshwater wetland, but other wetlands can contain salty water, or a mixture of both salty and fresh.

Pantanal

Fed by tributaries of the Paraguay River, the Pantanal has the highest concentration of wildlife in South America. It is a seasonal wetland that largely dries out during the dry season, leaving pools and small lakes, and flooding again when rainfall resumes. Among its grasses, rushes, and other plant life, many animals make their home.

Paradoxical frog
The tadpoles of the paradoxical frog start off very large, up to 10.7 in (27 cm) long but shrink as they develop into adults. Fully grown frogs, which hide in the murky water, are smaller–only up to 3 in (7.5 cm) long.

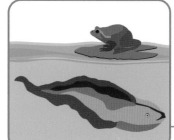

Freshwater habitats

There are two types of freshwater habitat. Lotic habitats include flowing water, such as in rivers or streams, whereas lentic habitats include calm or standing water, such as in lakes or ponds. From birds swooping in and out to slow-swimming fish, the diverse organisms in these habitats spend their time in different parts of the water. While some stay at the bottom, others thrive closer to the surface.

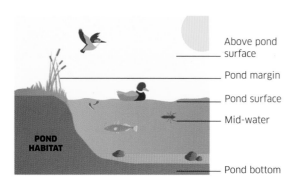

- Above pond surface
- Pond margin
- Pond surface
- Mid-water
- Pond bottom

POND HABITAT

Giant water lily
The largest member of the lily family, the giant water lily opens its white, fragrant flowers only at night. The flowers turn pink after being pollinated by beetles.

Jabiru stork
This large bird with a long upturned black bill wades in shallow water.

Giant lily pad
Stretching up to 9.8 ft (3 m) across, the lily pads of the giant water lily are strong enough to support a small child.

Jaguar
These big cats are strong swimmers and often wade through the water hunting for prey to crush with their powerful jaws.

Caiman
Millions of this crocodile species live in the Pantanal, snapping up snakes, amphibians, and fish such as piranhas for food.

South American lungfish
This large air-breathing fish swims in floodwater. To survive in times of drought, it burrows in the mud and surrounds itself with a waterproof layer of mucus.

Chiquitano cichlid
These small fish have special teeth in their throats that enable them to grind down the shells of snails.

Spotfin hatchetfish
Strong fins allow these fish to jump above the water to catch prey such as insects

54,000 sq miles (140,000 sq km)—the **minimum estimated size of the Pantanal.**

440 fish species or more **migrate between ocean and freshwater** habitats.

135

Roseate spoonbill
These birds use their spoon-shaped bills to forage under the water. They get their pink color from the crustaceans they eat.

Capybara
The world's largest rodent, the capybara is a semiaquatic mammal that feeds on land but sometimes hides in the water.

Goby attaches itself to the rock

Climbing fish
The Nopili rock-climbing goby lives in flood- and landslide-prone streams in Hawaii and on other volcanic islands. In order to travel upstream to breed, the goby has developed a special sucker that allows it to stick to the rocks behind waterfalls and propel its body upward to reach the river beyond.

Wattled jacana
This resourceful bird can carry its chicks tucked under its wings when crossing flooded areas. Its long toes allow it to perch on floating vegetation.

Giant river otter
These sociable mammals are at home on land and in the water and can grow up to 6 ft (1.8 m) long.

Humbug catfish
Found in soft, sandy areas at the bottom of swamps, this fish burrows into the sediment for protection.

Green anaconda
This gigantic, semiaquatic snake crushes and swallows its prey whole, before slowly digesting it.

Freshwater stingray
The eyes of this flat fish sit on the top of its body, with its mouth and gill slits underneath.

Red-bellied piranha
Schools of 20 or more piranhas often swim together, using their razor-sharp teeth to hunt small fish and insects.

Serpae tetra
These colorful, flame-colored fish hide from predators in plants.

Coastal habitats

Away from the murky depths of the open ocean lie richer, shallower habitats, where a diverse range of marine creatures thrives close to both the ocean surface and the shifting shorelines of the coast.

The strip of land where the ocean meets the shore is a dynamic, ever-changing environment, which provides a range of habitats for organisms. Tides ebb and flow and waves crash onto the shore, creating unique challenges for the animals and plants that live here. Further out to sea, corals and green algae provide the foundation for many complex ecosystems. Human activity, from oil spills to ocean warming and acidification caused by climate change, has negatively impacted these habitats.

○ TYPES OF SHORE

From rocky beaches to sandy shores and mudflats, the seashore, where the ocean meets the land, can take many forms. The type of shore and its geology—whether it is hard, soft, rocky, sandy, or muddy—determines the type of organisms that can live there.

Sandy shore
Sometimes called soft shores, these types of coasts can be made of sand, muddy sand, or mudflats. Most animals live under the surface, hiding in the sediment.

Rocky shore
These harder shores can include dramatic boulder beaches, cliffs, and rock pools. They house a wealth of organisms, such as algae, lichens, barnacles, and seabirds.

○ ROCKY SHORE LIFE

Rocky shores are home to many life forms that have ways to survive the relentless incoming and outgoing tides. Organisms must contend with the force of the waves, the risk of drying out, and changes in the salinity in rockpools on hotter and cooler days. Plants are rare as it is difficult for them to set roots, but many different seaweeds thrive.

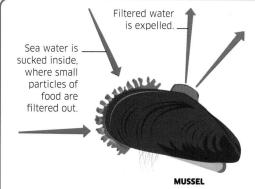

Filtered water is expelled.

Sea water is sucked inside, where small particles of food are filtered out.

MUSSEL

Filter feeding
Many creatures that attach themselves to the shore get their food by filter feeding. Some, such as mussels, inhale water using their gills, then filter out the food.

Limpets
These aquatic snails cling onto the upper parts of exposed rocky shores using a strong, muscular foot.

Oystercatcher
These bright-beaked shorebirds use their pointed beak to open the hard shells of the mussels and cockles they eat.

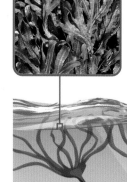

Seaweeds
These slimy organisms are algae and have no roots but cling onto rocky surfaces using special suckers called holdfasts.

Tidal zonation
Marine organisms live in several distinct zones on the seashore. Areas higher up the shore are never completely submerged, whereas the parts closest to the sea are submerged most of the time. In the middle sits a zone that experiences a variety of conditions—it is sometimes submerged, sometimes not.

Sea stars
These spiny creatures use rows of tiny tube feet to crawl on the seabed. If they lose one of their pointy arms to a predator, some species of stars are able to regrow them.

Crabs
Protected by tough exterior skeletons, crabs scuttle along the seafloor, searching for food. They can survive both underwater and out of the water, as long as their gills stay wet.

492 ft (150 m)—the **typical depth of the continental shelf,** the shallow marine zone around continents that hosts a huge diversity of ocean life.

25 percent of all known marine species are found within or close by coral reefs.

137

Mangrove forests
Tropical mangrove trees have roots that are adapted to grow in the intertidal zone, and which can also protect the coast from storms.

Seagrass meadows
Underwater meadows of flowering plants called seagrasses are home to many animals, such as large, grazing manatees.

Kelp forests
Dense forests of tall brown algae growing in cool shallow waters near the shore provide shelter and nutrients for many organisms.

SHALLOW SEAS

Many key underwater spaces are found on or close to the coast, in zones filled with leafy plants and algae. These habitats are rich in life—often serving as nurseries for the young of many fish, such as seahorses. Many also prevent the coastline from eroding and can take up and store carbon.

CORAL REEFS

The most diverse marine habitats on Earth, coral reefs are huge structures that can stretch for miles. Simple animals called corals cling to the seabed and provide a base for other creatures to build their homes around them. Despite their importance, coral numbers have reduced in recent years due to climate change.

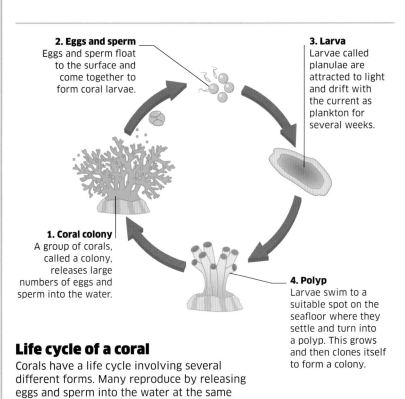

2. Eggs and sperm
Eggs and sperm float to the surface and come together to form coral larvae.

3. Larva
Larvae called planulae are attracted to light and drift with the current as plankton for several weeks.

1. Coral colony
A group of corals, called a colony, releases large numbers of eggs and sperm into the water.

4. Polyp
Larvae swim to a suitable spot on the seafloor where they settle and turn into a polyp. This grows and then clones itself to form a colony.

Life cycle of a coral

Corals have a life cycle involving several different forms. Many reproduce by releasing eggs and sperm into the water at the same time as other corals in mass-spawning events.

ROCKY CORAL

The backbone of most reefs is formed from hard corals, such as this brain coral. They absorb minerals from the water and use these to build tough limestone skeletons to protect their soft bodies. These also shelter algae, which produce nutrients for the coral.

Reef animals

The animals that live in the reefs are often bright and colorful tropical fish and invertebrates that each play their own unique role in the ecosystem. Some swim together in groups, others hide in the seabed, and many are able to disguise themselves from predators by mimicking their surroundings.

Moorish idol
These stripy tropical fish move around in groups called shoals, a strategy that helps them feed and hide from predators.

White-tip reef shark
Living in caves in the day, these sharks hunt at night, gobbling up octopuses and fish hiding in the crevices of the reef.

Cleaner wrasse
This small fish eats parasites and dead skin from the mouth and the skin of other fish, cleaning them in the process.

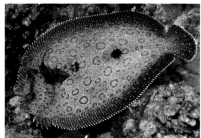

Peacock flounder
The eyes of this flatfish move during its life, until they are both on one side, allowing the fish to settle into the sand.

Biting reef worm
This worm buries itself in the seafloor popping up dramatically to slice unsuspecting prey with its scissorlike jaws.

Flamboyant cuttlefish
Usually camouflaged on the seabed, this cuttlefish displays its dazzling colors only during courtship or when fighting.

Diving down

The zone where air and water meet is an important habitat for birds. In the North Sea around Scotland's Shetland Islands, northern gannets and boobies soar high above the waters, scanning the surface waters for fish.

When they select their prey, they plunge-dive into the chilly sea at speeds of up to 78 ft/s (24 m/s) Once they have breached the surface, gannets use their webbed feet and wings to propel themselves underwater toward their prey.

140 life on earth ○ **THE OPEN OCEAN**

90 percent of the ocean's water is in the midnight zone, whereas the majority of the ocean's animals live in the sunlight zone.

The open ocean

Extending from shallow, coastal seas to the deepest parts of the ocean floor, the open ocean is the largest biome on Earth—containing more life than anywhere else.

Earth's vast oceans accommodate many different habitats—from sunny surface waters to murky trenches on the ocean floor. These habitats alter most dramatically with depth, as conditions such as temperature, pressure, light, and oxygen levels change. To classify these, scientists refer to a vertical slice of the ocean as the water column and split this into several key zones.

Ocean zones

The zones of the ocean are not all equal. Near the ocean surface, the waters teem with life—from tiny plankton to predatory sharks. However, the deeper you go, the harder it is for creatures to thrive and only a few specially adapted animals are found.

Who lives where

Ocean-dwelling creatures can be grouped according to where they live in the ocean water column but also by how they get around. Pleuston are forms of life such as the Portuguese man o'war that live at the surface of the ocean, where air and water meet. Plankton, such as algae and tiny microscopic animals, live below them and drift with the currents, whereas nekton move around by swimming against currents. This group includes most fish and whales. Right at the bottom, the benthos, such as crabs, sit, crawl, or creep on the ocean floor.

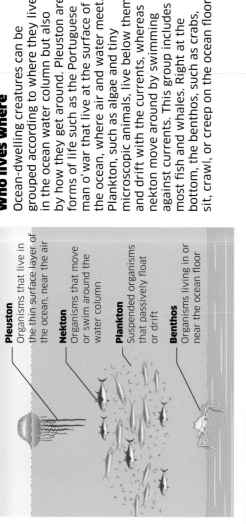

Pleuston
Organisms that live in the thin surface layer of the ocean, near the air

Nekton
Organisms that move or swim around the water column

Plankton
Suspended organisms that passively float or drift

Benthos
Organisms living in or near the ocean floor

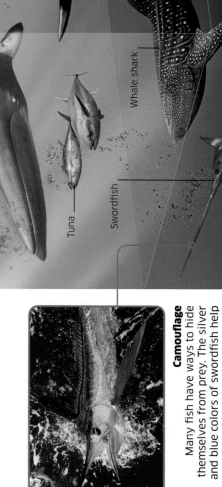

Moorish idol

Royal angelfish

Bleeker's parrotfish

Coconut octopus

Blacktip reef shark

Lionfish

Regal blue tang

Yellow longnose butterfly fish

Clownfish

Reef octopus

Manta ray

Gray whale

Whale shark

Helmet jellyfish

Bottlenose dolphin

Green sea turtle

Tuna

Swordfish

Sunlight zone
0–660 ft (0–200 m)
This bright, warm surface layer is oxygen-rich and full of life. It is dominated by plankton, including algae that use sunlight to produce their food. These form the base of most ocean food chains, consumed by many fish and mammals.

Camouflage
Many fish have ways to hide themselves from prey. The silver and blue colors of swordfish help them blend in with the sunlit ocean by making their bodies highly reflective.

27,000 ft (8,229 m)—**the depth at which one of deepest-known living fish was found** by scientists, in 2018, **a snailfish** called *Pseudoliparis swirei.*

36,201 ft (11,034 m)—**the** depth of the Mariana **Trench, the deepest place** in the ocean.

141

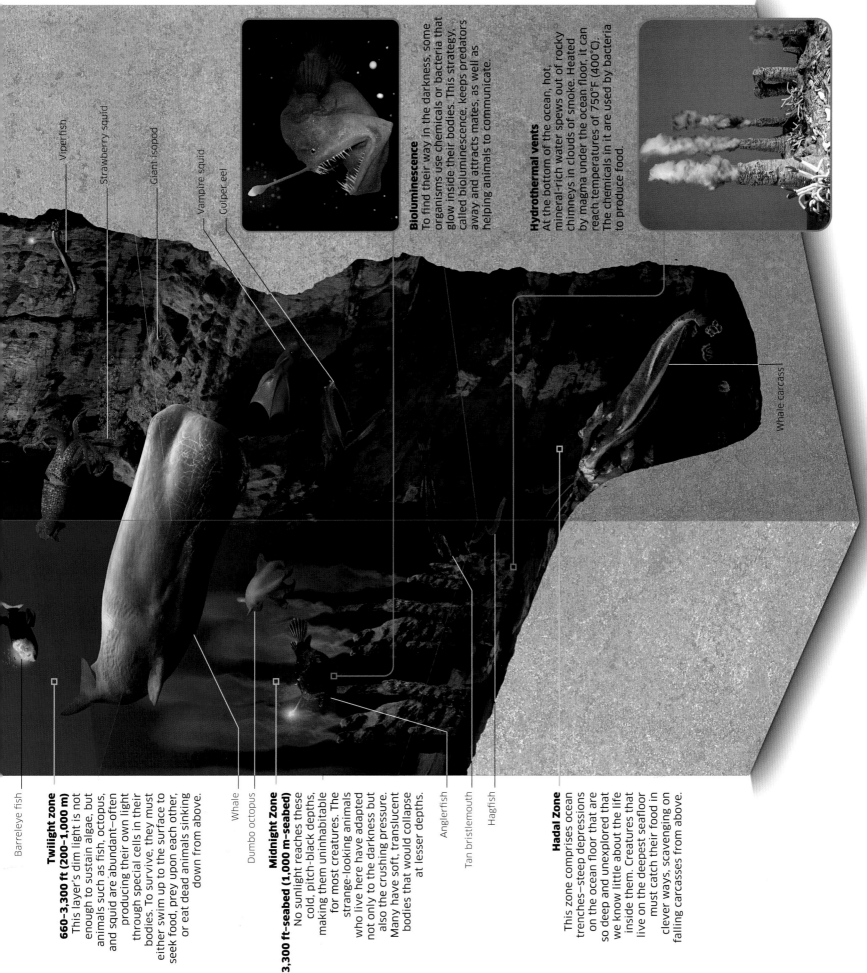

Bioluminescence
To find their way in the darkness, some organisms use chemicals or bacteria that glow inside their bodies. This strategy, called bioluminescence, keeps predators away and attracts mates, as well as helping animals to communicate.

Hydrothermal vents
At the bottom of the ocean, hot, mineral-rich water spews out of rocky chimneys in clouds of smoke. Heated by magma under the ocean floor, it can reach temperatures of 750°F (400°C). The chemicals in it are used by bacteria to produce food.

Viperfish

Strawberry squid

Giant isopod

Vampire squid

Gulper eel

Whale carcass

Barreleye fish

Twilight zone
660–3,300 ft (200–1,000 m)
This layer's dim light is not enough to sustain algae, but animals such as fish, octopus, and squid are abundant—often producing their own light through special cells in their bodies. To survive, they must either swim up to the surface to seek food, prey upon each other, or eat dead animals sinking down from above.

Whale

Dumbo octopus

Midnight Zone
3,300 ft–seabed (1,000 m–seabed)
No sunlight reaches these cold, pitch-black depths, making them uninhabitable for most creatures. The strange-looking animals who live here have adapted not only to the darkness but also to the crushing pressure. Many have soft, translucent bodies that would collapse at lesser depths.

Anglerfish

Tan bristlemouth

Hagfish

Hadal Zone
This zone comprises ocean trenches—steep depressions on the ocean floor that are so deep and unexplored that we know little about the life inside them. Creatures that live on the deepest seafloor must catch their food in clever ways, scavenging on falling carcasses from above.

Ecosystems

All around the world, communities of plants, animals, and microorganisms interact with each other and their habitats to form unique ecosystems.

Ecosystems involve all organisms—from the smallest bacteria to large, fearsome hunters such as lions. All of these are linked together in a food chain. Energy and nutrients move through the ecosystem as animals feed. Healthy ecosystems need balanced food chains that are sustainable and in which nutrients are continually recycled.

Ecological niches

Every organism plays a role in its community—known as a niche. Koalas have a very specific niche, spending almost all their lives in eucalyptus trees in Australia, feeding on the leaves. Species such as koalas that live in narrow niches are called specialists.

Savanna food chain

Life in the tropical grasslands of Africa depends on a balance of food sources. At the bottom of the food chain are plants. Herbivores feed on grasses and shrubs, gaining energy from them. Carnivorous predators and scavengers feast on their meat, while decomposers break down waste.

1 Primary producer
Food chains begin with a producer, an organism that makes its own food. Plants, such as this finger grass, make their food from the sun through photosynthesis.

2 Primary consumer
Zebras are herbivores with a diet that is nine-tenths grasses and one-tenth leaves and buds. As they feed on producers, they are known as consumers. Other consumers include elephants and water buffalo.

Oxpecker
These birds feed on ticks and other parasites that live on zebras' skin. This is a mutualistic relationship, in which both organisms benefit.

Bristly, stripy mane

Herbivores have different stomachs from carnivores—often bigger and with several chambers to help them break down the tough cellulose in plants.

10 gigatons—the amount of carbon dioxide transferred by phytoplankton from the atmosphere to the ocean each year.

143

Zebra herd
Large herds of zebras roam the grasslands in search of food and water. Being in a herd helps individual zebras hide from predators.

Antelope
Like zebras, antelopes are browsers who munch on leaves and grasses. They are preyed upon by secondary consumers such as lions and cheetahs.

Vulture
From above, these birds of prey carefully scan the landscape in search of carcasses. Their populations around the world are threatened by poisons from agriculture, including drugs fed to livestock.

Acacia tree
These umbrella-shaped trees are producers that get their shape partly as a result of giraffes eating leaves on their lower branches.

Scavenger 4
Patiently waiting for animals to die or be killed before they feed on them, hyenas and vultures act as scavengers. They play a vital role in keeping ecosystems free of carcasses and disease by consuming meat that would otherwise be left to rot.

Versatile feeders
Sometimes hyenas hunt in packs instead of scavenging.

Decomposer 5
Dung beetles are one of the savanna's recyclers, feeding on half-digested grass in herbivore dung. They roll the dung into balls, which they bury to feed themselves and their young. The nutrients from the dung are released back into the environment.

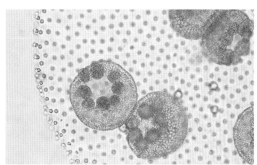

Grassy ground
Grasses make up most of the savanna, along with scattered trees and shrubs. They produce their own energy—made from the sun by their long green leaves.

3 Secondary consumer
Lions are proficient hunters, able to pounce on speedy herbivores such as zebras. Like cheetahs and snakes, they are carnivores—eating only meat. As these predators feed on primary consumers, they are known as secondary consumers.

Fragile food chains
When one element of a food chain is threatened, it can put the entire ecosystem at risk. Tiny organisms floating on the water's surface are the primary producers of ocean food chains, feeding animals such as whales, fish, and crustaceans. However, rising sea temperatures are threatening these phytoplankton and the web of aquatic life that depends on them.

144 life on earth ∘ **THREATS TO HABITATS**

110 million tons (100 million metric tons) of **aquatic life**, such as fish and mollusks, are **taken from the wild every year**.

DEFORESTATION

Forests play a crucial role in Earth's carbon cycle, capturing carbon dioxide and releasing oxygen into the air. But Earth is losing forests at an alarming rate due to human activities. This loss of trees is contributing to and accelerating global warming, as well as destroying precious ecosystems. By 2011, more than half of the world's original, natural forests had been cut down, mainly to make space for farmland, and the rate of deforestation has accelerated since then.

FOREST LOSS

Forests cover around 30 percent of Earth's land surface but are continuously being removed and degraded. The world's remaining forests face many threats, such as illegal logging, and land lost to agricultural crops such as palm oil. The trees planted for timber and palm oil harvesting do not make up for the loss of original forests, as they are nowhere near as rich in animals, plants, and microorganisms.

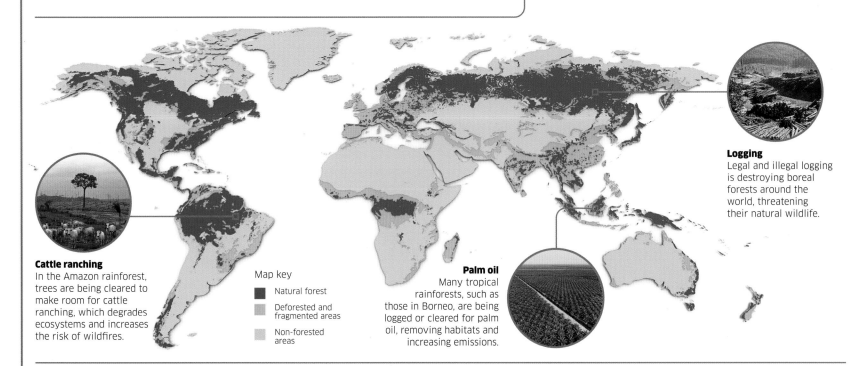

Logging
Legal and illegal logging is destroying boreal forests around the world, threatening their natural wildlife.

Cattle ranching
In the Amazon rainforest, trees are being cleared to make room for cattle ranching, which degrades ecosystems and increases the risk of wildfires.

Map key

- ■ Natural forest
- ▨ Deforested and fragmented areas
- ▨ Non-forested areas

Palm oil
Many tropical rainforests, such as those in Borneo, are being logged or cleared for palm oil, removing habitats and increasing emissions.

Amazon tipping point

The world's largest rainforest, the Amazon is heavily threatened by human activity, especially fires to clear land for agriculture. Currently, water is constantly recycled through the forest's trees, which triggers the rainfall needed to sustain it. But if too many trees are lost or damaged, this process will be disrupted—a crucial tipping point, after which the forest will no longer be able to survive. It would then turn into a grassland, releasing lots of stored carbon dioxide into the atmosphere.

Habitat fragmentation

Plants and animals are not just losing their habitats but are seeing them transformed into a number of smaller patches. When biomes such as forests become fragmented, the movements of animals are restricted, as many are reluctant or unable to cross other habitats or human areas. Habitats are most vulnerable at the edges; therefore, lots of smaller habitats are more at risk. Forest edges also dry out more easily, causing fires to spread quickly.

Threats to habitats

Oceans, forests, grasslands—humans are altering every habitat on Earth, either through direct destruction or the effects of climate change caused by human activity. These actions threaten the survival of many species of plants and animals.

As human activity continues to take over more and more of the planet's surface, it is having a negative effect on habitats, affecting the soil, and pushing wildlife into increasingly small pockets of land. Climate change is also putting pressure on ecosystems all around the world, causing habitats to flood, heat up, and in many cases go into decline. Urgent action is needed to prevent this and stop the loss of biodiversity.

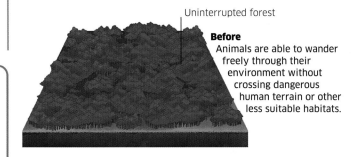

Uninterrupted forest

Before
Animals are able to wander freely through their environment without crossing dangerous human terrain or other less suitable habitats.

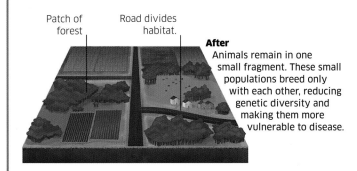

Patch of forest

Road divides habitat.

After
Animals remain in one small fragment. These small populations breed only with each other, reducing genetic diversity and making them more vulnerable to disease.

4.02 in (102 mm)—the average sea level rise since 1993.

34,000 sq miles (88,000 sq km)—the amount of forest estimated to be lost globally every year, one football field every two seconds.

145

RISING SEA LEVELS

Island habitats, which contain around 20 percent of the world's land biodiversity, are very vulnerable to the effects of climate change. As ice sheets melt and warm seawater expands, the resulting sea level rise is affecting low-lying atolls—submerging large areas and entire ecosystems. Scientists modeling climate change predict that tens of thousands of islands will be submerged if the sea level continues to rise.

Atolls in peril
Both humans and wildlife in Pacific islands, such as the Marshall Islands, are under threat due to sea level rise. Entire nations could be below the sea by 2030.

Atoll animals
Some animals, such as this coconut crab, live on very low-lying island atolls, a habitat threatened by sea level rise, and could become extinct when their habitat is flooded.

OCEANS AND CLIMATE CHANGE

Oceans play a key role in regulating Earth's climate by absorbing carbon dioxide. However, as it dissolves in seawater, it increases the acidity of the ocean. This acidification, combined with the heat oceans absorb, causes many problems—bleaching corals and damaging hard-bodied creatures. Fish are unable to adapt to warmer waters, whereas large masses of algae thrive, making areas toxic to other life.

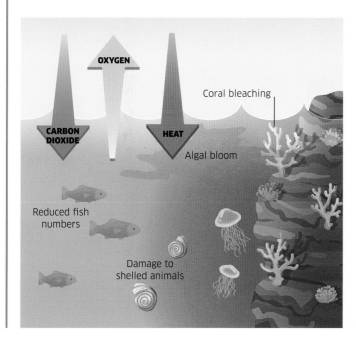

OXYGEN
CARBON DIOXIDE
HEAT
Coral bleaching
Algal bloom
Reduced fish numbers
Damage to shelled animals

DESERTIFICATION

In many arid regions, a combination of poor farming practices and climate change is leading to desertification. Actions such as removing natural vegetation can degrade the soil, causing drought and a loss of wildlife, as seen here in Mauritania. Scientists estimate that 186,000 miles (300,000 km) of land on southern Europe's coast is undergoing desertification.

BIODIVERSITY LOSS

Human intervention and climate change are altering ecosystems and causing species to become extinct at worrying rates. Loss of certain species could have a knock-on effect to entire ecosystems. If global warming reaches 3.6°F (2°C) above preindustrial levels by 2100, scientists predict that the risks of extinction and ecosystem collapse will escalate rapidly.

Mongoose

Buffel grass

Invasive species

Organisms that are not indigenous or native to a area are often introduced by humans and can damage habitats. On tropical islands, mongooses threaten native species, as well as carrying disease. In arid regions, invasive buffel grass can spread rapidly, displacing native species and helping the spread of wildfires.

NUMBER OF SPECIES CLASSIFIED AS ENDANGERED OR CRITICALLY ENDANGERED

FISH
AMPHIBIANS
REPTILES
BIRDS

800
700
600
500
400
300
200
100
0

1996 2021 | 1996 2021 | 1996 2021 | 1996 2021

Poaching

The illegal wildlife trade poses a huge threat to many species as poaching of elephant tusks and tiger skin and bones grows. Each year, at least 20,000 African elephants are illegally killed for their tusks. Governments around the world have implemented bans on the elephant ivory trade to try and address this.

Decline in animal species

Ensuring the biodiversity of Earth means having a wide range of living things across habitats, but species numbers are declining. The International Union for the Conservation of Nature (IUCN) classifies the risk to each animal species, from least threatened to extinct. The number of species in the two most endangered categories has increased rapidly in the past decades.

146 life on earth ○ **PLANTS UNDER THREAT**

Two-fifths of the estimated 500,000 land plants are currently considered to be at risk of extinction.

Plants under threat

Providing not only the oxygen humans and animals breathe but also medicines and food, plants are precious to life on Earth.

Plants are vital to every ecosystem across the globe, often the base of the food web for a wide variety of animals. But they face a range of major threats— such as habitat loss, being overexploited by humans, pollution, and climate change. In an effort to conserve plants for the future, scientists are storing their seeds to preserve genetic diversity.

TITAN ARUM
Amorphophallus titanum
Location: Sumatran rainforest
Height: 10 ft (3 m)

Easily recognized by its powerful smell of rotten flesh, designed to attract flies, this plant generates its own heat by storing energy in a giant underground organ. Mass deforestation has made it endangered.

Titan arum has a large underground organ called a corm that can weigh

110 lb (50 kg).

VENUS FLYTRAP
Dionaea muscipula
Location: North and South Carolina
Height: 4 in (10 cm)

The leaves of this carnivorous plant snap shut to trap insects inside, with stiff interlocking bristles ensuring its victim can't escape. Overcollection, habitat destruction, and fires are some of the threats it faces.

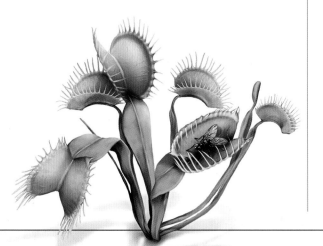

ESCARPMENT CYCAD
Encephalartos brevifoliolatus
Location: Extinct in the wild
Stem height: 8.2 in (2.5 m)

Once found in the savannas but now only in gardens, this palm-like plant has leaves with tips that roll up into curled structures to protect the growing tips. As the plant photosynthesizes and grows, the leaves unfurl.

A stout woody trunk supports the plant's leaves.

Titan arum's tall spike is the largest cluster of flowers that stick together to form a stem in the world.

WOLLEMI PINE
Wollemia nobilis
Location: Wollemi National Park, Australia
Height: 131 ft (40 m)

With its pointed, needle-like leaves, this conifer used to be thought to be extinct. It was previously known only from fossils, some dating back nearly to the time of the dinosaurs, until it was discovered in 1994 in an Australian rainforest. Today, it is critically endangered, with fewer than 100 plants remaining.

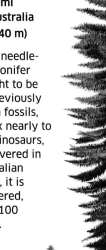

65 plant species are thought to have gone extinct in North America since European settlers arrived.

9,200 The number of tree species thought to still be undiscovered. Many will already be threatened before scientists find them.

147

SANDER'S PAPHIOPEDILUM
Paphiopedilum sanderianum
Location: Borneo
Petal length: Up to 3.2 ft (1 m)

This tropical orchid uses its remarkably long, thin, curled petals to lure pollinators. Once thought to be extinct, this rare plant is now confined to the boundaries of a national park in Malaysia.

FOUR-PETAL PAWPAW
Asimina tetramera
Location: Florida
Height: Up to 15 ft (4.5 m)

Scientists are looking into ways to conserve this highly endangered shrub. Because its seeds cannot easily be dried and stored, they have come up with a way of preserving its tissues in liquid nitrogen.

ALULA
Brighamia insignis
Location: Hawaii
Stem height: Up to 16 ft (5 m)

This critically endangered Hawaiian plant has a stout, succulent stem and sweet-smelling, trumpet-shaped flowers that are favored by moths. Feral animals, invasive weeds, and natural disturbances such as landslides, as well as climate change, have made this plant vulnerable to extinction.

TAHINA PALM
Tahina spectabilis
Location: Northwestern Madagascar
Frond diameter: Up to 15 ft (4.6 m)

This gigantic, critically endangered palm was only discovered in 2006. It is a slow-growing palm that produces flowers once before dying. Only one population remains, but its seeds are being stored for the future.

SEA URCHIN CACTUS
Astrophytum asterias
Location: Northwestern Madagascar
Height: Up to 4 in (10 cm)

This slow-growing, spineless succulent produces bright yellow flowers. Illegal collection, habitat destruction, and invasive species have left only a handful of wild populations, but it is also conserved in botanical gardens.

QUEEN OF THE ANDES
Puya raimondii
Location: Peru and Bolivia
Stalk height: 30 ft (10 m)

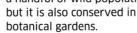

Known as Queen of the Andes, this plant grows high up in mountains above 13,000 ft (4,000 m). It is endangered, with only three populations in the wild. Climate change and fires connected to land clearance are its biggest threats.

ATTENBOROUGH'S PITCHER
Nepenthes attenboroughii
Location: Palawan, the Philippines
Height: 5 ft (1.5 m)

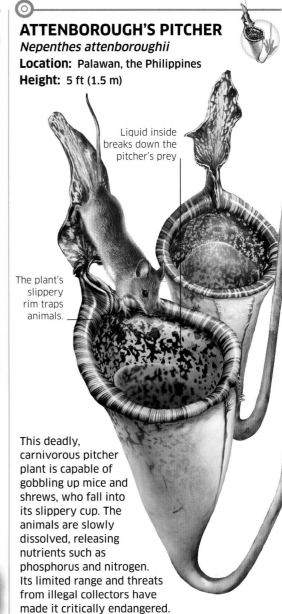

Liquid inside breaks down the pitcher's prey

The plant's slippery rim traps animals.

This deadly, carnivorous pitcher plant is capable of gobbling up mice and shrews, who fall into its slippery cup. The animals are slowly dissolved, releasing nutrients such as phosphorus and nitrogen. Its limited range and threats from illegal collectors have made it critically endangered.

DRAGON BLOOD TREE
Dracaena cinnabari
Location: Morocco and nearby islands
Height: Up to 66 ft (20 m)

This umbrella-shaped tree has stiff leaves and white, fragrant flowers. Excessive harvesting of the red resin on its bark, which is used in varnishes and stains and gives the tree its name, has contributed to its decline.

HAINAN GIBBON
Nomascus hainanus
Location: Hainan Island, China
Length: Up to 19 in (49 cm)

This is one of the world's most endangered primates. Although there were around 2,000 gibbons in the 1950s, by the 1980s only eight remained. Thanks to conservation efforts, including local people preventing poaching, there are now around 33 individuals.

Soft fur
Female Hainan gibbons have golden fur, whereas males are almost entirely black in color.

Animal conservation

While human activities have contributed to shrinking habitats and changing environmental conditions, many animals–from parrots to pandas–have been brought back from the brink of extinction.

Creatures around the world are feeling the effects of climate change and humans encroaching on their environment, but there have been some successful efforts to turn the tide on their decline. These have included creating wildlife reserves, banning hunting, removing invasive species, and community-driven initiatives such as ecotourism.

BLUE IGUANA
Cyclura lewisi
Location: Grand Cayman island, Caribbean
Length: Up to 59 in (1.5 m)

From tens of thousands of individuals before European colonization to fewer than 25 in 2002, these large, solitary lizards were decimated by human land clearance and vehicle traffic. A breeding program has since restored the population to around 1,000, but threats remain.

ARABIAN ORYX
Oryx leucoryx
Location: Arabian peninsula
Size: Up to 63 in (160 cm)

This regal antelope became extinct in the wild in 1972 due to uncontrolled hunting, but captive oryx have been reintroduced to the wild since the 1980s. Today, there are more than 1,200 wild individuals, and as many as 7,000 in captivity.

Shovel-like hooves
Wide hooves enable the oryx to travel across shifting desert sands and dig cool holes in the sand to rest in.

GIANT BLUE CLAM
Tridacna gigas
Location: Indo-Pacific Ocean
Length: Up to 3.3 ft (1 m)

These clams weigh more than 30 stone (200 kg) and are the largest living mollusks. They have been harvested for food and as part of the aquarium trade. Their trade is now regulated, but they are still classified as vulnerable.

INDUS RIVER DOLPHIN
Platanista gangetica
Location: Indus River, Pakistan
Length: Up to 8.2 ft (2.5 m)

These dolphins live in muddy river habitats that have been severely fragmented by irrigation dams. With the help of local communities and ecotourism, their numbers have increased, but they are still threatened.

GIANT MANTA RAY
Mobula birostris
Location: Tropical–subtropical oceans
Wingspan: Up to 29 ft (9 m)

The largest ray in the world is threatened by hunting, overfishing, global warming, and even collisions with ships. Strict regulations and ecotourism are helping these endangered animals recover.

TIGER
Panthera tigris
Location: South and east Asia
Length: Up to 9.19 ft (2.8 m)

Poaching, habitat loss, and conflict with people are among the causes of tigers declining from 100,000 a century ago to just 3,200 in 2010. But recent conservation efforts have allowed populations to increase by 40 percent between 2015 and 2021.

NASSAU GROUPER
Epinephelus striatus
Location: Atlantic Ocean
Size: Up to 39 in (100 cm)

Once the most important reef fish in the Caribbean, the Nassau grouper has seen its population severely decline in recent decades due to overfishing. Laws banning fishing during the spawning season have helped the groupers recover.

KAKAPO
Strigops habroptilus
Location: New Zealand
Size: 25 in (64 cm)

A nocturnal, flightless parrot, the kakapo's ground-dwelling nature made it an easy target for hunters. With land clearance and new predators, this led to only 51 birds remaining in 1995. Monitoring the birds has helped the population bounce back to around 200.

Kakapos can live to be
90 years old,
making them one of the longest-living bird species in the world.

CALIFORNIA CONDOR
Gymnogyps californianus
Location: California, US
Wingspan: Up to 9.8 ft (3 m)

The California condor is the largest flying land bird in North America, but very nearly reached extinction in 1987, when only 27 birds remained. Subsequent efforts to reintroduce captive birds were successful and led to a population of 300 wild birds in 2021.

Broad wings
Outspread black wing feathers have a fingerlike appearance.

PANAMANIAN GOLDEN FROG
Atelopus zeteki
Location: Panama, South Central America
Size: Up to 2.5 in (6.3 cm)

Fungal disease and the illegal pet trade threaten this tiny, toadlike frog, which has a highly toxic, vibrant yellow skin to ward off predators. It is probably extinct in the wild, but several breeding programs aim to reintroduce the species to its natural habitat.

GIANT PANDA
Ailuropoda melanoleuca
Location: East Asia
Height: Up to 6 ft (1.8 m)

Huge efforts to halt the decline of these bamboo-loving giants, who numbered only 1,114 in the 1980s, led to the creation of 67 reserves and wildlife corridors in China. Now, 20 populations remain, but they are still fragmented and only about 1,800 of these iconic animals are left in the wild.

EARTH AND US

Humans have been on Earth for just a small fraction of its history, but our time on the planet has changed it forever. Using its resources, we have built settlements, grown food, and found ways to power our modern lives. However, human activity can harm the planet and we must reduce its impact.

HUMANS ON EARTH

Modern humans appeared on Earth relatively recently and, at first, had little impact on the world around them. But some 11,000 years ago, people discovered farming and began to transform their environment. Then, just over two centuries ago, we learned how to harness energy to create a new, industry-based way of life. Industrialization has driven economic and population growth, which is accelerating the impact humans have on Earth.

OUT OF AFRICA

Our earliest ancestors evolved in Africa more than 4 million years ago. They were not humans, but they walked upright, unlike their ape relatives. The first humans—belonging to the group *Homo*—appeared some 2 million years later. Our own species, *Homo sapiens*, evolved in Africa about 300,000 years ago and eventually started spreading across the world.

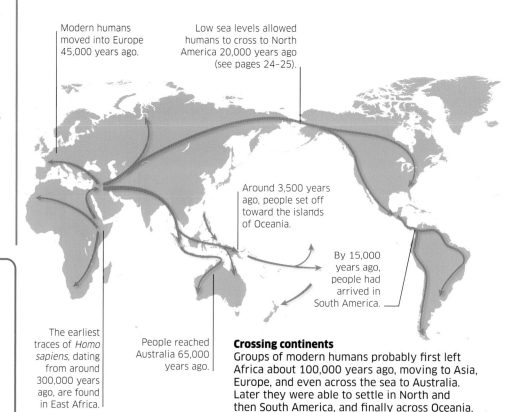

Modern humans moved into Europe 45,000 years ago.

Low sea levels allowed humans to cross to North America 20,000 years ago (see pages 24–25).

Around 3,500 years ago, people set off toward the islands of Oceania.

By 15,000 years ago, people had arrived in South America.

The earliest traces of *Homo sapiens*, dating from around 300,000 years ago, are found in East Africa.

People reached Australia 65,000 years ago.

Crossing continents
Groups of modern humans probably first left Africa about 100,000 years ago, moving to Asia, Europe, and even across the sea to Australia. Later they were able to settle in North and then South America, and finally across Oceania.

THE FIRST FARMERS

Early humans lived by hunting wild animals and seeds, roots, and berries. Eventually, people in West Asia discovered that they could collect the seeds of useful plants and cultivate them as crops. By 9,000 years ago, these pioneer farmers were producing enough food to support people with different skills, such as potters and metalworkers, who built and lived in the first towns. Animals were tamed and domesticated.

Wheat and barley
The first farmers in West Asia grew early types of wheat and barley, used to make bread.

Rice
Early Chinese farmers started growing rice on the banks of the Yangtze River.

Pigs
Around this time, pigs were domesticated in West Asia, and in China, too, for meat.

Zebu cattle
Some 2,000 years after people started keeping cattle in West Asia, this species was common in South Asia.

Corn
Farmers in Mexico discovered how to cultivate edible types of corn.

Sunflowers
In North America, people grew crops like sunflowers but still relied on hunting.

   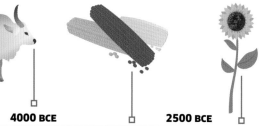 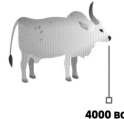

8000 BCE	6000 BCE	4000 BCE	2500 BCE

9000 BCE	7000 BCE	5000 BCE	3000 BCE	2000 BCE

Goats and sheep
In West Asia, the first animals to be tamed and kept for meat, milk, and skins were goats and sheep.

Potatoes
By this time, potatoes of different kinds were probably being grown in Peru in South America.

Taro
People in New Guinea began to grow taro, a starchy root vegetable with edible leaves.

Horses
Wild horses in Central Asia were turned into essential domestic animals.

Llamas
In the Andes of South America, llamas were used for wool and for transporting goods.

Sorghum
In Africa, farmers began to plant sorghum (a grain), as well as millet, yam, and peanuts.

THE INDUSTRIAL REVOLUTION

For thousands of years most people worked on the land. But in the 18th century, the building of factories for the production of commodities such as cotton cloth led to a massive growth of towns. The factories housed machines, driven first by water power and then by steam engines fueled by coal. This industrial revolution marked the start of a new phase in humanity's impact on the environment.

Factory town

By the 19th century, many towns in Europe and North America were dominated by huge factories. Workers lived in small, cramped houses, and many suffered from diseases caused by pollution, poverty, and harsh conditions.

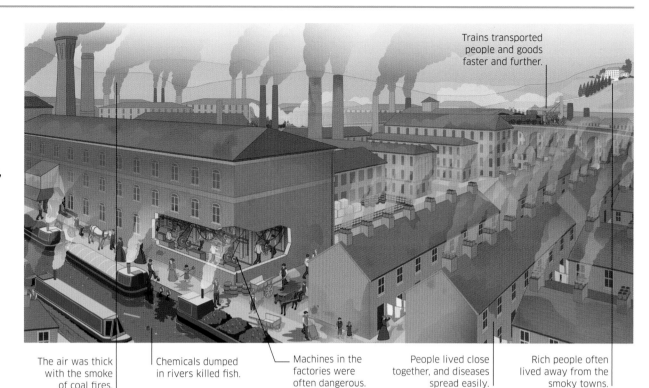

Trains transported people and goods faster and further.

The air was thick with the smoke of coal fires.

Chemicals dumped in rivers killed fish.

Machines in the factories were often dangerous.

People lived close together, and diseases spread easily.

Rich people often lived away from the smoky towns.

THE RELENTLESS RISE

At first, industrialization affected only a few parts of the world, but by the 1950s, it had spread around much of the globe. Increased wealth led to population growth and more demand for industrial products, accelerating the process. As this graph shows, as production increased, so did pollution and the destruction of wildlife. We have entered a new era, when humanity has become the main factor shaping life on Earth.

Key (average global rise)

- Production measured in Gross Domestic Product (GDP)
- Population
- Carbon dioxide concentration
- Surface temperature, northern hemisphere
- Freshwater use
- Species extinctions

Production

Industrial production all over the world has risen dramatically in the years since 1950. It is measured in terms of the market value of everything that is produced (GDP).

Population

The products of industry raise living standards, and this in turn leads to a growth in population. More people means an increase in demand and more production.

Carbon dioxide

Industry, transportation, and our homes all use energy, most of which is produced by burning fossil fuels. This releases greenhouses gases which lead to global warming.

Slowing down?
Population growth will probably slow down, as birth rates continue to go down compared to the 1950s.

INCREASE

Extinct toad
The golden toad is one of several amphibians declared extinct in the last 20 years.

Temperature

Carbon dioxide in the atmosphere helps to keep the world warm. As levels of the gas have risen, data from the northern hemisphere has shown an increase in average temperature, causing climate change.

Water

Fresh water is a vital resource for life on Earth. The ever-rising rate of water use by humans is a measure of our growing impact on the natural environment.

Extinctions

The rate at which plant and animal species go extinct is increasing every day as human activities destroy the wild places that they rely upon for survival.

1950   1970   1990   2010   2030

154 earth and us ∘ **FARMING**

26 percent of the world's population works in agriculture, although some countries have far more farm workers than others.

Farming

Today, the world is home to nearly 8 billion people and this number is rapidly rising. All of these humans require food, most of which is produced by agriculture.

There are many different types of farms—from large commercial farms that churn out huge amounts of produce to sell around the world to small subsistence farms where the farmers grow only enough to feed themselves and their families. Whether rearing animals or sowing crops, all types of agriculture have an impact on the land they use. To feed the growing global population, the farms of the future must use techniques that are more sustainable and do not damage the Earth.

Commercial farming

Some modern farms are owned by large businesses and are designed to produce food cheaply and efficiently, and may use some of the methods shown here. Many of these can negatively impact the environment, which could affect our ability to produce more food in the future.

Monoculture
For increased efficiency, many farms constantly grow just one crop across large expanses of land. This lack of diversity reduces the nutrients in the soil.

Machinery
Modern farming uses many machines, which can efficiently harvest large fields of a crop.

Methane emitters
Livestock, such as cows, produce significant amounts of methane, a greenhouse gas, as part of their normal digestive processes. They are often packed together into small spaces—a method known as factory farming.

Irrigation
To make their crops grow, farms supply them with water through sprayers or pipes along the ground. This uses large amounts of water—an increasingly scarce resource.

Antibiotics
Animals are given drugs to prevent infections and sometimes to boost their growth. Overuse of these in agriculture has led to higher levels of antibiotic resistance—meaning these medicines are now less effective at treating both humans and animals.

Pesticides
Chemicals designed to kill pests, such as weeds and crop-munching insects, are routinely sprayed on crops, but these can harm wildlife and upset the balance of ecosystems.

Agricultural runoff
Rainwater can carry artificial fertilizers and manure from farms into nearby rivers and streams, polluting the water.

Genetically modified crops

Scientists can modify the genes (building blocks) of plants to create new, improved varieties, such as golden rice (left), which was designed to include more nutrients than regular rice. Genetically modified (GM) foods are controversial, as some people worry about their effects on human health and wider ecosystems and biodiversity.

Food insecurity

In 2018, around a quarter of the world's population was affected by moderate or severe food insecurity—when people do not have enough food to stay healthy. Climate change and drought are worsening the situation, along with historic problems, such as swarms of locusts preying on crops.

570 million—the estimated number of farms around the world.

One-third of all the food produced globally is either spoiled before it reaches the consumer or wasted.

70 percent of all the fresh water humans use is used in agriculture.

155

Agroforestry
Crops grown among trees and shrubs benefit from less soil erosion and more water and nutrients in the soil.

Compost heaps
Composting farm and food waste to produce fertilizer naturally enriches the soil.

Hedgerows
Leafy hedgerows shelter crops, livestock, and wildlife, providing safe habitats and protecting them from the wind.

Hydroponics
Growing plants without soil in nutrient-rich water can save space and water and take place in any part of the world. Similar soil-free methods, such as aquaponics, raise aquatic animals alongside plants.

Rewilding
Returning areas of land to a more natural state can encourage plants and wildlife to thrive.

Bees
Insects such as bees are one of the most important pollinators of plants and crops.

Fallow field
Leaving some land free from crops for a period of time allows the soil to recover its nutrients.

Mixed crops and poultry
The plants and animals support each other, meaning fewer chemical fertilizers and pesticides are required.

Crop rotation
Growing a range of different crops avoids exhausting the soil and controls weeds, pests, and diseases.

Drone sprayers
These automated machines can be used to precisely spray water where it is needed, as well as to dispense seeds and animal feed.

Sustainable farming
Lots of farmers are now looking to develop more sustainable farming practices and methods that are profitable, environmentally sound, and benefit local communities. These often involve using traditional techniques for managing the land as well as making the most of new technological advances.

Underwater farms
Nemo's Garden is made up of air-filled pods anchored to the seabed near Italy. These bubbles are free of pests and recycle their water. Underwater farms are one of several ways we may one day sustainably produce more food.

Living with the land

Spiraling up the hillsides in dizzying layers, the Yuanyang rice terraces of Yunnan province in China form a complex agricultural system that has been cultivated for more than 1,300 years.

Carved out of the mountains by the indigenous Hani people, the terraces use a clever engineering system of ditches and canals that distributes water to every level to irrigate the red rice crop. This ancient method of terrace farming works in harmony with nature and is found in many parts of China and Southeast Asia.

158   earth and us ○ **POPULATION**

2007 The year that the **number of people** living in **urban areas** overtook those living in **rural areas** for the **first time globally**.

Population

Almost eight billion people live on Earth today. The population is rising, moving into cities, and increasing consumption.

People who study population are called demographers. They research impacts such as how population growth is putting increasing pressure on Earth's resources, from energy and raw materials to food and water. They also study migration patterns to understand why people move from one country to another, or within a country, from rural communities to ever larger cities.

RISING NUMBERS

From around 10,000 years BCE, when people began to settle and farm, the global population grew very slowly. It was during the Industrial Revolution in the middle of the 18th century that this accelerated, as economic growth and scientific advances increased life expectancy as well as birth rates.

The Industrial Revolution takes off in Europe and then the US.

Average global life expectancy is 30 years of age.

1760   1800   1840   1880   1920   1960   2000

Year

Growth over time

Global population has increased from 770 million in 1760 to almost 8 billion in 2022. Growth has slightly slowed since the 1960s but is still increasing by around 81 million people (about 1 percent) a year.

By 1987, the global population is five billion, double what it was in 1950.

Between 1850 and 1950 the population of the world doubles.

Population (billions)

8
7
6
5
4
3
2
1
0

DISTRIBUTION AND DENSITY

The global population is unevenly distributed. Urban areas have the highest density (number of people in an area), while rural areas the lowest. In 2022, China had the world's largest population, at 1.45 billion people, with India expected to overtake it by 2026.

Population density (people per sq km)

0–1	2–5
6–10	11–20
21–50	51–100
101–200	above 200

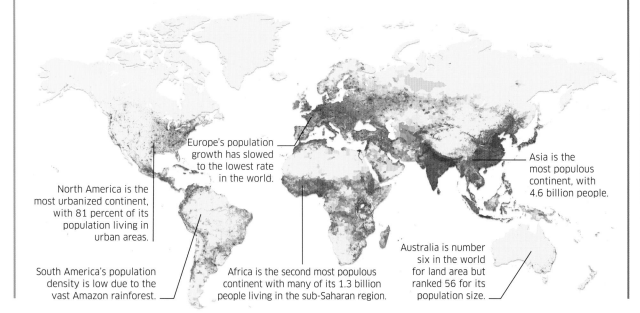

Europe's population growth has slowed to the lowest rate in the world.

North America is the most urbanized continent, with 81 percent of its population living in urban areas.

South America's population density is low due to the vast Amazon rainforest.

Africa is the second most populous continent with many of its 1.3 billion people living in the sub-Saharan region.

Asia is the most populous continent, with 4.6 billion people.

Australia is number six in the world for land area but ranked 56 for its population size.

COUNTRY PATTERNS

Changes in a country's population are mainly influenced by a change in the balance of birth and death rates. Typically, lower-income countries have younger, rapidly growing populations. In higher-income nations, improvements in health care and family planning may result in a stable population, or even population decline.

Slow and steady
Malaysia is a newly emerging economy and has a stable population. Population growth has halved since 1990, and it is now growing at just 1.3 percent a year.

Young and growing
Uganda has a very young population, with a high growth rate of 3.3 percent a year. Someone is born every 19 seconds, which has put its growing population on track to reach more than 100 million by 2050.

Old and shrinking
Japan, a higher-income country, has one of the oldest populations in the world. Since 2011, it has been shrinking. Life expectancy in Japan is 85 years, compared to the global average of 72 years.

Global life expectancy increased from 30 years of age pre-1900 to 73 years of age in 2020.

50 per cent—the proportion of people in Niger who are under 15 years old, making it the country with the world's youngest population.

159

INCREASING CONSUMPTION

Human strain on the Earth's natural resources cannot be measured by population alone. Demographers also study consumption—the volume of natural resources that an individual person uses, which is broadly dictated by where they live and their lifestyle.

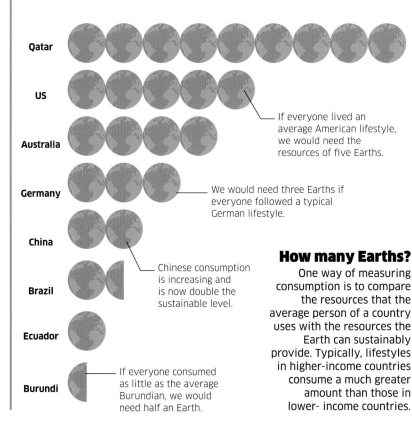

Qatar

US

If everyone lived an average American lifestyle, we would need the resources of five Earths.

Australia

Germany

We would need three Earths if everyone followed a typical German lifestyle.

China

Chinese consumption is increasing and is now double the sustainable level.

Brazil

Ecuador

Burundi

If everyone consumed as little as the average Burundian, we would need half an Earth.

How many Earths?

One way of measuring consumption is to compare the resources that the average person of a country uses with the resources the Earth can sustainably provide. Typically, lifestyles in higher-income countries consume a much greater amount than those in lower-income countries.

URBANIZATION

For the last 30 years, populations in cities have been growing faster than anywhere else in the world. Rural to urban migration is a key factor, as people swap agricultural lives for urban ones. Since 2007, more than 50 percent of the world's population lives in cities.

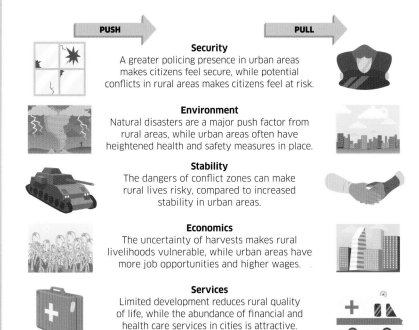

PUSH   PULL

Security
A greater policing presence in urban areas makes citizens feel secure, while potential conflicts in rural areas makes citizens feel at risk.

Environment
Natural disasters are a major push factor from rural areas, while urban areas often have heightened health and safety measures in place.

Stability
The dangers of conflict zones can make rural lives risky, compared to increased stability in urban areas.

Economics
The uncertainty of harvests makes rural livelihoods vulnerable, while urban areas have more job opportunities and higher wages.

Services
Limited development reduces rural quality of life, while the abundance of financial and health care services in cities is attractive.

Push and pull

Migration from rural to urban regions is due to a combination of push and pull factors. Push factors motivate people to leave their current lives, while pull factors makes city life more appealing.

MEGACITIES

Cities with more than 10 million people are known as "megacities." Today, urbanization is greatest in higher-income countries, but in many lower-income countries undergoing urbanization, the biggest cities keep getting bigger.

Now and in the future
Megacities in Asia and Africa are growing the fastest. These graphs compare the top five biggest cities in 2021 with those predicted for 2035.

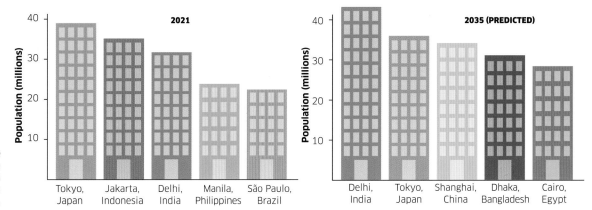

2021 — Population (millions): Tokyo, Japan; Jakarta, Indonesia; Delhi, India; Manila, Philippines; São Paulo, Brazil

2035 (PREDICTED) — Population (millions): Delhi, India; Tokyo, Japan; Shanghai, China; Dhaka, Bangladesh; Cairo, Egypt

Tokyo
The original megacity and still the most populous city in the world in 2022 is Tokyo, Japan, at 37 million people. This capital city's wider metropolitan area is home to 30 percent of Japan's population. However, as the population of this country shrinks, Tokyo's population growth is also coming to an end.

Copenhill

Designed to help Copenhagen become the world's first carbon-neutral capital, Amager Ressource Center in Denmark is a power plant that burns waste to produce energy and also a ski slope. It has a hiking trail along its roof and the highest climbing wall in the world at 280 ft (85 m) tall.

Central business district
As well as people, cities are home to thriving businesses that provide economic stability.

Sustainable skycrapers
Smart technologies are being used to create better high-rise buildings that use clever designs to direct energy only where it is needed, reducing waste.

Garden walkways
Open green spaces, such as the high line in New York City, can be created all over cities, often by transforming industrial zones. They provide important places for people to socialize and relax.

Living walls
Plants provide habitats for many birds, animals, and insects, increasing biodiversity within urban areas.

Amenities
Public buildings such as hospitals, libraries, and doctor's offices are located within residential areas.

Community gardens
These small plots can help counteract the environmental impacts of transporting food over long distances.

Electric charging point
These fixed features recharge electric cars and make it easier for residents to use sustainable vehicles.

Solar lighting
Unlike conventional street lighting, which demands lots of energy and is expensive to maintain, solar lighting is efficient and environmentally friendly.

Drainage
Enhanced technology can monitor water systems and detect leaks sooner, meaning fewer water shortages.

Cycle lanes
Safe, accessible lanes for bikes encourage citizens to cycle rather than use their car—reducing traffic and improving air quality.

56.6 percent of the world's population (4.46 billion people) lived in either towns or cities in 2021.

London was ranked as **the most sustainable city,** according to the 2018 Sustainable Cities Index.

161

Sustainable cities

Imagine city centers that are free of smog, full of thriving green ecosystems, and have more pedestrians and cyclists than cars.

Home to billions of the world's people, cities consume huge amounts of resources each day and have a large ecological footprint. They are constantly growing, as more and more people move to urban areas—creating some megacities that are home to more than 10 million people. All around the world, people and governments are driving efforts to transform these bustling urban centers into sustainable communities that are better for both the environment and the residents who live there.

Vertical forests
Adding leafy plants to buildings, such as in the Bosco Verticale complex in Milan, Italy, has many benefits. The leaves absorb heat, cooling the buildings and surrounding area, as well as improving the air quality.

Living sustainably

Cities have to provide homes, jobs, power, and facilities for large populations, but there are ways these elements can be made more sustainable. These can include environmentally friendly transportation, using renewable energy as a power source, and innovative green architecture.

Solar panels
Harnessing renewable energy directly from the sun, these help fulfill energy demands in cities.

Affordable housing
To meet the needs of all residents, housing must be varied, of good quality, and affordable.

Leafy balconies
As well as releasing oxygen into the atmosphere, green spaces full of plants can improve well-being.

Permeable pavements
Designed to prevent flooding, these allow water to run through them into an underlying stone reservoir, from where it slowly spreads to the soil below.

Recycling bins
These collect many types of cans, plastics, paper, and other materials so they can be recycled into new goods.

Electric transportation
Vehicles powered by electricity rather than fossil fuels do not emit harmful gases into the atmosphere.

Tree-shaded parks
In addition to providing cool outdoor areas, trees intercept rainwater on their leaves and pull up water from the ground, reducing the risk of flooding.

Public transportation
Often making use of space underground, efficient trains and other forms of public transportation can carry a lot of passengers, producing fewer emissions than cars.

162 earth and us ○ **CONNECTED WORLD**

A total of **2.9 billion people**—or **37 percent of the global population**—have **never used the internet**, of whom **96 percent live in lower-income countries**.

Connected world

In the 21st century, our lives have become more connected than ever. Expanding transportation networks allow us to travel and transport goods faster and reach remote areas more easily, while digital connections mean we can exchange information almost instantly wherever we are.

But this connectivity comes at a cost to our planet. Road transportation, for example, relies on energy from fossil fuels, such as oil and gas. Burning these contributes to greenhouse gas emissions that are causing Earth's temperature to rise. They are also responsible for air pollution. The storage and streaming of digital information is powered by electricity, which also contributes to an increase in greenhouse gases.

COMMUNICATION SATELLITES

Many of our day-to-day activities now rely on satellites tens of thousands of miles (km) above us in the atmosphere. They are essential to the way we communicate, travel, work, and receive news. Today, there are more than 8,000 satellites orbiting Earth, half of which are no longer operational and have become space debris.

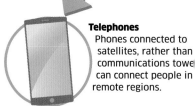

TV and radio
Broadcast satellites transmit audio and visual information to satellite dishes on homes and other buildings.

Telephones
Phones connected to satellites, rather than communications towe[r] can connect people in remote regions.

THE CLOUD

Software or files that are used on the internet are stored in large servers, referred to as "the cloud." Transferring and storing digital information requires large amounts of electricity to power and cool cloud servers, leaving a big carbon footprint. Yet, in many ways, digital technology is helping to reduce carbon emissions by cutting down the number of trips made by people and goods.

Renewable data storage

Using renewable energy resources can reduce the emissions from cloud data centers. These solar panels are built in the Apple Data Center in North Carolina, which uses entirely renewable energy, minimizing its impact on the environment. Solar and wind energy are being used to power other data centers around the world, from Denmark to China.

Streaming

As more and more people stream films and music, play games, and use data stored in the cloud, the impact of our digital lives on the environment is beginning to rival that of our nondigital lives. For example, streaming viral songs—which are played millions of times from a cloud server—can generate comparable emissions to flying.

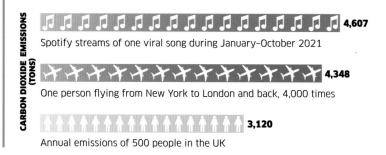

CARBON DIOXIDE EMISSIONS (TONS)

4,607
Spotify streams of one viral song during January–October 2021

4,348
One person flying from New York to London and back, 4,000 times

3,120
Annual emissions of 500 people in the UK

TRANSPORTATION CONNECTIONS

The transportation of goods by road, rail, sea, and air has been key to economic growth around the world and within countries. Transportation is also essential for carrying people to school, work, and on vacation. Today, more and more cities are developing sustainable transportation systems that reduce greenhouse gas emissions and air pollution from burning fossil fuels.

Charging machines
Enabling electric vehicles (EVs) to charge while they park encourages low-emission transportation.

Electric cars
Vehicles running on electricity do not produce any direct air pollution, keeping the local air clean.

Green mobility hubs

In many places, city authorities are finding new ways to link sustainable methods of transportation, such as trams, buses, and trains. Cycle lanes encourage people to leave their car at home, while pedestrianized streets keep cars out of city centers and the air cleaner.

Roads

Road networks are constantly growing, to link communities. Highways seek to streamline road systems, taking traffic around or over cities, and making trips quicker. But these roads also cut through natural habitats, degrading ecosystems and reducing biodiversity.

10 percent—the increase in the number of people **using the internet during the COVID-19 pandemic in 2020**, the largest annual increase in a decade.

1971 The year that computer scientist **Ray Tomlinson** sent the **first-ever email**.

163

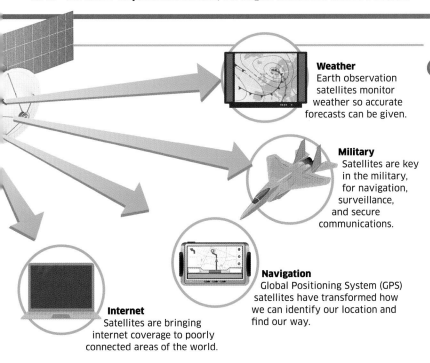

Weather
Earth observation satellites monitor weather so accurate forecasts can be given.

Military
Satellites are key in the military, for navigation, surveillance, and secure communications.

Navigation
Global Positioning System (GPS) satellites have transformed how we can identify our location and find our way.

Internet
Satellites are bringing internet coverage to poorly connected areas of the world.

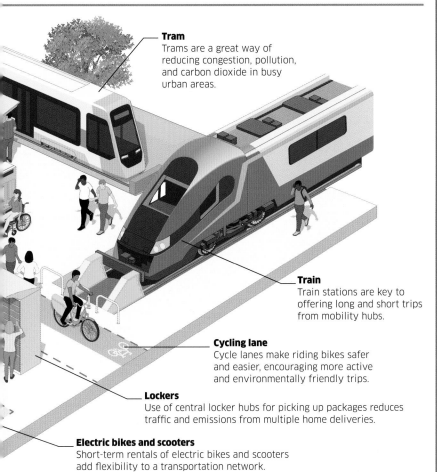

Tram
Trams are a great way of reducing congestion, pollution, and carbon dioxide in busy urban areas.

Train
Train stations are key to offering long and short trips from mobility hubs.

Cycling lane
Cycle lanes make riding bikes safer and easier, encouraging more active and environmentally friendly trips.

Lockers
Use of central locker hubs for picking up packages reduces traffic and emissions from multiple home deliveries.

Electric bikes and scooters
Short-term rentals of electric bikes and scooters add flexibility to a transportation network.

Wildlife corridor

Building wildlife corridors, like this one over a highway in Germany, preserves connections between ecosystems. It enables animals to roam and reduces the numbers of road deaths. In Germany, 75 percent of known wolf deaths are caused by collisions with vehicles.

◎ INSTANT CONNECTIONS

Today, many activities that people did face-to-face now happen online, at near-instant speeds across long distances. This digital revolution began in higher-income countries and is spreading around the world, changing the way we interact with each other. Many devices can connect with each other online, from desktop computers, laptops, and tablets to cell phones and smartwatches.

Cell phones

From banking to shopping, modern phones connect people and companies worldwide faster than ever before. The ability to use cell phones to transfer money, instead of traveling to banks, has revolutionized the economy in many countries, such as Kenya (pictured), where 96 percent of households have a mobile money account.

Email

Electronic mail, or email, has transformed communication in our personal lives, at educational institutions, and when conducting business. More than 300 billion emails are sent globally every day from around four billion email user accounts. Sending fewer emails would save energy.

1. Sender
The sender opens an email computer program, then enters the message and the receiver's email address.

2. Sender email server
The email reaches a server, which then checks a database for the receiver's email address.

3. Receiver email server
Once the email address is recognized, it is transferred to a second server using the internet.

4. Receiver
Finally, the email arrives in the receiver's inbox. They click on it to open and read it.

Internet

The internet has caused a huge shift in the lives of people with access to the web. During the COVID-19 pandemic, the internet played a huge role in enabling people to communicate with friends and family when lockdowns kept them apart.

Shopping
Online shopping is very popular. Some companies are experimenting with drone technology to make deliveries faster and greener.

Social media
Our social lives have moved online. The most popular social media network in 2022, Facebook, has 2.4 billion users, more than the population of China.

Lithium extraction
One of many minerals needed to create complex goods such as electric car batteries, lithium can be extracted from briny pools on salt flats. When the water evaporates from these (such as the above site in Chile), lithium and other minerals are left behind.

Extracting resources
Many resources, such as coal, oil, and natural gas, are found beneath the earth or sea. Known as fossil fuels, these burn easily and release a lot of energy, but also emit harmful greenhouse gases. Extracting them can be difficult and dangerous and may scar the landscape indefinitely. Other ways of getting energy use renewable resources that cannot be used up, such as the wind. These have less environmental impact.

Mining uranium
Dug out of the Earth, uranium is used as fuel in nuclear power stations. The process does not releas[e] emissions, but creates dangerous radioactive was[te]

Coal mining
These black nuggets are mined by digging shafts down through layers of rock or by creating massive holes in the ground, a method known as open-cast mining.

Oil extraction
A liquid fuel, oil is trapped in the small spaces within rocks. Oil rigs are built to drill down through the Earth (including the underwater seabed too) and pump it out.

Fracking
This technique injects liquid at high pressure into fissures in order to extract gas and oil from shale rock. It uses a lot of water, creates pollution, and may trigger mini earthquakes.

Energy

Energy is a vital resource—used in homes, as well as to power industry, businesses, and transportation. Harnessing the resources of the Earth allows us to meet our ever-increasing demand for it.

There are many different ways we can convert Earth's resources into energy, whether by burning fuels mined from the ground or by using the power of the sun. However, resources are unevenly distributed between countries. Some are not only finite—meaning they will eventually be used up—but also cause harm to the environment by releasing high levels of greenhouse gases into the atmosphere.

Layers of sediment   Trapped oil

Ancient animals
When creatures die, their bodies land on the seabed.

Oil forms
As layers build up, pressure and heat converts them to oil.

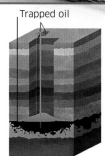

Fuel is extracted
Humans can drill down to the fuel deposits.

Fossil fuels
Coal, oil, and natural gas are known as fossil fuels, because they developed from the remains of dead plants and animals. Over millions of years, tiny plankton decompose into natural gas and oil, while plants become coal—all fuels we can burn to release energy. However, their long formation process means there is only a limited supply of them.

100 times **more energy is consumed by a person in the world's wealthiest nations** than by someone in one of the poorest countries.

Countries such as **Iceland, Paraguay, and Albania** get **100 percent of their electricity from renewable sources**.

165

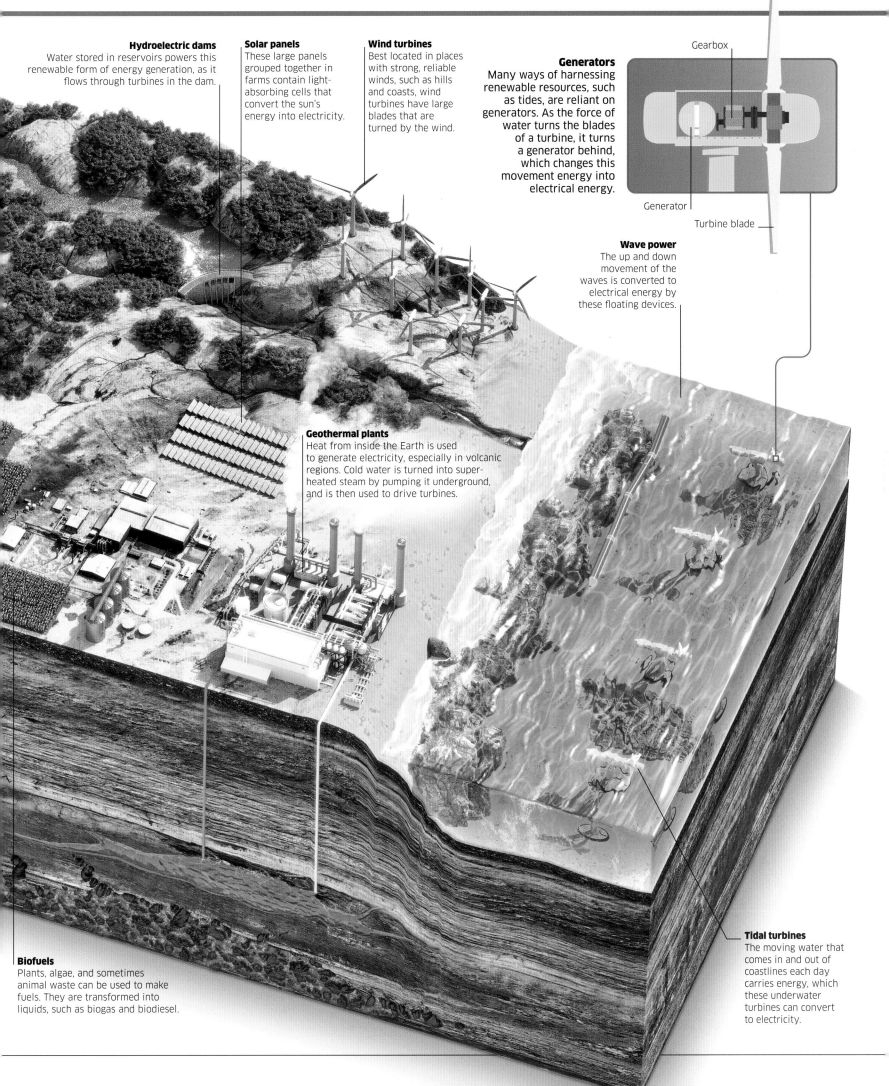

Hydroelectric dams
Water stored in reservoirs powers this renewable form of energy generation, as it flows through turbines in the dam.

Solar panels
These large panels grouped together in farms contain light-absorbing cells that convert the sun's energy into electricity.

Wind turbines
Best located in places with strong, reliable winds, such as hills and coasts, wind turbines have large blades that are turned by the wind.

Generators
Many ways of harnessing renewable resources, such as tides, are reliant on generators. As the force of water turns the blades of a turbine, it turns a generator behind, which changes this movement energy into electrical energy.

Gearbox

Generator

Turbine blade

Wave power
The up and down movement of the waves is converted to electrical energy by these floating devices.

Geothermal plants
Heat from inside the Earth is used to generate electricity, especially in volcanic regions. Cold water is turned into super-heated steam by pumping it underground, and is then used to drive turbines.

Biofuels
Plants, algae, and sometimes animal waste can be used to make fuels. They are transformed into liquids, such as biogas and biodiesel.

Tidal turbines
The moving water that comes in and out of coastlines each day carries energy, which these underwater turbines can convert to electricity.

80 percent of **global trade** involves **transnational corporations.**

2 billion tons of **goods were shipped by containers** in 2017.

Globalization

The world today is increasingly interconnected, with economies, cultures, and people coming together more than ever before. And as just a few companies and brands grow bigger, the world seems to get smaller.

Globalization is not new. Countries have been trading with each other for thousands of years, and there has been large-scale global trade since at least the 17th century. But trade today is more international than ever, dominated by transnational corporations (based in two or more countries). Advances in technology mean that ideas and knowledge can be exchanged instantly, but some argue that globalization is responsible for rising inequality and environmental damage.

SHRINKING WORLD

Globalization means that across the world, people can buy the same fast food, soft drinks, and clothes and watch the same movies and TV shows. This is mainly possible because of improved transportation and digital technology in the last 50 years, making it cheaper and easier to sell products around the world.

The whole world on your phone
Many of the world's largest companies are technology giants, whose business it is to help the world get connected. American company Google has developed apps that allow users to view almost any location in the world. Camera-equipped cars, such as this one in Kenya, take 360-degree images, which are then uploaded and can be searched for online.

Supercontainers
Giant container ships, up to 1,300 ft (400 m) long, have made it much easier and cheaper to carry goods across the seas and are vital to today's global economy. These monster vessels can carry more than 20,000 containers; one fully laden ship can hold around 40,000 family-size cars.

GLOBAL FASHION

Companies often locate different parts of their business in different parts of the world. In the fashion industry, especially, clothes are often designed, marketed, and sold in higher-income countries such as the UK and US but manufactured in lower-income countries, where workers can be paid less and raw materials are cheaper.

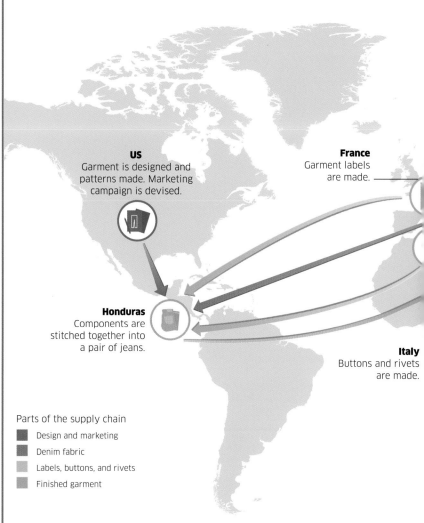

US
Garment is designed and patterns made. Marketing campaign is devised.

France
Garment labels are made.

Honduras
Components are stitched together into a pair of jeans.

Italy
Buttons and rivets are made.

Parts of the supply chain
- Design and marketing
- Denim fabric
- Labels, buttons, and rivets
- Finished garment

MAKING GLOBAL MORE LOCAL

One of the consequences of globalization is less cultural diversity, as communities and markets become less distinct from each other. Some corporations have found ways around this with "glocalization." This means keeping the advantages of a global operation while tailoring products to suit local tastes.

Mc-Glocal
Food giant McDonald's has adopted the "Think global, act local" concept with huge success. Its "glocal" offerings include "McArabia" flatbreads in Arab countries, teriyaki burgers in Japan, and kosher Big Macs without cheese in Israel.

38,000 The approximate number of **McDonald's restaurants** worldwide, **employing 1 million people**.

500,000 miles (805,000 km)—the **estimated distance** traveled by a **smartphone** during its manufacture.

167

The journey of jeans

The steps to create a product from scratch and get it into the stores is called the supply chain. The process of turning a raw material such as cotton into a finished pair of designer jeans might involve 10 or more countries. While this complex sequence makes financial sense for a manufacturer, it is less good news for the environment, with different materials crossing the globe, generating emissions, and leaving a considerable carbon footprint.

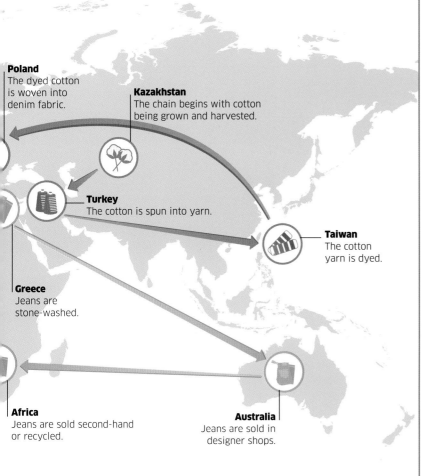

Poland
The dyed cotton is woven into denim fabric.

Kazakhstan
The chain begins with cotton being grown and harvested.

Turkey
The cotton is spun into yarn.

Taiwan
The cotton yarn is dyed.

Greece
Jeans are stone-washed.

Africa
Jeans are sold second-hand or recycled.

Australia
Jeans are sold in designer shops.

Fast fashion

Around 80 billion garments are produced each year to meet the demand for "fast fashion"—cheap clothes that are worn only a few times before being thrown away to make room for new, more fashionable items. To keep prices low for the consumer, clothes are made in countries where labor costs are cheap and environmental standards are low.

Dumped in the desert
An estimated 101 million tons (92 million metric tons) of clothes are thrown away every year. Unwanted garments often end up in landfill sites in lower-income countries. This dump in Chile's Atacama Desert contains second-hand and unsold clothes from across Europe and the US.

Thirsty industry

The fashion trade uses 2 percent of the world's fresh water—only the agricultural industry uses more. When water is siphoned off to irrigate cotton fields, areas can become deserts, with people no longer able to grow crops, catch fish, or raise livestock. The Aral Sea in Central Asia has shrunk by 90 percent because the rivers that once fed it have been diverted to provide water for cotton farms.

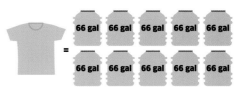

Cotton T-shirt
To make just one cotton T-shirt, the process requires 660 gallons (2,500 liters) of water.

Polyester T-shirt
A polyester T-shirt can be made using just 92.5 gallons (350 liters) of water. However, polyester causes other environmental problems. It is made of tiny plastic fibers that pollute rivers and oceans.

GLOBALIZATION CHALLENGES

Critics of globalization say that although it is probably creating more wealth worldwide, the only real winners are a few huge corporations based in higher-income countries. In addition, a more connected world makes it easier for harmful things, such as infectious diseases or invasive plant and animals species, to spread unchecked.

Anti-globalization
Campaigners such as these French students claim that globalization means greater inequality between rich and poor countries. Corporations may take advantage of lower environmental standards in lower-income countries, leading to increased pollution, landfill, and harmful emissions.

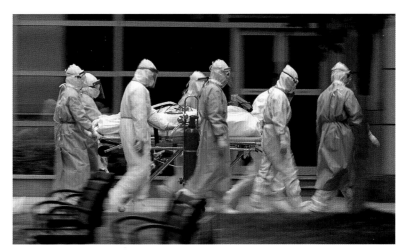

Spread of a pandemic
When the virus COVID-19 was first identified in China in December 2019, medical workers tried to contain the spread of the virus. But in our hyper-connected world, this was impossible. By the end of that year, air travelers had carried COVID to five surrounding countries. At the end of January 2020, 25 nations were affected—and just eight weeks later, 183 countries were reporting COVID-19 outbreaks.

Industrial zone

The snow-covered peak of Mount Fuji, Japan's highest volcano, looms over the factories of Shizuoka prefecture's industrial zone.

Part of a larger industrial region running along the southern coast of Japan's main island, Honshu, Shizuoka is known for its manufacturing, especially motorcycles and musical instruments. In this densely populated region, heavy industry contrasts sharply with its natural features. The iconic Mount Fuji is a young volcano on the Ring of Fire, an active tectonic zone that causes frequent earthquakes in Japan.

170 earth and us ∘ **COASTAL LIVING**

1 billion people around the world live on **land that is less than 33 ft (10 m) above current high-tide sea levels.**

Coastal living

Humans have lived by the coast for thousands of years—fishing for food, building great trading ports to send ships across the ocean, and marveling at its natural beauty.

Today, many of the world's most densely populated cities are on the coast, and key industries such as tourism, shipping, and energy rely on the coastal environment. However, many stretches are under threat from rising sea levels and extreme weather events. All around the world, countries are finding new ways to reduce the effects of erosion and flooding on their coastline.

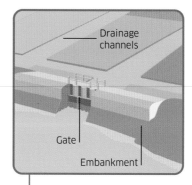

How polders work
Originally designed in The Netherlands, polders are low-lying pieces of land ringed by embankments, which have often been reclaimed from the sea. Gates or pumps in the embankments can be used to drain the water from the land through a series of channels, helping protect it from flooding.

Drainage channels

Gate

Embankment

Polders
Built in low-lying areas, such as Bangladesh, polders pump water off low-lying land so that it can still be used for agriculture and homes.

Managed retreat
In some cases, existing defenses are removed and the sea is allowed to flood the land. Eventually, this land becomes marshland—a new habitat for wildlife.

Mangroves
These coastal trees have complex underwater root systems that stabilize shoreline sediments and prevent them from being washed away.

Oyster breakwater
Artificial structures near the shore provide a new habitat where oysters can grow and form a protective reef.

Sinking cities
Some parts of Jakarta, the capital of Indonesia, are sinking at a rate of up to 10 in (25 cm) per year, making it the world's fastest sinking city. The city is sinking due to too much groundwater being extracted for use, lowering the ground level, as well as the impact of rising sea levels. As 50 percent of Jakarta is now below sea level, the government has outlined plans to build a new capital city inland.

Living sea walls
Sea walls are usually flat and featureless, but they can be made to work in harmony with natural ecosystems. Adding habitat features to sea walls, such as rock pools, gaps, and grooves, allows a range of creatures to live there.

For every 0.4 in (1 cm) rise in global sea level, another **six million people are under threat from coastal flooding** around the planet.

25 percent of **mangrove forests have been lost** within the past 40 years.

171

Coastal defenses

To prevent settlements and beaches from being swept away, coastlines can be managed in different ways. Approaches can be classified as either hard-engineering, such as groynes and sea walls, or soft-engineering, including planting grasses to stabilize dunes. The former tend to be expensive, short-term options that have a huge impact on the landscape and are often unsustainable, while the latter make use of more natural processes.

Threatened homes

Coastal homes around the world are at risk of destruction—from this cliffside house in Norfolk, UK, to huge swathes of low-lying countries, such as Bangladesh, where it is estimated up to 13.3 million people may become displaced by 2050. The impacts of sea level rises and extreme weather are likely to be most severe in the poorest countries.

Adapting cities
Cities on the coast have many ways to prevent the sea from destroying them—from building barriers and sea walls to creating new green spaces on the coast to serve as natural buffers during periods of flooding.

Dune nourishment
Eroded areas of beaches and sand dunes can be stabilized using hardy dune grasses, such as marram grass, as well as fencing.

Reprofiling
Materials, such as sand and shingle from the seabed or lower down the beach, can be redistributed to the upper part of the beach to reshape it and slow the waves.

Groynes
Long structures built at right angles to the coast trap sediment carried along the shore by the waves, helping to slow erosion.

Beach nourishment
Sand can be pumped up from the seabed to extend a beach artificially.

Sea wall
Usually constructed out of concrete, these vast structures often encircle coastal cities and other developments and are built either slightly out to sea or directly on the coast. Although they are expensive barriers to build and maintain, they can be very effective at preventing flooding. In 2004, a large sea wall in the Maldives shielded Malé Island from a tsunami.

Gabions
Wire cages filled with rocks, gabions are usually found at the foot of cliffs and are a cheap and easy method of reducing beach and shore erosion. Boulders can also be piled up along the coast to form rock armor.

Coastal livelihoods

Coastal areas are popular places to live, visit, and work, and many people depend on the coast for their livelihoods. Whole industries, such as fishing, shipping, and tourism employ millions of people, many of whose jobs may soon be at risk due to threats to the coast from climate change and human exploitation.

172 earth and us • **TOURISM**

In 2019, the **Middle East** had the fastest growth in **tourist arrivals**.

5.9 million people worked in tourism in the US in 2019.

Tourism

Leisure travel provides employment for people around the world, but mass tourism can pose challenges to local people, economies, and environments.

When people visit places for fun or travel for business, the money they spend in destination countries can help create jobs, boost incomes, and improve living standards. However, intensive tourism can damage or even destroy local habitats. When tourist resorts expand, they can increase demand for resources such as homes and water, restricting what is available to local residents. There is a fine balance to be struck between the benefits of tourism and its potential harms.

A GROWING INDUSTRY

Prior to the COVID-19 pandemic, the tourist industry was one of the largest and fastest-growing industries in the world. In 2019, more than 1.4 billion international tourist trips were made by people around the world, and the industry as a whole was worth almost $1.5 trillion dollars. Europe is consistently the most popular tourist destination in the world, receiving 744 million visitors in 2019.

Boom in tourist numbers

The United Nations World Tourism Organization (UNWTO) estimates that 70 years ago, there were just 25 million tourist trips worldwide. Since then, this number has increased 56 times. There are a variety of reasons behind this rapid growth, including flights becoming cheaper and people having more disposable income and paid leisure time.

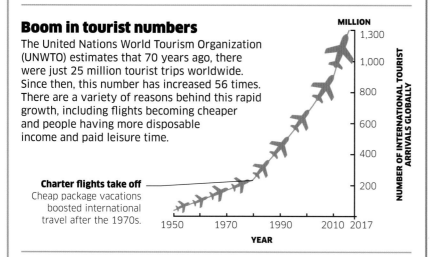

MILLION

NUMBER OF INTERNATIONAL TOURIST ARRIVALS GLOBALLY

1,300
1,000
800
600
400
200

Charter flights take off
Cheap package vacations boosted international travel after the 1970s.

1950   1970   1990   2010 2017
YEAR

Jobs in tourism

In 2019, 334 million people were employed in the tourist industry. Jobs in tourism provide income and security, but employment is often seasonal, leaving some people with no income during the quieter months of the year. Extreme weather, wars, or events such as the COVID-19 pandemic that disrupt travel can devastate the economies of places that are heavily dependent on tourism, such as the Caribbean islands.

% OF TOTAL EMPLOYMENT PROVIDED BY TOURISM

100
75
50
25
0

Antigua and Barbuda | Aruba | St. Lucia | US Virgin Islands | British Virgin Islands

CARIBBEAN TOURIST DESTINATIONS

TYPES OF TOURISM

Many different forms of tourism cater for travelers' preferences. Some people opt for beach vacations, while others prefer outdoor adventures, such as walking or skiing. Governments often favor mass tourism (when large numbers of people visit the same place at any one time) as it creates jobs and generates more income. This is also usually the cheapest way to go on vacation. However, mass tourism can cause increased pollution, traffic congestion, the disappearance of traditional landscapes, and higher emissions.

Outward bound

Hill-walking trails in mountainous regions attract outdoor enthusiasts. In the Snowdonia National Park in North Wales, UK, tourism has created more than 5,000 jobs and brought in money to boost the local economy. However, the number of visitors has caused environmental degradation. The sheer number of tourists in natural beauty spots limits the unspoiled appeal that encourages people to visit these sites in the first place.

Lining up for the top
Walkers crowd the peak of Mount Snowdon, Wales, as they wait to climb to the summit.

Footpath erosion

Overuse of popular footpaths can cause the area around the path to wear away over long periods of time.

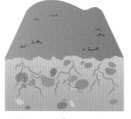 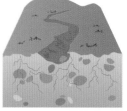 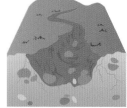

1 Unused footpath
Vegetation forms a level surface. Roots bind the soil together and keep the earth stable.

2 Worn footpath
Trampling compacts the soil and reduces the vegetation. A gully forms, accelerating soil erosion.

3 Deepening gully
Walkers use the areas at the side of the footpath where plants grow, widening the gully.

Busy beach
Beaches may become overcrowded, especially during the school breaks.

Beach tourism

Coastal locations tend to be cooler than inland areas in summer. Many people flock to the beach so that they can cool down in the sea and enjoy a variety of seaside activities. However, the increased noise and litter that arises can disturb local residents and endanger wildlife on land and in the water. The development of new beach resorts may be viewed as an eyesore.

6 percent—the amount **emissions** dropped in **2020**, when travel was **restricted**.

50 percent of all **international tourists** visit **European countries**.

1949 was the year of the first **jet-powered flight**, beginning the **age of tourism**.

173

The environmental impact

Tourism is estimated to account for 8–11 percent of global greenhouse gas emissions. Flying is one of the key contributors because the carbon dioxide, vapor trails, soot particles, and other pollutants planes release at high altitudes trap the heat that radiates from the Earth's surface.

Air transportation
Cheaper and more frequent flights have made it easier to travel abroad but have drastically increased the emissions from air travel.

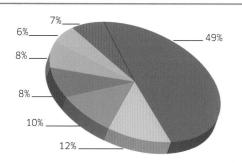

7%
6%
8%
8%
10%
12%
49%

Tourism emissions
Transportation is by some way the largest source of emissions from the tourism industry. In 2018, the US was the largest producer of transport emissions, followed by China and Germany.

- Transportation
- Goods
- Food & beverage
- Agriculture
- Services
- Accommodation
- Other

SUSTAINABLE TOURISM

As awareness of the environmental impact of tourism has grown, new sustainable practices have started to be applied to all forms of tourism and in every region of the world. Sustainable tourism seeks to ensure that tourist activities do not disrupt local ecosystems and biodiversity, promotes respect for the natural environment and host communities, and provides stable employment to local people.

Canoeing in Costa Rica
Eco-tourism aims to reduce the impact that tourism has on the natural environment and protect local wildlife. In Costa Rica, small groups explore the rainforest by canoe, a method of transportation that does not produce emissions and causes no damage to the area's ecosystem. Tourism can encourage wildlife conservation efforts too.

Coral
Sunscreen causes bleaching, deforms and kills new coral

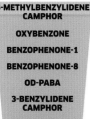

Dolphins
Accumulates in tissue and can be transferred to young

4-METHYLBENZYLIDENE CAMPHOR
OXYBENZONE
BENZOPHENONE-1
BENZOPHENONE-8
OD-PABA
3-BENZYLIDENE CAMPHOR
NANO-TITANIUM DIOXIDE
NANO-ZINC OXIDE
OCTINOXATE
OCTOCRYLENE

Mussels
It causes defects in young

Fish
Decreases fertility, and causes female characteristics to occur in male fish

Toxic sunscreen
When in the water, sunscreen can wash off skin and into the sea. The chemicals contained in the protective balm can be hazardous to coral and other marine life.

Extreme environments

In recent years, the warmer temperatures and melting ice caused by climate change have made it possible to reach destinations whose extreme environments had previously made them inhospitable or inaccessible.

Antarctic cruise
As the polar ice caps melt, it has become possible for people to visit this frozen landscape, but high numbers of tourists may harm the continent's delicate ecosystem.

Sports tourism

One of the fastest-growing forms of leisure travel is sports tourism. Tourists travel to compete on championship courses, while major sporting events attract thousands of spectators and provide a huge boost to local economies.

Desert golf
Sports tourism can lead to overdevelopment. This golf course in the Las Vegas desert uses precious water resources to create its lawns and water features.

174 earth and us ∘ POLLUTION

By the year **2050**, there will be more **pieces of plastic** in the sea than **fish**.

73 percent—the amount of **beach litter** worldwide that is **made of plastic**.

Pollution

When the environment is damaged by the addition of something harmful, it becomes polluted.

Pollution is caused by human activity. It can affect all aspects of the environment, including the water, land, and air. In recent years, great efforts have been made to limit the impact by attempting to control the release of harmful emissions into the air, treat wastewater, and reduce and recycle solid waste. However, the scale of the problem continues to grow. High levels of air pollution are common in large cities worldwide, while land and sea pollution damage animal habitats and pose an urgent threat to biodiversity.

⊙ TYPES OF POLLUTION

Some forms of pollution, such as plastic waste or contaminated water, are clearly visible. Air and noise pollution may be less obvious, but they still pose a threat to nearby ecosystems. Every living thing is vulnerable to the effects of pollution, each of which affects the environment in a different way.

Land pollution

When plastic and other waste accumulates in a single place, such as this vast garbage dump in Tokyo, Japan, harmful substances can seep into the earth. There, the toxins mix with chemical waste from mines and factories, polluting the soil and groundwater. This can poison plants, animals, and people.

Noise pollution

Unwanted sounds can harm the health of living things. Sources of noise pollution include road and air traffic, building sites, and noisy events. In areas near airports, where the sound of planes taking off and landing is extremely loud, it can be hard to sleep. At sea, the noise of large ships can disrupt animal behavior.

Light pollution

Bright, artificial light illuminates the night sky, obscuring the stars. This can harm newly hatched turtles, who mistake the lights for the moon's reflection on water and head inland instead of swimming out to sea. City lights are dangerous to migrating birds, disrupting their flight paths and causing them to collide with buildings.

Water pollution

When harmful substances flow into rivers, lakes, or the sea, they pollute the water. One major pollutant is oil, which is toxic and sticks to the fur or feathers of water creatures, making them less able to float and keep warm.

Eutrophication

If too many nutrient-rich substances enter a body of water, they can stimulate the rapid growth of algae, which then smothers all the other aquatic animals and plants in the water.

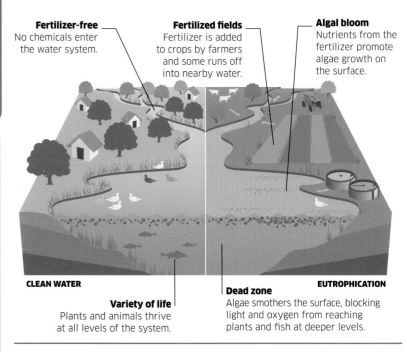

Fertilizer-free
No chemicals enter the water system.

Fertilized fields
Fertilizer is added to crops by farmers and some runs off into nearby water.

Algal bloom
Nutrients from the fertilizer promote algae growth on the surface.

CLEAN WATER

Variety of life
Plants and animals thrive at all levels of the system.

Dead zone
Algae smothers the surface, blocking light and oxygen from reaching plants and fish at deeper levels.

EUTROPHICATION

Air pollution

Many industrial processes, including manufacturing, transportation, and electricity generation from coal, release harmful gases, ash, and soot into the air. These gases can spread for hundreds of miles, making the air harder to breathe and causing conditions such as asthma and heart disease.

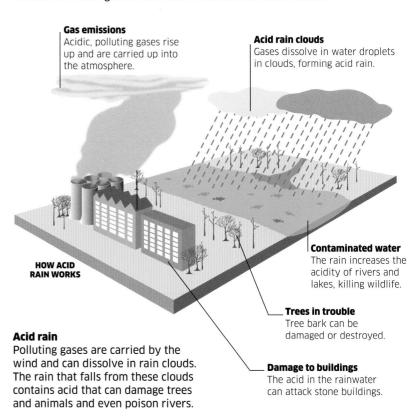

Gas emissions
Acidic, polluting gases rise up and are carried up into the atmosphere.

Acid rain clouds
Gases dissolve in water droplets in clouds, forming acid rain.

HOW ACID RAIN WORKS

Contaminated water
The rain increases the acidity of rivers and lakes, killing wildlife.

Trees in trouble
Tree bark can be damaged or destroyed.

Damage to buildings
The acid in the rainwater can attack stone buildings.

Acid rain

Polluting gases are carried by the wind and can dissolve in rain clouds. The rain that falls from these clouds contains acid that can damage trees and animals and even poison rivers.

80 percent of **people** live under **light-polluted** skies.

2.2 billion tons (2 billion metric tons) of waste is produced **every year** worldwide.

7 million–the number of **people** estimated to die each year as a direct result of breathing **polluted air**.

175

THE PROBLEM WITH PLASTIC

Each year, around 331 million tons (300 million metric tons) of plastic are made. It is in almost everything we use, but it takes a very long time to break down and is difficult to recycle. Many plastic products are designed to be used only once, which means that plastic waste accumulates rapidly. Plastic pollution has now spread to every corner of the Earth, from the heights of Mount Everest to the deepest ocean trenches.

AVERAGE NUMBER OF YEARS FOR PLASTIC TO DEGRADE

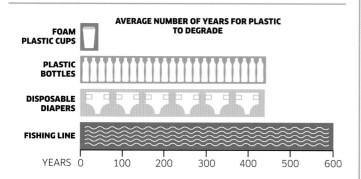

FOAM PLASTIC CUPS	
PLASTIC BOTTLES	
DISPOSABLE DIAPERS	
FISHING LINE	

YEARS 0   100   200   300   400   500   600

A very long life

Unlike organic materials, plastic, which is made from fossil fuels, takes years or even centuries to biodegrade (decompose). A thin, foam-plastic drinking cup might take 15 years to be broken down by the action of sunlight and microbes, while a strong strand of fishing line could still be intact after 600 years.

Ocean plastics

Earth's oceans are especially vulnerable to plastic pollution. Plastic ends up in the ocean in a number of ways, including from fishing and shipping, runoff from waste sites, or food and drink packaging. Some of it creates huge, floating waste patches, and plastic in the water poses a deadly threat to marine life. Animals can get entangled in discarded fishing lines, or, as in the case of this octopus, become trapped inside plastic items on the seabed.

Microplastics

Microplastics are fragments of plastic, less than 0.2 in (5 mm) across, about the size of a sesame seed. They are formed when waves break down larger pieces of plastic. It is likely that there are now trillions of particles floating in the world's oceans. When marine animals ingest microplastics, these particles enter the food chain–which means that many humans are regularly ingesting microplastics in the food they eat.

POLLUTION-BUSTING INNOVATION

The only lasting solution to the problems caused by pollution is to curb our worst polluting habits: stop burning fossil fuels, reduce emissions, and limit how much plastic we use. However, technology and innovation can also play a part in reducing the impacts of pollution. These are some recent initiatives that are helping to restore our environment.

Replacing bottles

At a typical big city marathon, up to a million plastic bottles are handed out and discarded. One alternative is drinks capsules made from seaweed. Users can safely swallow the capsules, or suck out the water and discard the casing, which breaks down within a month.

Ocean Cleanup

The Ocean Cleanup organization develops technologies to rid the world's oceans of plastic. One system currently in use, nicknamed "Jenny," is a U-shaped, 2625 ft (800 m) long floating barrier, which is pulled through the water by two boats. Plastic gathers inside the barrier, where it is collected and sent for recycling.

Purifying paint

In Mexico City, artists from the Absolut Street Trees initiative have created giant murals using paint that purifies the environment. When it is exposed to sunlight, this paint produces a chemical reaction that releases oxygen into the air. The project's creators estimate that the murals will neutralize an amount of pollution equivalent to the emissions created by 60,000 vehicles each year.

Plastic school

Australian charity Classroom of Hope and Finnish company Block Solutions teamed up on the Indonesian island of Lombok to build a school out of eco-blocks. Made from recycled plastic and wood, the blocks are quick to assemble–the school took six days to build.

176 earth and us ○ BUILDING THE FUTURE

95 percent—the potential **saving of energy** if a new house is built to the fully insulated **Passive House Standard**.

Building the future

While the main forces behind climate change and environmental destruction are large corporations, there are also actions that we, as individuals, can take to counter the harm.

Governments all over the world are tackling the world's problems by promoting new technology such as wind turbines and solar farms. These massive projects are vital, but the things we do as individual people are just as important. We can all reduce the energy we use, the things we think we need, and the waste we generate. We can shop more wisely and take more care of the things we buy. And we can support the campaigners who fight to make the world a better, more beautiful place.

FIGHTING BACK

When we know something is wrong, it is important to speak out. In the past, many issues have been brought to public attention by activists, who highlight what is happening and campaign for change. They may be opposed by big business or even national governments, making their campaigns seem hopeless, but history shows that they often win in the end.

Rachel Carson
The American scientist and writer Rachel Carson (1907–1964) studied the effects of artificial pesticides, especially DDT (dichloro-diphenyl-trichloroethane) on the natural world. She showed how they led to polluted streams and soil, and could travel through food chains once eaten by animals. She wrote about this in her hugely influential book *Silent Spring*. Eight years after her death, DDT was banned in the USA.

The Chipko movement
Faced with the destruction of their local forests by logging in the 1970s, village women in the hills of northern India used their own bodies to defend the trees. After several days, the loggers were forced to give up. The campaign spread and became so successful that, in 1980, the Indian government made logging there illegal.

Vaness Nakate
In 2019, Vanessa Nakate started her own one-woman climate protest in Uganda, aiming to highlight the disastrous impact of climate change in Africa. For months, she campaigned alone but gradually gained support and is now a regular speaker at international events, alongside other activists, including Greta Thunberg.

WHAT CAN WE DO?

We can all help by remembering the three Rs—reduce, reuse, and recycle. This means reducing the amount of energy, water, and other resources we use every day. It means getting the most value out of any possessions we have—if necessary by getting them repaired instead of replacing them, and by selling or donating things we don't need. And when they cannot be repaired any more, we can try to make sure they are recycled instead of polluting our environment.

Use less water
A lot of water is wasted in toilets. To reduce this, fill a plastic bottle with water and a few stones, and put it in the cistern to decrease its capacity. A one-liter bottle saves a liter of water with every flush.

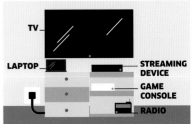

Use less energy
Whenever you leave an electrical device on standby, it keeps on using energy. So if you are not using it, switch it off at the plug. You could save up to 16 percent of your home's energy use.

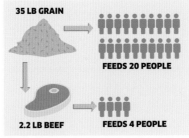

Eat less meat
If 35 lb (16 kg) of grain is fed to cattle, it turns into 2.2 lb (1 kg) of beef—enough for four people. But if we eat the grain instead of feeding it to cattle, the same amount feeds 20. We must eat less meat.

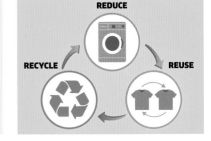

Reduce, reuse, and recycle
Clothes last longer if we wash them less frequently. This also saves energy. We can pass them on to others if we grow out of them, and finally recycle their fabric when they are worn out.

THE FUTURE

In recent years, people in higher-income countries rarely worried about wasting or throwing things away if they had the money to replace them. But the environmental crisis shows that we need to think differently and focus on using resources as efficiently as we can. New technology can help, making our homes, our eating habits, and even our waste processing kinder to the environment.

Smart homes

In the future, homes may be equipped with "smart" appliances that help prevent waste. A smart refrigerator, for example, monitors its contents and sends updates to a phone, prompting the owner to use food before it becomes inedible and has to be thrown away.

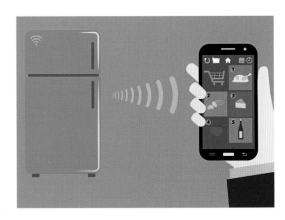

30 percent of the world's **energy** was generated from **renewable sources** in 2021.

6.6 million new **electric vehicles** were sold worldwide in 2021.

32 The **number of countries** where **plastic bags** are **banned**, 18 of which are in **Africa**.

177

Shop wisely

Are the things that you buy produced in ways that do not damage the environment? Check by looking for labels that certify how they were sourced or made and which materials were used or not used.

Sustainable seafood
This logo shows that a fishery is well managed with healthy fish stocks.

Eco-friendly wood
Look for a Forest Stewardship Council logo on wood products.

Fair traders
The Fairtrade logo shows producers were paid and treated fairly.

Palm-oil products
This label signifies sustainable, responsibly sourced palm oil.

Rainforest Alliance
Choosing products with this label helps protect the world's rainforests.

Cruelty-free
A leaping bunny shows that the product was not tested on animals.

◎ GREENER LIVING

Reducing the amount of energy we use can help tackle climate change. We can all help reduce energy use in our homes by the way we behave. We can wear more clothes in winter, so we can turn the heating down. We can keep the house warmer by insulating them and turning off lights that are not needed. Clothes can be washed at lower temperatures and dried on a clothes line instead of using a tumble dryer.

Home improvements
Reducing our energy use saves money, which can be used to help pay for energy-saving improvements to the home. These could include LED lighting, roof insulation, and even solar panels.

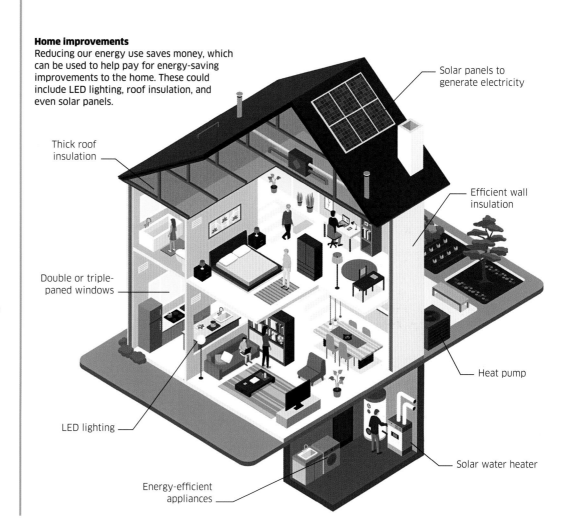

- Solar panels to generate electricity
- Thick roof insulation
- Efficient wall insulation
- Double or triple-paned windows
- Heat pump
- LED lighting
- Solar water heater
- Energy-efficient appliances

Artificial meat

Rearing animals for meat has a much bigger impact on the environment than producing plant foods. But artificial meat products can be grown in a laboratory with far less waste. In the future, we will be able to use this technology to produce burgers and other meat products in factories.

Cell collection
Specific cells are removed from an animal in a painless procedure. Only a few animals are needed and are not harmed by the process.

Cell culture
The cells are cultured in a laboratory to make them multiply. They double over and over, until there are enough cells for the next production stage.

Tissue growth
The cell culture is placed in a large machine called a bioreactor, where it is grown into fibers that resemble animal muscle tissue—the main form of edible meat.

Processing into food
Finally, the tissue is processed into food products such as burgers, which are traditionally made of ground meat along with other ingredients.

Tackling plastic

Waste plastic is a huge global problem. Currently, only 20 percent of the plastic we use is recycled—the rest is thrown away. But new ways of treating waste plastic using chemicals can turn it into a form of oil. This can be used to make more products, which can then be recycled in the same way. This no-waste approach to production is known as a circular economy.

- Consumers use the products and throw them away.
- Waste plastic is collected and sorted.
- The mixed materials are used to make new products.
- **CIRCULAR ECONOMY**
- Chemicals and heat are used to turn the plastic into oil.
- The material is added to other raw materials.
- The oil is purified so it can be used as a raw material.

EARTH'S CONTINENTS

The landmasses on Earth form seven continents, each with its own combination of landscapes, geological features, and wildlife. Humans have divided six of the continents into countries, all with diverse populations and cultures.

CONTINENTS AND OCEANS

Earth's continents are huge slabs of ancient rock separated by broad expanses of younger, heavier rock that form the ocean floors. The Atlantic Ocean is very slowly expanding while the Pacific Ocean is shrinking, and this is gradually pushing the American continents further away from Europe and Africa.

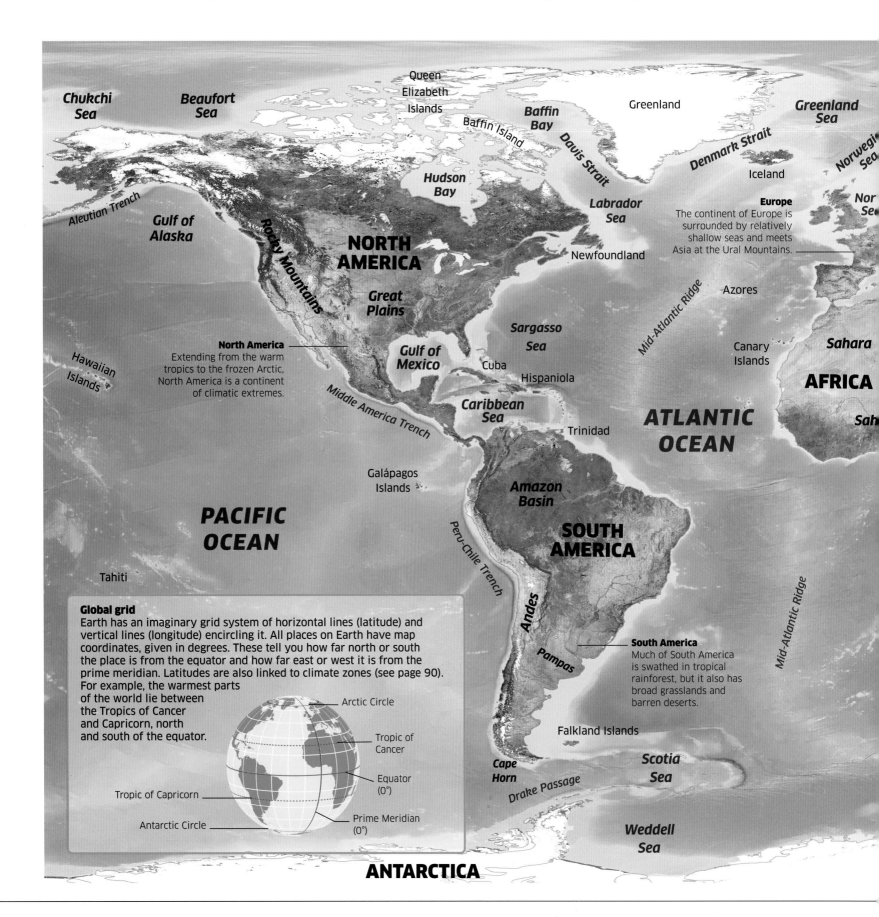

Chukchi Sea

Beaufort Sea

Queen Elizabeth Islands

Baffin Island

Baffin Bay

Greenland

Greenland Sea

Davis Strait

Denmark Strait

Iceland

Norwegian Sea

Hudson Bay

Labrador Sea

Europe
The continent of Europe is surrounded by relatively shallow seas and meets Asia at the Ural Mountains.

Nor Se

Aleutian Trench

Gulf of Alaska

Rocky Mountains

NORTH AMERICA

Newfoundland

Mid-Atlantic Ridge

Azores

Great Plains

Sargasso Sea

Canary Islands

Sahara

North America
Extending from the warm tropics to the frozen Arctic, North America is a continent of climatic extremes.

Gulf of Mexico

Cuba

Hispaniola

AFRICA

Sah

Hawaiian Islands

Middle America Trench

Caribbean Sea

Trinidad

ATLANTIC OCEAN

Galápagos Islands

Amazon Basin

PACIFIC OCEAN

Peru-Chile Trench

SOUTH AMERICA

Tahiti

Andes

Mid-Atlantic Ridge

Global grid
Earth has an imaginary grid system of horizontal lines (latitude) and vertical lines (longitude) encircling it. All places on Earth have map coordinates, given in degrees. These tell you how far north or south the place is from the equator and how far east or west it is from the prime meridian. Latitudes are also linked to climate zones (see page 90). For example, the warmest parts of the world lie between the Tropics of Cancer and Capricorn, north and south of the equator.

Pampas

South America
Much of South America is swathed in tropical rainforest, but it also has broad grasslands and barren deserts.

Arctic Circle

Tropic of Cancer

Equator (0°)

Tropic of Capricorn

Antarctic Circle

Prime Meridian (0°)

Falkland Islands

Cape Horn

Drake Passage

Scotia Sea

Weddell Sea

ANTARCTICA

The 7 continents

take up 29 percent of Earth's surface, while sea and fresh water cover 71 percent.

Highest and lowest land points

The highest mountain peaks soar more than 4.97 miles (8 km) above the average coastal level of the world's oceans—known as sea level. Some of the lowest places on land lie below sea level, but since they are cut off from the ocean, they have not been flooded by sea water.

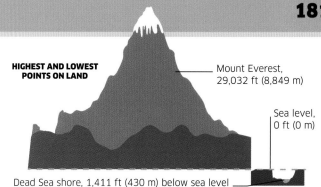

HIGHEST AND LOWEST POINTS ON LAND

Mount Everest, 29,032 ft (8,849 m)

Sea level, 0 ft (0 m)

Dead Sea shore, 1,411 ft (430 m) below sea level

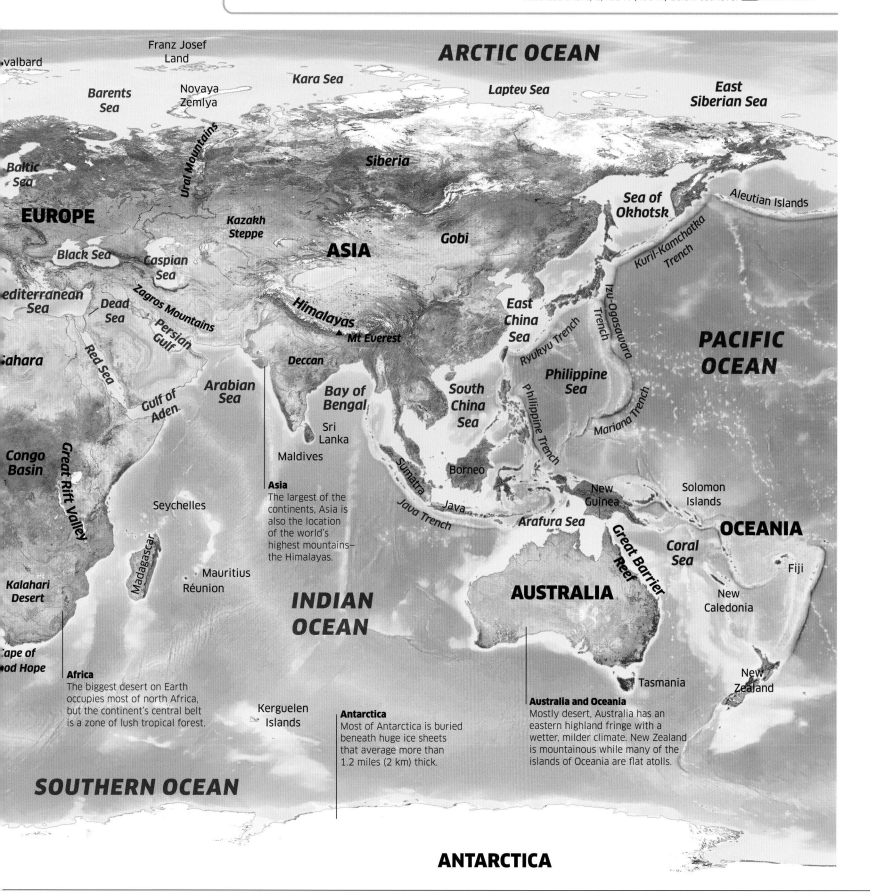

Svalbard

Franz Josef Land

ARCTIC OCEAN

Barents Sea

Novaya Zemlya

Kara Sea

Laptev Sea

East Siberian Sea

Baltic Sea

Ural Mountains

Siberia

Sea of Okhotsk

Aleutian Islands

EUROPE

Kazakh Steppe

Gobi

Kuril-Kamchatka Trench

Black Sea

Caspian Sea

ASIA

Mediterranean Sea

Dead Sea

Zagros Mountains

Himalayas

East China Sea

Izu-Ogasawara Trench

PACIFIC OCEAN

Persian Gulf

▲ Mt Everest

Ryukyu Trench

Sahara

Red Sea

Deccan

Philippine Sea

Gulf of Aden

Arabian Sea

Bay of Bengal

South China Sea

Philippine Trench

Mariana Trench

Sri Lanka

Congo Basin

Great Rift Valley

Maldives

Asia
The largest of the continents, Asia is also the location of the world's highest mountains—the Himalayas.

Borneo

Sumatra

Java

New Guinea

Solomon Islands

OCEANIA

Seychelles

Java Trench

Arafura Sea

Coral Sea

Madagascar

Mauritius

Réunion

Great Barrier Reef

Fiji

Kalahari Desert

INDIAN OCEAN

AUSTRALIA

New Caledonia

Cape of Good Hope

Africa
The biggest desert on Earth occupies most of north Africa, but the continent's central belt is a zone of lush tropical forest.

Kerguelen Islands

Antarctica
Most of Antarctica is buried beneath huge ice sheets that average more than 1.2 miles (2 km) thick.

Tasmania

New Zealand

Australia and Oceania
Mostly desert, Australia has an eastern highland fringe with a wetter, milder climate. New Zealand is mountainous while many of the islands of Oceania are flat atolls.

SOUTHERN OCEAN

ANTARCTICA

Rocky Mountains
Extending 3,000 miles (4,800 km) from north to south, the Rocky Mountains dominate the western side of North America. They were pushed up by massive earth movements that forced parts of the Pacific Ocean floor beneath the continent, between 80 and 55 million years ago. The pressure folded and fractured the rocks into jagged mountain peaks, such as the Grand Tetons, seen here towering over herds of grazing buffalo.

Monument Valley
This majestic desert landscape in southwestern US was formed by ancient rivers eroding a broad sandstone plateau over millions of years. The highest of the surviving rocky mesas, buttes, and pinnacles tower 1,000 ft (300 m) above the dry valley floor.

Great Plains
During the age of giant dinosaurs, the central region of North America was a shallow sea. It is now a vast, open plain, originally wild prairie grassland but now mainly farmland. Powerful thunderstorms sweep across it in summer.

Yucatán sinkholes
On the Yucatán Peninsula in Mexico, sinkholes known as cenotes have formed in the rock, carved out by acidity in the water that trickles into them through the limestone. They are dotted around the rim of a prehistoric meteorite impact crater (see page 23).

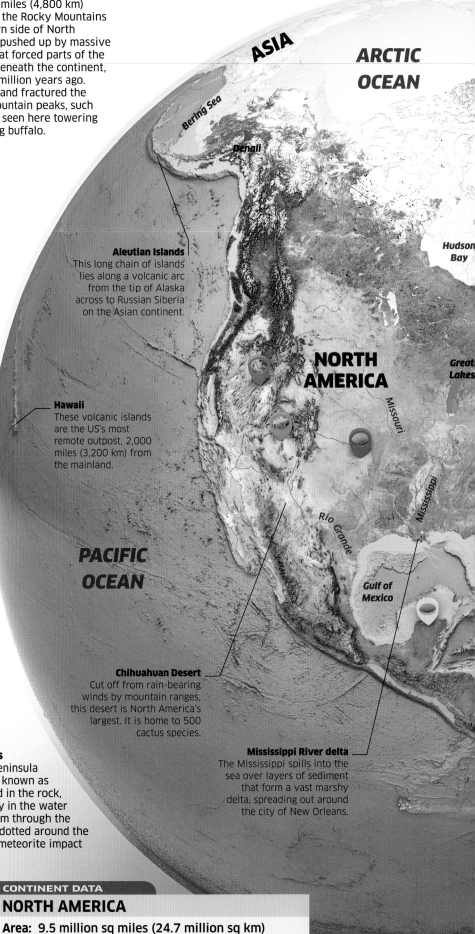

ASIA

ARCTIC OCEAN

Bering Sea

Denali

Hudson Bay

Aleutian Islands
This long chain of islands lies along a volcanic arc from the tip of Alaska across to Russian Siberia on the Asian continent.

NORTH AMERICA

Great Lakes

Hawaii
These volcanic islands are the US's most remote outpost, 2,000 miles (3,200 km) from the mainland.

Missouri

Mississippi

PACIFIC OCEAN

Río Grande

Gulf of Mexico

Chihuahuan Desert
Cut off from rain-bearing winds by mountain ranges, this desert is North America's largest. It is home to 500 cactus species.

Mississippi River delta
The Mississippi spills into the sea over layers of sediment that form a vast marshy delta, spreading out around the city of New Orleans.

CONTINENT DATA
NORTH AMERICA
Area: 9.5 million sq miles (24.7 million sq km)

Population: 600 million

Highest point: Denali 20,310 ft (6,190 m)

2,340 miles (3,766 km)—the **length** of the **Mississippi River** from its **source** at Lake Itasca to the **sea**.

53 ft (16 m)—the **difference** between **high** and **low tide** in the **Bay of Fundy** in Canada, the greatest in the world.

183

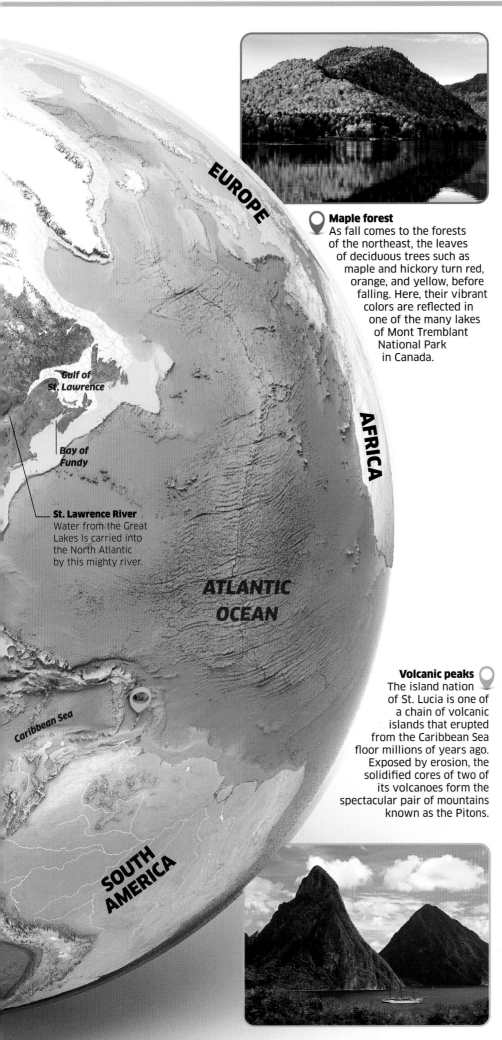

Maple forest
As fall comes to the forests of the northeast, the leaves of deciduous trees such as maple and hickory turn red, orange, and yellow, before falling. Here, their vibrant colors are reflected in one of the many lakes of Mont Tremblant National Park in Canada.

EUROPE

AFRICA

Gulf of St. Lawrence

Bay of Fundy

St. Lawrence River
Water from the Great Lakes is carried into the North Atlantic by this mighty river.

ATLANTIC OCEAN

Caribbean Sea

SOUTH AMERICA

Volcanic peaks
The island nation of St. Lucia is one of a chain of volcanic islands that erupted from the Caribbean Sea floor millions of years ago. Exposed by erosion, the solidified cores of two of its volcanoes form the spectacular pair of mountains known as the Pitons.

North America

Lying north of the equator, North America extends from the lush forests of Central America to the icy wastes of the high Arctic.

The continent has a western spine of mountain ranges that overlook its Pacific shore, which sits along the Ring of Fire and at times shakes from earthquakes. To the east of the mountains, much of the landscape is open prairie. Chilly tundra and vast evergreen conifer forests cover its northernmost parts, while in the east deciduous trees grow across rolling hills. To the south, dry deserts give way to humid rainforest, marshy deltas, alligator-filled swamps, and the tropical islands of the Caribbean.

Protecting the land

The Indigenous peoples who made up North America's original population lived in close contact with nature for thousands of years. Today, their descendants demand the right to manage their native lands and are at the forefront of efforts to protect the environment. This group is protesting against an oil pipeline planned close to a river in North Dakota.

Destructive hurricanes

The hurricanes that build up in the tropical Atlantic each year sweep west into the Caribbean and Gulf of Mexico. Here they batter islands and coasts, flooding them with storm surges that are like wind-driven tsunamis. This satellite image shows Hurricane Katrina spinning toward New Orleans, which it devastated in August 2005.

184 earth's continents ○ **SOUTH AMERICA**

5,500 miles (8,900 km)—the **length** of the **Andes Mountains** from north to south.

South America

A continent of lush tropical rainforests, parched deserts, grassy plains, and rugged mountains, South America has some of the most varied, dramatic landscapes on the planet.

Much of the northern half of South America is shaped by the mighty Amazon River and its many tributaries, which drain a vast area of lowland swathed in dense rainforest. The western edge is quite different—a high ridge of mountains that stops rain from getting to the southeastern regions, creating the Pampas grasslands and the near-deserts of Patagonia. Situated along the Ring of Fire (see page 48), the west coast is at risk of earthquakes and volcanic eruptions.

CONTINENT DATA	
SOUTH AMERICA	
Area:	6.9 million sq miles (17.8 million sq km)
Population:	438 million
Highest point:	Aconcagua 22,841 ft (6,962 m)

Amazonian biodiversity

The tropical rainforests of Amazonia support more types of wild plant and animal than any other habitat on Earth. There are at least 16,000 different species of trees, and well over 2.5 million species of insects. This immense biodiversity is a natural marvel. Its vast untapped resources, including plants thought to have medicinal use, place the region under threat, in addition to the threat posed by logging.

Colorful birds
One in every five of the world's bird species lives in the Amazon rainforests. They include these red-and-green macaws, seen gathering vital minerals from a seam (layer) of clay exposed on a riverbank.

Scaly hunter
The warm climate of the Amazon is ideal for reptiles like Catesby's snail-eater, a snake that hunts snails and slugs in trees and plants.

Desert stargazing

The Atacama in Chile is the world's driest hot desert. Its reliably cloudless skies and lack of light pollution make it perfect for studying the night sky. Several observatories operate here, such as La Silla, which houses different types of giant telescopes inside its many domes.

NORTH AMERICA

Galápagos Islands
This cluster of remote volcanic islands is famous for its unique wildlife.

PACIFIC OCEAN

Andes Mountains
Forced up along the continent's western edge, the Andes form the longest mountain range on Earth. With an average height of 13,100 ft (4,000 m), they are a challenging habitat for animals. These llamas on a plateau near Huayna Potosí, a peak in Bolivia, are adapted to breathe at high altitudes.

SOUTHERN OCEAN

4,000 miles (6,400 km)—the estimated **length** of the **Amazon River**, **competing** with the Nile for "longest river in the world."

2.6 million sq miles (6.7 **million** sq km)—the **vast, but shrinking, area** covered by the Amazon **rainforest**.

185

ATLANTIC OCEAN

Caribbean Sea

AFRICA

Amazon

Amazon

SOUTH AMERICA

Atacama Desert

Aconcagua

Parana

Pampas

Patagonia

ANTARCTICA

Mount Roraima
More than 100 imposing table-topped mountains, called tepuis, tower over the tropical forests of northern South America. The highest is Mount Roraima in Venezuela, with sheer sandstone cliffs that rise above the clouds. Many of the animal species that live on its flat summit can be found nowhere else.

Amazon River
The biggest river in the world, the Amazon carries up to a fifth of the world's river water. Its waters and rainforest-covered shores are home to a rich variety of wildlife, including Amazon river dolphins like the one seen here.

Sugarloaf Mountain, Rio
Rising above Rio de Janeiro in Brazil, this dramatic peak emerged as the surrounding softer rock weathered away, leaving just a cone-shaped granite core standing.

Iguaçu Falls
Tumbling over massive stepped slabs of hard basalt rock on the border of Brazil and Argentina, the Iguaçu Falls are some of the most spectacular on Earth. There are around 300 falls here, including the ones forming the section known as the Devil's Throat, seen above.

Cape Horn
Part of the Tierra del Fuego archipelago, this rocky headland overlooks the Drake Passage, the stormy strait between South America and Antarctica.

Marble Caves
Outcrops of pure marble on the edge of a large lake in the Patagonian Andes have been carved into a complex of caves by wave action. Minerals carried downstream from glaciers tint the lake water, which reflects in the gray marble, giving everything a turquoise shimmer.

Stockholm archipelago
The Baltic coastline is dotted with islands. Nearly 30,000 of them are clustered east of Stockholm, Sweden. During the Ice Age, they were weighed down by a massive ice sheet. When that melted, the islands began slowly rising out of the water, a process that continues today.

Coastal caves
The Algarve in southern Portugal is famous for its spectacular rock formations. Created by the erosion of sedimentary rock by waves and rainwater, these coastal caves form huge arches spanning the shallow water.

The Alps
Formed by the Italian peninsula pushing north against the rest of Europe, this rugged range contains some 80 peaks that are over 13,000 ft (4,000 m) high, including the pyramid-shaped Matterhorn.

Matterhorn, 14,692 ft (4,478 m)

Limestone gorge
In the south of France, the Verdon River has carved a dramatic gorge through the limestone landscape. More than 15 miles (24 km) long, it is 2,300 ft (700 m) deep in places, making it the biggest such canyon in Europe.

ARCTIC OCEAN

NORTH AMERICA

Scandinavian Mountains
Much older than the Alps, this range stretches along most of the Scandinavian Peninsula.

Volcanic Iceland
Iceland is a landscape of dark basalt rock, volcanoes, hot springs, and geysers.

British Isles
Once connected to mainland Europe, Britain became separated from it some 9,000 years ago.

Norwegian Sea

Barents Sea

North Sea

Baltic Sea

Volga

ATLANTIC OCEAN

EUROPE

Volga

Ural Mountains

Danube

Black Sea

Mt. Elbrus

Caspian Sea

Mediterranean Sea

Strait of Gibraltar
More than 5 million years ago, the Mediterranean became closed off from the Atlantic and nearly evaporated. Then this narrow strait opened up again, connecting the two seas but dividing Europe from Africa.

The Bosporus
Separating Europe from Asia, this narrow strait allows sea water to flow between the Black Sea and the Mediterranean.

AFRICA

2,194 miles (3,531 km)—the **length** of the **Volga**, Europe's longest **river**.

1 mile (1.6 km)—the **maximum width** of the **Danube River**.

187

CONTINENT DATA

EUROPE

Area: 3.9 million sq miles (10.2 million sq km)

Population: 748 million

Highest point: Mt. Elbrus 18,510 ft (5,642 m)

Eurasian landmass
Europe forms a vast landmass with Asia, divided by the Ural mountains. Two countries, Russia and Turkey, straddle both continents.

ASIA

INDIAN OCEAN

Europe

From the Mediterranean Sea to the Arctic shores of Scandinavia, Europe has a varied landscape of high mountains, rich farmland, and rolling plains.

Lying on the western side of the great landmass of Eurasia, Europe benefits from steady winds that carry mild, rain-bearing air from the Atlantic Ocean. This gives much of the continent a temperate climate ideal for farming. Once covered in dense forest, the European Plain–which stretches across the continent between mountain ranges to the south and north–is today mainly farmland. Despite this, Europe still has many regions of wilderness, which provide refuges for its native wildlife.

Enclosed seas

Europe is almost surrounded by oceans and seas. Many of its seas are connected to the Atlantic Ocean, but some are virtually cut off. The Baltic and Black seas have a lower salt content than the ocean because so many big rivers flow into them, making them brackish. The Mediterranean is saltier than the Atlantic because the warm sunshine makes its water evaporate, leaving the salt behind.

Water salinity

Salt content of water is shown in parts per thousand (ppt). Less than 0.5 ppt is fresh water, anything above 50 ppt is extremely salty (briny).

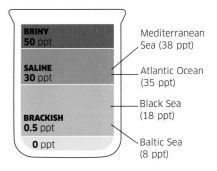

BRINY 50 ppt

SALINE 30 ppt

BRACKISH 0.5 ppt

0 ppt

Mediterranean Sea (38 ppt)

Atlantic Ocean (35 ppt)

Black Sea (18 ppt)

Baltic Sea (8 ppt)

The Danube River
More than 1,770 miles (2,850 km) long, the Danube is Europe's second-longest river, after the Volga. Where it flows into the Black Sea, it has formed the Danube Delta, a marshy landscape that supports a rich variety of wildlife, including these pelicans.

Wild wolves

Once widespread, Eurasian gray wolves were all but wiped out in Europe by many centuries of persecution. A few survived in northern and eastern Europe, however. Since the 1980s, legal protection has allowed them to return to many of their former habitats. Wolves now thrive in the wilder regions of Poland, Germany, Romania, Greece, the Alps, and northern Spain as well as in Norway, Sweden, Finland, and Russia.

All built up

Europe is one of the most densely populated regions in the world, with civilizations extending back nearly four thousand years. The density of settlement in some parts is evident in this satellite image of Europe by night, showing the lights of many large cities and industrial regions.

188 earth's continents ○ **AFRICA**

3.5 million sq miles (9.2 **million** sq km)—the **approximate** area **covered** by the **Sahara Desert**, an area bigger than Australia.

Africa

A huge, mainly tropical continent, Africa is dominated by a vast desert, dry grasslands, and a broad central belt of steamy rainforest. The Mediterranean Sea separates it from Europe, and the Red Sea from Asia.

Some North African countries cover huge tracts of desert, where farming is impossible and few people can live. Further south, the climate is more suited to farming, although many areas, such as the Sahel, are threatened by climate change turning grassland to desert. To the east of the tropical forests lie the highlands of Ethiopia and the deep lakes of the African Rift Valley, with their spectacular colonies of flamingos. In the far south, a Mediterranean-type climate supports the rich plant life of the Cape Floral Kingdom. South of this region, the Indian Ocean meets the Atlantic at Cape Agulhas.

Solar power revolution

The drier parts of Africa get more hours of sunshine than almost any other region, making them ideal places to generate electricity from sunlight. Some countries, such as South Africa, Morocco, and Egypt, have built large-scale solar power plants. Small-scale projects provide electricity in rural areas, such as for these solar-powered street lights in a village in Guinea.

Wildlife reserves

Threatened by poaching and habitat loss, some of Africa's big animals are relatively safe within large wildlife reserves such as Serengeti and Maasai Mara. These tropical grasslands support some of the most spectacular wildlife on Earth, including lions, wildebeest, hyenas, antelopes, and giraffes.

Young population

Compared to other continents, Africa has an exceptionally young population. At least 60 percent of its people are below the age of 25. This is because it is common to have many children and because today fewer children die at a very young age. In Africa as a whole, the median age is 19 years, but it varies greatly from country to country—in Niger, it is only 15 years; in South Africa it is 27.

SCHOOL CHILDREN IN SOWETO, SOUTH AFRICA

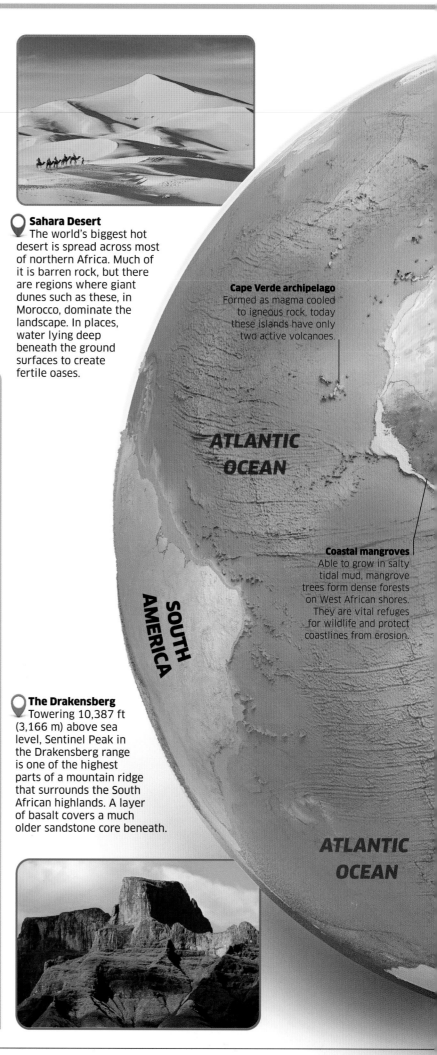

Sahara Desert
The world's biggest hot desert is spread across most of northern Africa. Much of it is barren rock, but there are regions where giant dunes such as these, in Morocco, dominate the landscape. In places, water lying deep beneath the ground surfaces to create fertile oases.

Cape Verde archipelago
Formed as magma cooled to igneous rock, today these islands have only two active volcanoes.

ATLANTIC OCEAN

SOUTH AMERICA

Coastal mangroves
Able to grow in salty tidal mud, mangrove trees form dense forests on West African shores. They are vital refuges for wildlife and protect coastlines from erosion.

The Drakensberg
Towering 10,387 ft (3,166 m) above sea level, Sentinel Peak in the Drakensberg range is one of the highest parts of a mountain ridge that surrounds the South African highlands. A layer of basalt covers a much older sandstone core beneath.

ATLANTIC OCEAN

7 million years ago—the time when our **earliest ancestors** appeared in **Africa**, long before evolving into modern humans.

121°F (49°C)—the **hottest temperature** recorded in Dallol in the **Afar Triangle**.

189

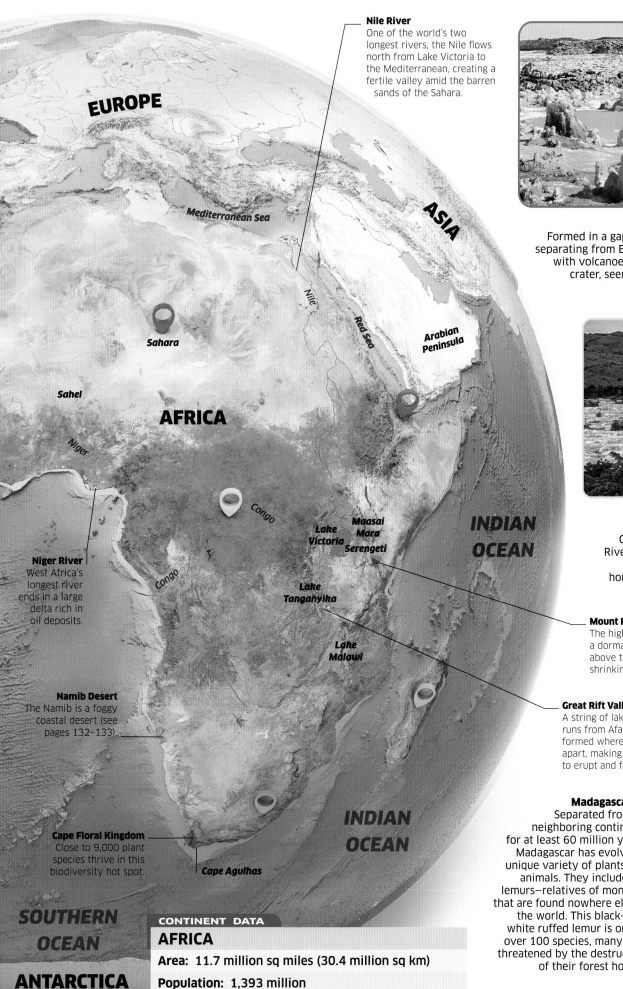

EUROPE

Mediterranean Sea

ASIA

Nile River
One of the world's two longest rivers, the Nile flows north from Lake Victoria to the Mediterranean, creating a fertile valley amid the barren sands of the Sahara.

Nile

Red Sea

Arabian Peninsula

Sahara

Sahel

AFRICA

Niger

Congo

Congo

Niger River
West Africa's longest river ends in a large delta rich in oil deposits.

Lake Victoria

Maasai Mara

Serengeti

INDIAN OCEAN

Lake Tanganyika

Lake Malawi

Namib Desert
The Namib is a foggy coastal desert (see pages 132–133).

INDIAN OCEAN

Cape Floral Kingdom
Close to 9,000 plant species thrive in this biodiversity hot spot.

Cape Agulhas

SOUTHERN OCEAN

ANTARCTICA

CONTINENT DATA

AFRICA

Area: 11.7 million sq miles (30.4 million sq km)

Population: 1,393 million

Highest point: Mt Kilimanjaro 19,341 ft (5,895 m)

Afar Triangle
Formed in a gap left where the Arabian plate is slowly separating from East Africa, the Afar is a depression dotted with volcanoes and boiling hot saline waters. The Dallol crater, seen here, lies 410 ft (125 m) below sea level and is one of the hottest places on Earth.

Congo River Basin
Rainwater from the tropical forests of Central Africa pours into the mighty Congo River. Altogether it drains 1.5 million sq miles (4 million sq km) of rainforest, which is home to gorillas, chimpanzees, and bonobos.

Mount Kilimanjaro
The highest mountain in Africa, Kilimanjaro is a dormant volcano. Its peak, which soars high above the plains of Tanzania, is capped with shrinking glaciers.

Great Rift Valley
A string of lakes lies along the Great Rift Valley, which runs from Afar to Lake Malawi. This depression has formed where a plate of the Earth's crust is pulling apart, making part of it sink and allowing magma to erupt and form volcanoes.

Madagascar
Separated from neighboring continents for at least 60 million years, Madagascar has evolved a unique variety of plants and animals. They include the lemurs—relatives of monkeys that are found nowhere else in the world. This black-and-white ruffed lemur is one of over 100 species, many now threatened by the destruction of their forest homes.

Asia

The largest continent, with the highest mountains and the biggest population, Asia extends from the icy Arctic shores of Siberia to the tropical islands of Indonesia.

Unlike most other continents, Asia is not fully surrounded by ocean. It forms part of a gigantic landmass with Europe, divided by the Ural and Caucasus mountain ranges. It also includes the Himalayas and Tibetan plateau, which lie at such a high altitude that they are sometimes called the Roof of the World. Much of the continent's interior is dry grassland and desert, while lush rainforests grow in the wilder parts of Southeast Asia. Here, and in large parts of China, terraced rice fields shape the landscape.

CONTINENT DATA

ASIA

Area: 17.2 million sq miles (44.6 million sq km)

Population: 4.7 billion

Highest point: Mt. Everest 29,032 ft (8,849 m)

Natural frontier
East of the Black Sea, a plate of Earth's crust carrying the Arabian Peninsula and Turkey has pushed north into Europe to create the Caucasus Mountains.

ARABIAN DESERT

GOBI DESERT

Hot and cold deserts

Asia has large areas of desert. In the south, the hot Arabian Desert is an extension of the Sahara. Further northeast, the Gobi Desert of northern China and Mongolia is much colder and much drier—it gets very little rain because it is cut off from the sea by the world's highest mountains. Nights are cold, even in hot deserts, because dry air doesn't retain heat.

Siberian tiger

The biggest of the big cats, tigers once ranged across Asia from Iran to Korea, and from Siberia to Java. Today, only scattered populations survive in remote forests, mostly in India, but also as far north as the Amur River in the Russian far east. These Siberian tigers have to cope with very cold, snowy winters but are well protected by their thick coats.

Dead Sea
In hot, dry climates, lakes can turn salty as their water evaporates and leaves dissolved minerals behind. The Dead Sea lies 1,412 ft (430 m) below sea level. Its shores are lined with glittering salt crystals and formations known as salt chimneys, left by the shrinking waters.

Deadly waves

Earthquakes on the ocean floor can generate huge, destructive waves called tsunamis. These have devastated some coastal regions, including around the Indian Ocean in 2004, and Japan in 2011. The 2004 tsunami was triggered by a massive earthquake off the coast of Sumatra, Indonesia. The waves that swept across the Indian Ocean killed at least 228,000 people.

ASIA

INDIA

THAILAND

SRI LANKA

MALAYSIA

INDONESIA

Epicenter

INDIAN OCEAN

Countries affected by the 2004 tsunami

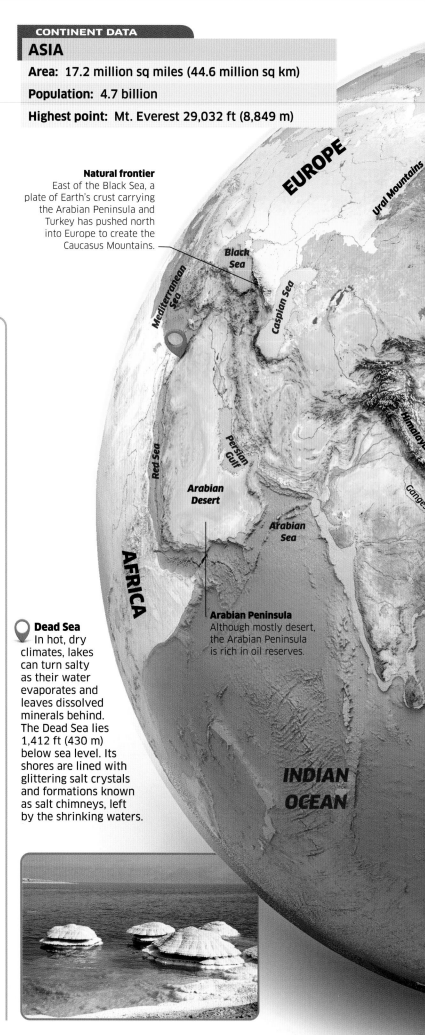

EUROPE

Ural Mountains

Black Sea

Caspian Sea

Mediterranean Sea

Red Sea

Persian Gulf

Himalayas

Ganges

Arabian Desert

Arabian Sea

AFRICA

Arabian Peninsula
Although mostly desert, the Arabian Peninsula is rich in oil reserves.

INDIAN OCEAN

14,370 ft (4,380 m)–the average **altitude** above sea level of the **Tibetan** plateau.

350 The **estimated** number of **Siberian tigers** left in the **wild**.

127 The number of **active** volcanoes in Indonesia.

191

ARCTIC OCEAN

Lena River
Flowing through Siberia from its source near Lake Baikal to the Arctic Ocean, the Lena is frozen for up to eight months of the year.

Oimyakon

Siberia

Lena

Zhangye Danxia
Tilted sandstone layers of many different colors have been eroded by wind and rain to create this dramatic landscape in northwest China. The rock layers get their colors depending on which minerals they contain.

Lake Baikal
Formed in a rift in the Earth's crust, this is the world's deepest lake (5,387 ft/1,642 m).

Amur

ASIA

Gobi Desert

Japan
Japan has a climate that ranges from very cold on its northernmost island, to subtropical in the far southern islands.

Tibetan Plateau

Everest

Brahmaputra

East China Sea

Ganges Delta
Sand and silt carried off the Himalayas by the Ganges and Brahmaputra rivers have created this colossal river delta in the Bay of Bengal. Its swampy channels support dense mangrove forests with their network of underwater roots.

Bay of Bengal

PACIFIC OCEAN

Philippine Sea

South China Sea

Ha Long Bay
This bay in northern Vietnam is dotted with more than 1,600 limestone islands, formed when the soft rock dissolved in water and was flooded by the sea. Most are shrouded with tropical forest, and many contain caves eroded by rainwater.

Borneo

Sumatra

Java

Indonesia
Made up of an estimated 18,000 islands scattered over more than 734,000 sq miles (1.9 million sq km) of ocean, including Sumatra, Java, and most of Borneo, Indonesia is the world's largest archipelago.

AUSTRALIA & OCEANIA

Mount Semeru
The highest of at least 45 active volcanoes on Java, Semeru is part of a long chain of volcanoes, called the Sunda Arc, extending through Java and Sumatra. This is one of the most active volcanic and earthquake zones on the planet, causing many catastrophic events, such as the 2004 Indonesian tsunami.

Cascade of pools

In the mountains of western Turkey, hot, mineral-rich springs near the city of Denizli have created a spectacular cascade known as Pamukkale.

The springs are fueled by volcanic activity deep below ground, where the hot water dissolves calcium carbonate from limestone rock. When the water is forced to the surface, contact with the air turns the calcium carbonate into the mineral travertine. Over time, this has built up the terraces, each with its own shallow turquoise pool of warm water. It has been a spa destination since the 2nd century BCE.

194 earth's continents ○ **AUSTRALIA AND OCEANIA**

1,381 ft (421 m)—the **depth** of Doubtful Sound/ Patea, the **deepest** of New Zealand's 14 **fjords**.

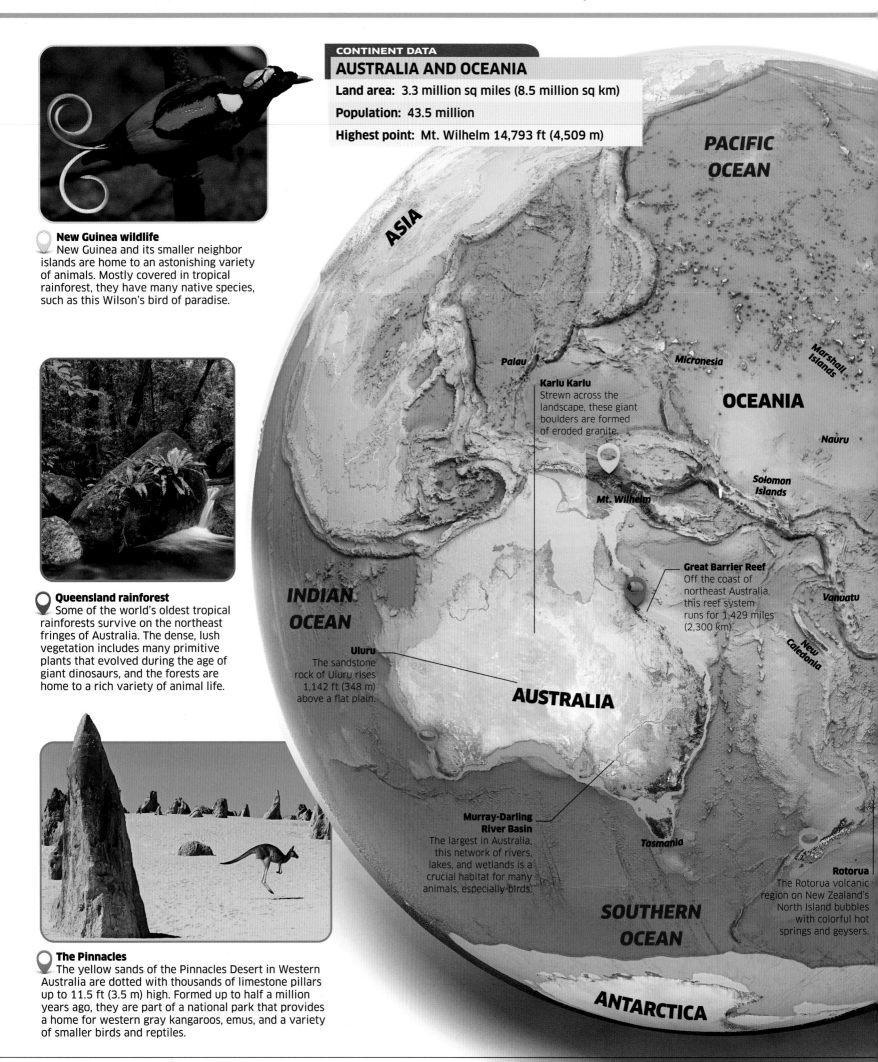

CONTINENT DATA

AUSTRALIA AND OCEANIA

Land area: 3.3 million sq miles (8.5 million sq km)

Population: 43.5 million

Highest point: Mt. Wilhelm 14,793 ft (4,509 m)

New Guinea wildlife
New Guinea and its smaller neighbor islands are home to an astonishing variety of animals. Mostly covered in tropical rainforest, they have many native species, such as this Wilson's bird of paradise.

Queensland rainforest
Some of the world's oldest tropical rainforests survive on the northeast fringes of Australia. The dense, lush vegetation includes many primitive plants that evolved during the age of giant dinosaurs, and the forests are home to a rich variety of animal life.

The Pinnacles
The yellow sands of the Pinnacles Desert in Western Australia are dotted with thousands of limestone pillars up to 11.5 ft (3.5 m) high. Formed up to half a million years ago, they are part of a national park that provides a home for western gray kangaroos, emus, and a variety of smaller birds and reptiles.

PACIFIC OCEAN

ASIA

Palau

Micronesia

Marshall Islands

Karlu Karlu
Strewn across the landscape, these giant boulders are formed of eroded granite.

OCEANIA

Nauru

Mt. Wilhelm

Solomon Islands

Great Barrier Reef
Off the coast of northeast Australia, this reef system runs for 1,429 miles (2,300 km)

Vanuatu

INDIAN OCEAN

New Caledonia

Uluru
The sandstone rock of Uluru rises 1,142 ft (348 m) above a flat plain.

AUSTRALIA

Murray-Darling River Basin
The largest in Australia, this network of rivers, lakes, and wetlands is a crucial habitat for many animals, especially birds.

Tasmania

Rotorua
The Rotorua volcanic region on New Zealand's North Island bubbles with colorful hot springs and geysers.

SOUTHERN OCEAN

ANTARCTICA

133,000 sq miles (344,400 sq km)—the **area** of sea **covered** by the **Great Barrier Reef**.

60,000 years ago—the time when the **first Aboriginal** and **Torres Strait Islander peoples** arrived in **Australia**.

195

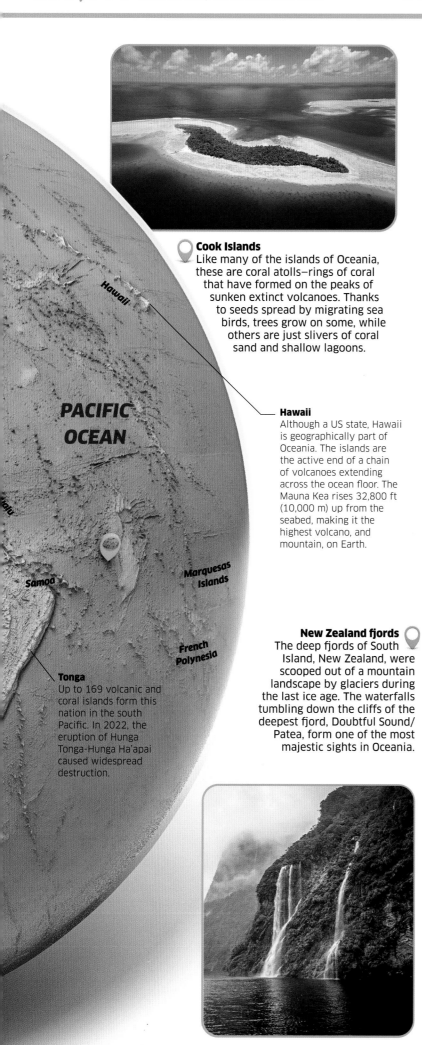

Australia and Oceania

Scattered over the vast expanse of the Pacific Ocean, this region consists of the countless coral islands of Oceania, the largely desert continent of Australia, and wetter, greener New Zealand.

Australia is a huge slab of ancient continental rock, once joined to South America and Antarctica. By contrast, the myriad islands of Oceania are nearly all based on volcanoes that erupted from the ocean floor. Mostly low and flat, these reef-ringed islands are at risk as sea levels rise as a result of climate change. To the south, New Zealand is a long range of volcanic mountains that straddles tectonic plates.

Cook Islands

Like many of the islands of Oceania, these are coral atolls—rings of coral that have formed on the peaks of sunken extinct volcanoes. Thanks to seeds spread by migrating sea birds, trees grow on some, while others are just slivers of coral sand and shallow lagoons.

PACIFIC OCEAN

Hawaii

Although a US state, Hawaii is geographically part of Oceania. The islands are the active end of a chain of volcanoes extending across the ocean floor. The Mauna Kea rises 32,800 ft (10,000 m) up from the seabed, making it the highest volcano, and mountain, on Earth.

Marquesas Islands

Samoa

French Polynesia

Tonga

Up to 169 volcanic and coral islands form this nation in the south Pacific. In 2022, the eruption of Hunga Tonga-Hunga Ha'apai caused widespread destruction.

New Zealand fjords

The deep fjords of South Island, New Zealand, were scooped out of a mountain landscape by glaciers during the last ice age. The waterfalls tumbling down the cliffs of the deepest fjord, Doubtful Sound/Patea, form one of the most majestic sights in Oceania.

Great Barrier Reef

Australia's Great Barrier Reef is the biggest coral reef complex on the planet, built by 600 types of coral and home to around 1,625 species of fish. But its future is threatened as sea temperatures rise.

Teeming with life
Where the reef is in good health and its corals alive, it swarms with colorful fish like these sea goldies.

Coral bleaching
If the water gets too warm, the corals turn white and may die, and this rich habitat will be lost.

Sacred sites

The intriguing giant granite boulders of Karlu Karlu and the spectacular monolith of Uluru are just two of many sites sacred to the Aboriginal peoples of Australia. After decades of ignorance and misuse, these sites and others have reverted to guardianship by local Aboriginal communities and are now protected areas.

KARLU KARLU GRANITE BOULDERS, NORTHERN AUSTRALIA

ULURU, SANDSTONE ROCK, CENTRAL AUSTRALIA

Flat, table-shaped tabular iceberg

Weddell Sea
Occupying a huge bay in the continent, the Weddell Sea is largely covered by floating sea ice dotted with huge tabular icebergs that have broken off Antarctic ice shelves. All the ice drifts clockwise around the Weddell Sea, driven by powerful winds. Orcas, minke whales, and several species of seals negotiate the ice.

South Pole marker
Backed by flags of nations that have scientific bases on Antarctica, this is the ceremonial South Pole. It doesn't stand that far from the geographic South Pole marker, which has to be relocated each year to mark the correct position, as the ice it sits on is moving.

Ross ice Shelf
Part of the West Antarctic ice sheet extending over the Ross Sea, the colossal Ross Ice Shelf covers an area the size of France. Its ice cliffs tower up to 164 ft (50 m) above the water and extend for more than 373 miles (600 km).

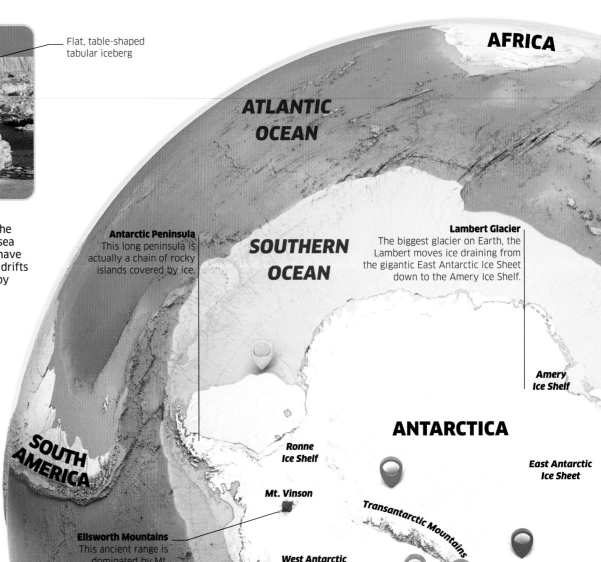

AFRICA

ATLANTIC OCEAN

SOUTHERN OCEAN

Antarctic Peninsula
This long peninsula is actually a chain of rocky islands covered by ice.

Lambert Glacier
The biggest glacier on Earth, the Lambert moves ice draining from the gigantic East Antarctic Ice Sheet down to the Amery Ice Shelf.

Amery Ice Shelf

SOUTH AMERICA

ANTARCTICA

Ronne Ice Shelf

East Antarctic Ice Sheet

Mt. Vinson

Ellsworth Mountains
This ancient range is dominated by Mt. Vinson, Antarctica's highest peak. The mountain rocks contain fossils from more than 250 million years ago, when Antarctica was not yet covered in ice.

West Antarctic Ice Sheet

Transantarctic Mountains

Ross Sea

SOUTHERN OCEAN

PACIFIC OCEAN

Mt. Erebus
An active volcano on an island at the edge of the Ross Ice Shelf, Erebus rises 12,447 ft (3,794 m) above sea level.

CONTINENT DATA
ANTARCTICA

Area: 5.5 million sq miles (14.2 million sq km)

Population: Up to 10,000 in summer

Highest point: Mt. Vinson 16,050 ft (4,892 m)

190 ft (58 m)–the amount by which **global sea levels** would **rise** if climate change **melted** the Antarctic **ice sheets**.

−128.6°F (−89.2°C)–the **lowest-ever temperature** recorded on Antarctica, at Vostok Station on the **East Antarctic Ice Sheet**. **197**

How icebergs are born

Huge glaciers creep slowly downhill off the Antarctic ice sheets, feeding ice shelves that extend out to sea. As the tide rises and falls beneath the floating ice, big chunks break off and float away as icebergs. Many break off as flat "tabular" icebergs, and some of these are gigantic–one that formed in 2021 was 105 miles (170 km) long.

Calved iceberg

Fracture is a sign that an iceberg might break off

Ice flow

Ice shelf
Enormous amounts of ice push forward to form an ice shelf. Near land, it rests on the seabed, but further out it floats.

Sea water erodes ice from beneath

Seabed

INDIAN OCEAN

Extent of sea ice
The sea ice surrounding Antarctica spreads further out in the colder months and reduces in size as ice floes melt during the Antarctic summer.

AUSTRALIA

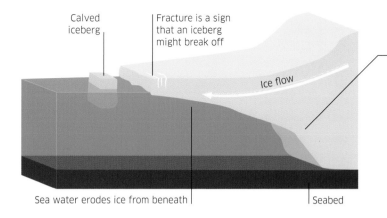

Penguin population

Five species of penguins breed on Antarctica. Four nest on shores in summer, but the biggest–the emperor penguin, seen here–breeds on the sea ice in winter. This gives its fluffy chicks the time they need to grow during the warmer months and be able to survive the following winter.

Ice fumaroles

Hot gases escaping from Antarctic volcanoes melt through the ice and snow to escape into the atmosphere. But the gases include water vapor, which freezes on contact with the cold air and builds up icy chimneys around the vents. These spectacular ice fumaroles can be up to 60 ft (18 m) tall.

Antarctica

The frozen continent of Antarctica is the coldest place on Earth. Apart from polar research scientists, it has no human population. Nearly all its wildlife lives on the shores of the stormy Southern Ocean.

Most of Antarctica is buried beneath a colossal sheet of ice up to 2.9 miles (4.7 km) deep–this thick layer makes Antarctica the highest of all continents. It is divided into the East and West Antarctic ice sheets, separated by the Transantarctic Mountains. The ice sheets extend out to sea as ice shelves, and in winter a vast area of ocean around Antarctica freezes over. Despite the cold, the ocean teems with life, including millions of penguins, seals, and whales.

McMurdo Dry Valleys

These barren valleys form one of the world's most extreme deserts. Very little snow falls, and it is soon blown away by powerful winds. The result is the nearest thing on Earth to conditions on the surface of Mars.

Antarctic research station

There are more than 80 scientific research stations on Antarctica, operated by different countries. Most are used only in summer. The French-Italian Concordia base, seen here, is one of the few that is occupied in winter, when it is completely cut off from the world.

The Arctic

Lying around the North Pole, the Arctic is a seasonally frozen ocean surrounded by the frosty northern fringes of three continents—Europe, Asia, and North America.

The Arctic region begins where the boreal forests of the north give way to treeless tundra. The landscape is frozen for much of the year, but, in the short Arctic summer, the snow and ice melt, giving low-growing plants a chance to flower in the thawed topsoil. The extent of the floating sea ice shifts with the seasons, too, expanding in winter and shrinking in summer. Many of the people living here belong to Inuit, Yu'pik, and other Indigenous groups who have been here for thousands of years.

REGIONAL DATA	
THE ARCTIC	
Area: 5.5 million sq miles (14.5 million sq km)	
Population: 4 million	
Highest point: Mt. Gunnbjørn 12,122 ft (3,695 m)	

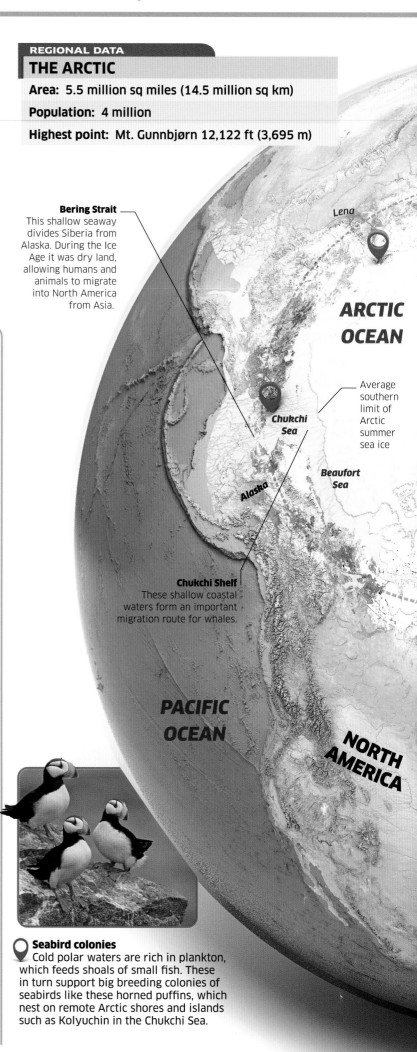

Bering Strait
This shallow seaway divides Siberia from Alaska. During the Ice Age it was dry land, allowing humans and animals to migrate into North America from Asia.

Lena

ARCTIC OCEAN

Average southern limit of Arctic summer sea ice

Chukchi Sea

Beaufort Sea

Alaska

Chukchi Shelf
These shallow coastal waters form an important migration route for whales.

PACIFIC OCEAN

NORTH AMERICA

Bleak future

Adapted for hunting seals on the Arctic sea ice, polar bears rely on the seas being frozen over for much of the year. But climate change is warming the Arctic at almost three times the global average rate, so the area of sea ice is shrinking. By 2100, if not before, the bears will have virtually nowhere to hunt and may face extinction.

Midnight sun and polar night

In winter, the Arctic is tilted away from the sun, so the area within the Arctic Circle endures months of darkness and icy chill. The opposite happens in summer, giving 24-hour daylight, but the sun's rays are so dispersed that temperatures stay low and some ice never melts.

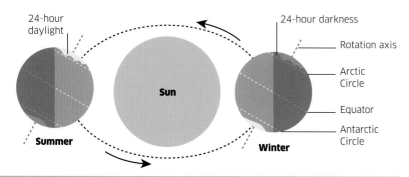

24-hour daylight

Sun

24-hour darkness

Rotation axis

Arctic Circle

Equator

Antarctic Circle

Summer

Winter

Arctic seaways

Early explorers set out to find navigable passages through Arctic islands and ice sheets. Today, icebreakers regularly clear the coastal sea routes around the Arctic Ocean. Climate change means less sea ice, and some want to see more ships using the routes. But this could increase the risk of seriously polluting the Arctic environment.

Seabird colonies
Cold polar waters are rich in plankton, which feeds shoals of small fish. These in turn support big breeding colonies of seabirds like these horned puffins, which nest on remote Arctic shores and islands such as Kolyuchin in the Chukchi Sea.

−93.3°F (−69.6°C)−the **lowest temperature** ever **recorded** in the **Arctic**.

8 ft (2.4 m)−the average **thickness** of floating **sea ice** at the North Pole.

199

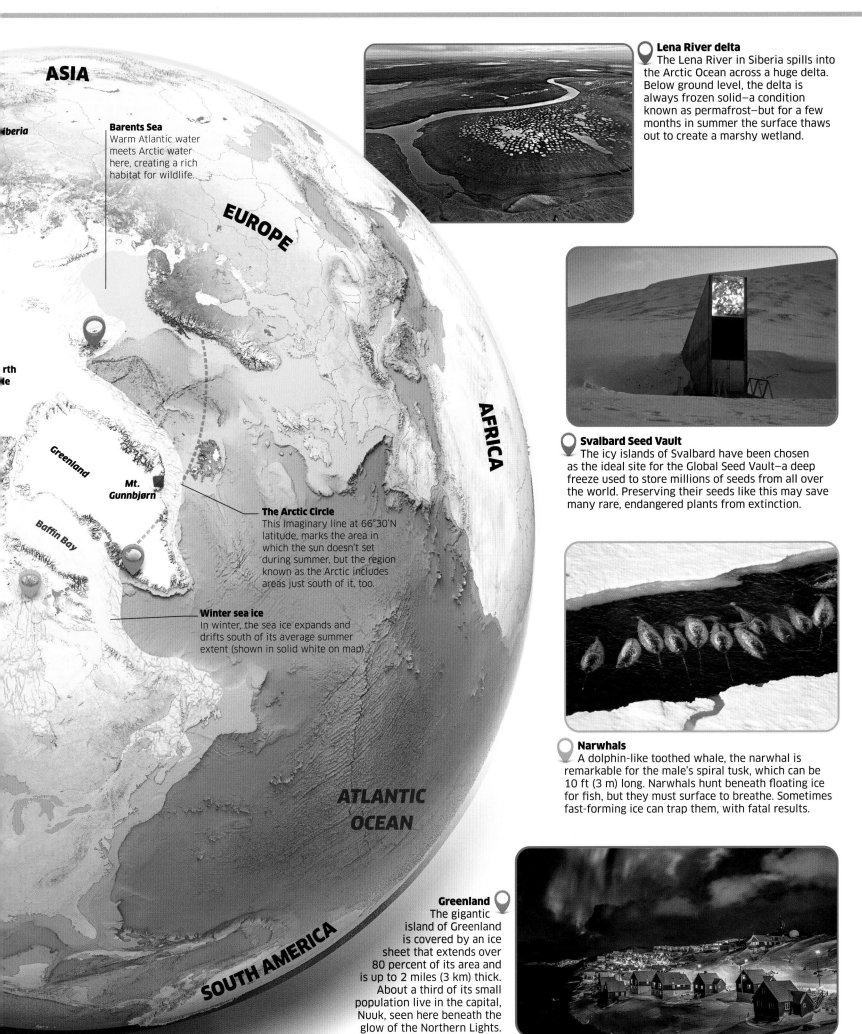

ASIA

EUROPE

AFRICA

Barents Sea
Warm Atlantic water meets Arctic water here, creating a rich habitat for wildlife.

Siberia

rth
le

Greenland

**Mt.
Gunnbjørn**

Baffin Bay

The Arctic Circle
This imaginary line at 66°30'N latitude, marks the area in which the sun doesn't set during summer, but the region known as the Arctic includes areas just south of it, too.

Winter sea ice
In winter, the sea ice expands and drifts south of its average summer extent (shown in solid white on map).

ATLANTIC
OCEAN

SOUTH AMERICA

Lena River delta
The Lena River in Siberia spills into the Arctic Ocean across a huge delta. Below ground level, the delta is always frozen solid—a condition known as permafrost—but for a few months in summer the surface thaws out to create a marshy wetland.

Svalbard Seed Vault
The icy islands of Svalbard have been chosen as the ideal site for the Global Seed Vault—a deep freeze used to store millions of seeds from all over the world. Preserving their seeds like this may save many rare, endangered plants from extinction.

Narwhals
A dolphin-like toothed whale, the narwhal is remarkable for the male's spiral tusk, which can be 10 ft (3 m) long. Narwhals hunt beneath floating ice for fish, but they must surface to breathe. Sometimes fast-forming ice can trap them, with fatal results.

Greenland
The gigantic island of Greenland is covered by an ice sheet that extends over 80 percent of its area and is up to 2 miles (3 km) thick. About a third of its small population live in the capital, Nuuk, seen here beneath the glow of the Northern Lights.

The world's **smallest country** is the **Vatican City**, at 0.17 sq miles (0.44 sq km).

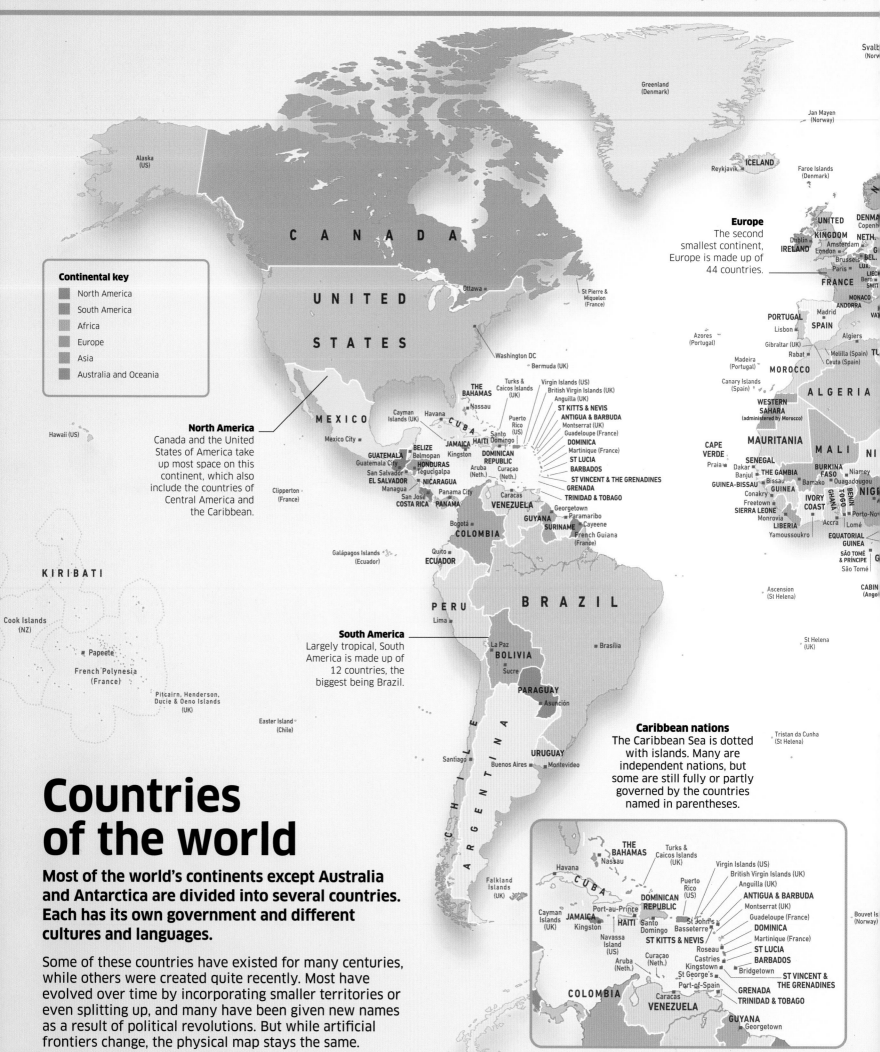

Continental key
- North America
- South America
- Africa
- Europe
- Asia
- Australia and Oceania

Alaska (US)

C A N A D A

Greenland (Denmark)

Jan Mayen (Norway)

Svalb (Norw

ICELAND
Reykjavik
Faroe Islands (Denmark)

Europe
The second smallest continent, Europe is made up of 44 countries.

UNITED KINGDOM
Dublin
IRELAND
London
Paris
FRANCE

DENMARK
Copenh
NETH.
Amsterdam
Brussels
BEL.
LUX.
Bern
SWIT

MONACO
ANDORRA
VA

PORTUGAL
Lisbon
Madrid
SPAIN

Azores (Portugal)
Algiers
MOROCCO

Madeira (Portugal)
Rabat
Gibraltar (UK)
Melilla (Spain)
Ceuta (Spain)
TU

Canary Islands (Spain)

WESTERN SAHARA (administered by Morocco)

ALGERIA

CAPE VERDE
Praia

MAURITANIA

MALI

Dakar
SENEGAL
Banjul
THE GAMBIA
BURKINA FASO
Niamey
NIG
GUINEA-BISSAU
Bissau
Bamako
Ouagadougou
Conakry
GUINEA
IVORY COAST
BENIN
TOGO
GHANA
Freetown
SIERRA LEONE
Monrovia
Accra
Porto-No
Lomé
LIBERIA
Yamoussoukro
EQUATORIAL GUINEA

SÃO TOMÉ & PRÍNCIPE
São Tomé
G

Ascension (St Helena)
CABIN (Ango

U N I T E D
S T A T E S

Ottawa
St Pierre & Miquelon (France)

Washington DC
Bermuda (UK)

Hawaii (US)

North America
Canada and the United States of America take up most space on this continent, which also include the countries of Central America and the Caribbean.

M E X I C O
Mexico City

Clipperton (France)

Cayman Islands (UK)
Havana
CUBA
THE BAHAMAS
Nassau

Turks & Caicos Islands (UK)
Virgin Islands (US)
British Virgin Islands (UK)
Anguilla (UK)
ST KITTS & NEVIS
ANTIGUA & BARBUDA
Montserrat (UK)
Guadeloupe (France)
Puerto Rico (US)
Santo Domingo
DOMINICA
GUATEMALA
BELIZE
Guatemala City
Belmopan
JAMAICA
HAITI
Kingston
DOMINICAN REPUBLIC
Martinique (France)
HONDURAS
ST LUCIA
San Salvador
Tegucigalpa
Aruba (Neth.)
Curaçao (Neth.)
BARBADOS
EL SALVADOR
NICARAGUA
ST VINCENT & THE GRENADINES
Managua
GRENADA
San José
PANAMA
Caracas
TRINIDAD & TOBAGO
COSTA RICA
Panama City
VENEZUELA
Georgetown
GUYANA
Paramaribo
SURINAME
Bogotá
Cayenne
COLOMBIA
French Guiana (France)

K I R I B A T I

Cook Islands (NZ)

Galápagos Islands (Ecuador)
Quito
ECUADOR

Papeete
French Polynesia (France)

Pitcairn, Henderson, Ducie & Oeno Islands (UK)

Easter Island (Chile)

P E R U
Lima

B R A Z I L

St Helena (UK)

South America
Largely tropical, South America is made up of 12 countries, the biggest being Brazil.

La Paz
BOLIVIA
Sucre
Brasília

Tristan da Cunha (St Helena)

PARAGUAY
Asunción

Caribbean nations
The Caribbean Sea is dotted with islands. Many are independent nations, but some are still fully or partly governed by the countries named in parentheses.

Santiago
CHILE
ARGENTINA
URUGUAY
Buenos Aires
Montevideo

Falkland Islands (UK)

Countries of the world

Most of the world's continents except Australia and Antarctica are divided into several countries. Each has its own government and different cultures and languages.

Some of these countries have existed for many centuries, while others were created quite recently. Most have evolved over time by incorporating smaller territories or even splitting up, and many have been given new names as a result of political revolutions. But while artificial frontiers change, the physical map stays the same.

THE BAHAMAS
Nassau
Havana
CUBA
Turks & Caicos Islands (UK)
Virgin Islands (US)
British Virgin Islands (UK)
Anguilla (UK)
ANTIGUA & BARBUDA
Montserrat (UK)
Puerto Rico (US)
Cayman Islands
JAMAICA
Port-au-Prince
DOMINICAN REPUBLIC
Guadeloupe (France)
Kingston
HAITI
Santo Domingo
St John's
Basseterre
DOMINICA
Navassa Island (US)
Martinique (France)
ST KITTS & NEVIS
ST LUCIA
Roseau
Aruba (Neth.)
Curaçao (Neth.)
Castries
BARBADOS
Kingstown
St George's
Bridgetown
Port-of-Spain
ST VINCENT & THE GRENADINES
COLOMBIA
GRENADA
TRINIDAD & TOBAGO
Caracas
VENEZUELA
GUYANA
Georgetown

Bouvet Is (Norway)

206 million—the number of **people** who live in **Nigeria**, which has the **largest population** of all African countries.

6.6 million sq miles (17 million sq km)—the **area** of **Russia**, the world's **largest** country.

201

Country abbreviations

BEL.	Belgium
BOS. & HERZ	Bosnia and Herzegovina
CZECHIA	Czechia (Czech Republic)
KOS.	Kosovo
LIECH.	Liechtenstein
LUX.	Luxembourg
N. MAC.	North Macedonia
MON.	Montenegro
NETH.	Netherlands
NZ	New Zealand
S.M.	San Marino
SLVN	Slovenia
SWITZ	Switzerland
U.A.E	United Arab Emirates
UK	United Kingdom
US	United States of America
VAT. CITY	Vatican City

Asia
The vast continent of Asia includes the economic powerhouses of China and Japan.

Africa
Africa is made up of 54 countries, more than any other continent. Algeria is the largest, and the Seychelles the smallest.

Australia and Oceania
This region consists of Australia, New Zealand, and thousands of mainly tropical islands, many of which form independent nations, spread across the Pacific Ocean.

Europe
The continent of Europe consists of many quite small but prosperous countries. Many belong to a federation called the European Union.

Antarctica
This icy landmass is a continent but not a country. It is jointly governed, but not owned, by the more than 50 countries that have signed the Antarctic Treaty.

Glossary

AGRICULTURE
The practice of farming–growing crops and raising livestock.

ALTITUDE
The vertical distance betwen an object and the Earth's surface or sea level.

AMPHIBIAN
A cold-blooded, backboned animal, such as a frog, that lives part of its life in water and part on land.

ANTIFREEZE
A substance used to lower the freezing point of a liquid. Some animals make antifreeze in their bodies to survive in subzero temperatures.

ASTHENOSPHERE
The soft layer of upper mantle on which the tectonic plates move.

ATMOSPHERE
The air that surrounds Earth, which contains gases such as nitrogen, oxygen, and carbon dioxide.

ATOM
The smallest particle of an element.

BACTERIA
Microscopic, one-celled organisms.

BEDROCK
The layer of solid rock below the soil.

BIODIVERSITY
The variety of all living things on Earth or in a particular area, measured by the numbers of different species.

BIOSPHERE
The parts of Earth where life exists.

CAMOUFLAGE
The ability of an organism to blend in with its environment.

CARBON FOOTPRINT
The total greenhouse gases released into the atmosphere by the activities of a person, company, or country.

CARNIVORE
An animal that eats other animals.

CLIMATE
The most common weather conditions in an area over a period of time.

COMPOUND
A chemical substance in which two or more elements have bonded together.

CONDENSATION
When a gas turns into a liquid.

CONTINENT
One of the seven large landmasses on Earth, mainly surrounded by sea.

CONTINENTAL SHELF
The submerged edge of a continent that lies beneath shallow coastal seas.

CONVERGENT BOUNDARY
Where two tectonic plates are moving together.

CRYOSPHERE
The parts of Earth's surface where the water is in solid, ice form.

DECIDUOUS
Trees or shrubs that shed their leaves every year, usually in fall.

DENSITY
The amount of matter that occupies a certain volume.

DISSOLUTION
The act of dissolving a substance.

DIVERGENT BOUNDARY
Where two tectonic plates are moving apart.

DNA
A material found in the cells of all organisms that carries instructions for how they will look and function.

DORMANT
Inactive at the moment, as if asleep.

DROUGHT
A long period with little or no rain, often leading to water shortages.

DYNAMO
A device that changes movement or mechanical energy into electrical energy.

ECOLOGICAL FOOTPRINT
The impact of a person or community on the environment, such as how much land or water they use.

ECOSYSTEM
A community of living organisms that interact with each other and with their environment.

ELEMENT
A simple substance made of atoms that are all of the same kind.

ELEVATION
The height of a place or object above land or sea level.

EMISSION
Something released into the air, such as gas, heat, or light.

ENERGY
The fuel or electricity used for power. Living things need energy to live and grow, which they usually get by eating other organisms or from sunlight.

EQUATOR
An imaginary circle around the center of Earth, dividing it into the northern and southern hemispheres (halves).

EVAPORATION
A process by which a liquid changes into a gas.

EVERGREEN
Plants that bear leaves and needles throughout the year.

EVOLUTION
The gradual process of change in living things between generations over millions of years.

EXTINCTION
The disappearance from Earth of the last living representative of a species.

FERTILIZER
A natural or artificial substance that is put on land to make plants grow better.

FIRE BREAK
A means to stop the spread of fire, such as a strip of open land in a forest.

FOSSIL
The preserved remains or traces of animals or plants from an earlier time.

FOSSIL FUEL
Formed from the remains of prehistoric organisms and burned to release energy; includes coal, oil, and gas.

FUNGUS
An organism that feeds on decaying matter and reproduces by releasing spores. A mushroom is the fruit of a fungus, growing above ground.

GALAXY
A collection of stars, gas, and dust held together by gravity.

GENE
One of the tiny units carried on DNA that determine what a living thing looks like and how it functions.

GENOME
An organism's complete set of DNA.

GEOTHERMAL
The internal heat of Earth.

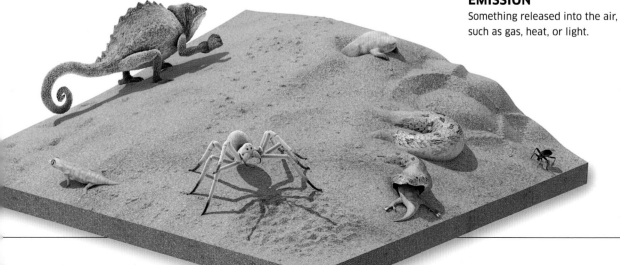

GLOBAL WARMING
The heating of Earth's climate.

GRAVITY
The force that attracts one object to another and prevents things from floating off into space.

GREENHOUSE GAS
A gas, such as carbon dioxide, that traps heat in Earth's atmosphere.

GROUNDWATER
Water present beneath Earth's surface in the rocks and soil.

GYRE
A circular pattern of ocean currents.

HABITAT
The area where an organism naturally makes its home.

HERBIVORE
An animal that feeds on plants.

HOT SPOT
A fixed point beneath Earth's surface where the mantle is particularly hot.

HYDROPONICS
A method of growing plants without soil, usually in water.

HYDROSPHERE
The total amount of water on a planet, both above and below the surface.

HYDROTHERMAL VENT
A crack in the ocean floor where very hot and chemical-rich water rises.

IRRIGATION
Supplying land with water so that crops and plants will grow.

JET STREAM
Narrow bands of strong wind in the upper levels of the atmosphere.

LATITUDE
Term used to indicate how far north or south a location is from the equator.

LIGHT-YEAR
The distance traveled by light in a vacuum in one year.

LIMESTONE
A rock made of calcium carbonate, formed from the shells of sea animals.

LITHOSPHERE
The solid upper part of Earth's mantle and the brittle outer crust.

LIVESTOCK
Domesticated animals, used for food, wool, and leather, or transportation.

MAGMA
Hot, liquid rock that is found beneath the Earth's surface.

MAGNETIC FIELD
The area around a magnet or electric current where magnetic force is felt.

MAMMAL
One of a group of warm-blooded, backboned animals, with females that feed their young with milk.

METHANE
A natural gas that burns easily and is used as fuel. It is a greenhouse gas.

MICROORGANISM
A tiny organism that can be seen only with the aid of a microscope.

MINERAL
A natural, inorganic substance. Most rocks are made from minerals.

MOLECULE
A group of atoms bonded together.

MOLTEN
Melted (in liquid form).

NEBULA
A cloud of gas and/or dust in space.

NUTRIENT
A substance essential for life to exist and grow.

ORBIT
The path taken by an object, such as a planet, that is circling around another.

ORGANISM
A living thing.

OXYGEN
A gas that is present in Earth's atmosphere and is essential to life.

OZONE LAYER
A thin part of Earth's atmosphere that absorbs most of the sun's harmful rays.

PARASITE
An organism that feeds on another, called the host, weakening it and sometimes eventually killing it.

PERMAFROST
A permanently frozen layer under Earth's surface.

PERMEABLE
Allows liquids or gases through it.

PESTICIDES
Any substance used by farmers to kill or repel insects that harm crops.

PHOTOSYNTHESIS
The process by which plants and some algae use the sun's energy to make food from carbon dioxide and water.

POLLUTANT
A substance that contaminates air, water, or soil.

POROUS
Has many small holes in it, through which water and air can pass.

PRECAMBRIAN
This vast span of time, between 4.6 billion and 542 million years ago, saw continents forming, our atmosphere developing, and early life evolving.

PRECIPITATION
Water that falls from the clouds to the ground, such as rain, snow, hail, and sleet.

PREHISTORIC
Existing before written records.

PRESSURE
The force that pushes against a particular area.

RESERVOIR
A place where water is stored.

RIDGE
A section of risen crust formed when two tectonic plates move apart, or a range of hills or mountains.

RIFT
A crack in Earth's crust where two tectonic plates are pulling apart.

SALINITY
The amount of salt dissolved in water.

SEAMOUNT
An underwater volcano that is not high enough to form an island.

SEDIMENT
Small bits of rock, sand, or mud that settle in layers, usually underwater.

SPECIES
A group of closely related living things that can breed together.

STAR
A massive sphere of glowing plasma (highly energized gas) that generates energy by nuclear fusion in its core.

STELLAR NURSERY
An area of dust and gas in space where stars are formed.

STORM SURGE
An abnormal rise in sea level caused by a storm.

SUBDUCTION
When one tectonic plate sinks beneath another.

SUBSISTENCE FARMING
Growing enough food for the farmer and their family to live on, not to sell.

SUBSPECIES
A smaller group within a species that is distinct from the rest, often due to geographical isolation.

SUPERCLUSTER
A large group of nearby galaxies and clusters of galaxies.

SUPERNOVA
An exploding giant star.

SUSTAINABLE
Able to continue over a period of time, without running out; the use of natural resources at a level that does not destroy the environment.

TECTONIC PLATES
Giant pieces of Earth's crust, which move around over millions of years.

TRADE WINDS
Winds on either side of the equator that blow east to west toward it.

TRANSFORM BOUNDARY
Where two tectonic plates are sliding past each other.

Index

Acknowledgments

The publisher would like to thank the following people for their assistance in the preparation of this book: Jemma Westing, Rob Perry, and Katy Jakeway for visualizing; Simon Mumford for maps; Dan Hooke for additional text; Jenny Sich and Sam Kennedy for editorial assistance; Laura Barwick and Myriam Megharbi for picture research; Hazel Beynon for proofreading; Elizabeth Wise for indexing; and Rachel Kenny for fact-checking.

Smithsonian Enterprises:
Kealy E. Gordon, Product Development Manager
Jill Corcoran, Director, Licensed Publishing
Brigid Ferraro, Vice President, Consumer and Education Products
Carol LeBlanc, President

The publisher would like to thank the following for their kind permission to reproduce their photographs: (Key: a-above; b-below/bottom; c-center; f-far; l-left; r-right; t-top)

2 Dorling Kindersley: 123RF.com: Corey A Ford (c). **Dreamstime.com:** Dorling Kindersley: Gary Hanna / Tuktop / Dreamstime.com (tl); Dorling Kindersley: Gary Hanna / Mattscott / Dreamstime.com (ca). **Shutterstock.com:** AndreAnita (c/capybara); Vadim Petrakov (bl); nounours (bc); Artur Bogacki (b); Standard store88 (cb); LUC KOHNEN (crb); Isarat (clb); Split Second Stock (cl). **5 Dorling Kindersley:** Jason Harding /Turbosquid/xfrog/cgmood (b). **Dreamstime.com:** Dorling Kindersley: Gary Hanna / Colin Young / Dreamstime.com (cl). **8 Alamy Stock Photo:** Matthew Banks (cla); Sergey Novikov (tr). **Dorling Kindersley:** Dreamstime.com: Mark Turner (tl). **9 Dorling Kindersley:** Colin Keates / Natural History Museum, London (tr). **naturepl.com:** Philippe Clement (cla). Science Photo Library: Martin Bond (clb); Duncan Shaw (bl). **10 Alamy Stock Photo:** Stocktrek Images, Inc. (cb). ESA: ESA and the Planck Collaboration (cl). **Millenium Simulation:** MPA / Virgo consortium (tr). **NASA:** ESA and the Hubble Heritage Team (STScI / AURA) (br). **11 ESA:** Hubble & NASA (tr). NASA: JPL-Caltech / STScI / CXC / SAO (tl). **12 ESO:** L. CALÇADA (tl). **14-15 solarsystemscope.com:** creativecommons.org /licenses / by / 4.0. **15 NASA:** H. Hammel, MIT, and NASA (cr). **16 Alamy Stock Photo:** Universal Images Group North America LLC (bl). **Dorling Kindersley:** 123RF.com: Boris Stromar / astrobobo (br). **Getty Images:** Richard Roscoe / StocktrekImages (cl). **naturepl.com:** Franco Banfi (cr). **Science Photo Library:** GREGOIRE CIRADE (clb). **16-17 Science Photo Library:** Mark Garlick (t). **17 Alamy Stock Photo:** Samuel Hess (br). **Science Photo Library:** Eckhard Slawik (cr). **18 Science Photo Library:** Richard Bizley (tl). **18-19 Dorling Kindersley:** Simon Mumford / Colorado Plateau Geosystems Inc. **19 Alamy Stock Photo:** Russotwins (tl). **Science Photo Library:** CAROLINA BIOLOGICAL SUPPLY COMPANY (ca). **20 Dorling Kindersley:** 123RF.com: Corey A Ford (cra). **21 Dorling Kindersley:** James Kuether (cra). **22 Dreamstime.com:** Paura (tl). **Getty Images:** Elizaveta Becker / ullstein bild (tr). **23 Alamy Stock Photo:** Susan E. Degginger (bl). **24 Shutterstock.com:** Mariusz Hajdarowicz (cr); Vac1 (bc). **24-25 Shutterstock.com:** Oleksii Liebiediev (b). **25 Shutterstock.com:** Kim dB (c); Michelle Holihan (cl); Ian Duffield (tr); Greens and Blues (cr); Rodrigo Lourezini (clb); Heliosphile (bl); L Galbraith (clb/pony). **26-27 Getty Images:** Fadil Aziz / AlcibbumPhotograph. **30 Alamy Stock Photo:** agefotostock (clb); Robbie Shone (cla). **Science Photo Library:** Alfred Pasieka (cb). **31 Alamy Stock Photo:** Greenshoots Communications (bl). **Science Photo Library:** NASA (br). **35 Alamy Stock Photo:** NOAA (tr). **36 Getty Images:** Stocktrek Images (ca). **37 Dorling Kindersley:** iStock: ratpack223 (br). **Shutterstock.com:** Vixit (tl). **38 naturepl.com:** Franco Banfi (tr). **39 Getty Images:** Arctic-Images (tc). **naturepl.com:** Doug Perrine (br). **40 Dorling Kindersley:** Simon Mumford / Colorado Plateau Geosystems Inc (cla). **Science Science Photo Library:** Natural History Museum, London (cr). **41 Alamy Stock Photo:** Zoonar GmbH (cla). Getty Images / iStock: DanielPrudek (tc); Thomas Faull (tr). **42 Alamy Stock Photo:** The Natural History Museum (tc). **43 Alamy Stock Photo:** Eric Nathan (cr). Getty Images: Richard Roscoe / StocktrekImages (tl). James St. John: (br).**44 Alamy Stock Photo:** Stuart Holroyd (bl). **DK/Simon Mumford/Getty Images:** Mike Hill (c). **46-47** Dosch Design. **48 Dorling Kindersley:** Dreamstime.com: Rob Kemp (cb); Harry Taylor / Natural History Museum, London (crb). **Getty Images / iStock:** KrimKate (cr). **Shutterstock.com:** Luca Renner Photgraphy (br). **49 Getty Images:** An Image is worth thousand words (cla); HUM Images (tr). **Science Photo Library:** Stephen & Donna O'meara (ca). **50-51 Shutterstock.com:** Emilio Morenatti / AP. **52 Alamy Stock Photo:** LOETSCHER CHLAUS (br). **Science Photo Library:**Jeremy Bishop (tl). **53 Alamy Stock Photo:** andrea federici (tr). **Dorling Kindersley:** 123RF.com: Paolo Gianfrancesco (br). **Science Photo Library:** Martin Rietze (bl). **54 Dorling Kindersley:** Getty Images: Kirsten Boos / EyeEm (bl); iStock: rusm (tl). **55 Dreamstime.com:** Dmitrii Pichugin (cr). **56 Depositphotos Inc:** rinderart (br). **Dorling Kindersley:** iStock: benedek (bc). **57 Alamy Stock Photo:** Danita Delimont (cr). **Dorling Kindersley:** Dreamstime.com: John.59 (tc); Colin Keates / Natural History Museum, London (clb/marble); Colin Keates / Natural History Museum, London (bc/slate); Colin Keates / Natural History Museum, London (bc/schist); Shutterstock: Aleksandr Pobedimskiy (crb). **Getty Images:** Ashley Cooper (c). **Shutterstock.com:** Genevieve_Andry (tl). **58 123RF.com:** gontar (cl). **Alamy Stock Photo:** Phil Degginger (ca). **Depositphotos Inc:** vvoennyy (cr). **Dorling Kindersley:** Ruth Jenkinson / HoltsGems (bl). **Dreamstime.com:** Vvoevale (crb); Vvoevale (br). **Shutterstock.com:** Branko Jovanovic (ca). **59 Depositphotos Inc:** Minakryn (bc). **Dorling Kindersley:** Dreamstime.com: Vlad3563 (cla); Ruth Jenkinson / HoltsGems (bc); Ruth Jenkinson / HoltsGems (tr); Ruth Jenkinson / HoltsGems (c/emerald); Tim Parmenter / Natural History Museum, London (cr); Ruth Jenkinson / HoltsGems (bl). **Dreamstime.com:** Roberto Junior (c/diamond); Ruslan Minakryn (cl); Vvoevale (ca); Björn Wylezich (crb). **Shutterstock.com:** Bjoern Wylezich (br). **62 Shutterstock.com:** Alex7370 (ca). **Science Photo Library:**Susumu Nishinaga (bl). **63 James St. John. 64-65 AirPano images. 66 Alamy Stock Photo:** REUTERS (tl). **67 Dorling Kindersley:** James Kuether (tl). **68 Dorling Kindersley:** iStock: cookelma (cr). **70 Getty Images:** PHILIPP ROHNER / 500px (cb); Marco Bottigelli (clb); SeppFriedhuber (bc); Alexandre Lamothe / EyeEm (br); Iñigo Fdz de Pinedo (crb). **U.S. Geological Survey:** Howard Perlman, USGS; globeillustration by Jack Cook, Woods Hole Oceanographic Institution; and Adam Nieman, data Igor Shiklamonov (cra). **71 Alamy Stock Photo:** Science History Images (tl). **74 Dorling Kindersley:** iStock: cookelma (br). **Getty Images:** Syed Almohdzar / EyeEm (bl). **75 Alamy Stock Photo:** D. Holden Bailey (tr). **76-77 Shutterstock.com:** Kuznetsova Julia. **78 Alamy Stock Photo:** Marshall Black (tr). **Getty Images:** Viaframe (br). **Shutterstock.com:** Ajdin Kamber (tc). **79 Depositphotos Inc:** desant7474 (cra). **Getty Images / iStock:** Jupiterimages (cla). **Getty Images:** zhouyousifang (br). **80 Alamy Stock Photo:** Hemis (bl). **81 Getty Images:** Matteo Colombo (tl). **82 Dreamstime.com:** Joachim Bago (br). **Getty Images:** Тихомир Димитров/ 500px (bl); Maksim Ozerov (cra); Wei Hao Ho (fbl); Suthida Loedchaiyapan / EyeEm (bc). **83 Alamy Stock Photo:** Gunter Marx / HI (cr). **Getty Images:** Artur Debat (br). **SuperStock:** John Warburton Lee (crb). **85 Alamy Stock Photo:** Album (c). **Dorling Kindersley:** Dynamo Limited (t). **86 Caroline Power. 87 Alamy Stock Photo:** Olivier DIGOIT (br/swell); Tom Uhlman (cl); PaulPaladin (br/ripples); Mesh (br/chop). **88 Alamy Stock Photo:** mauritius images GmbH (cl). **Shutterstock.com:** Kiichiro Sato / AP (cr). **90 Alamy Stock Photo:** ITPhoto (br); Mirosław Nowaczyk (bl). **Getty Images:** Daniel Nery / EyeEm (c). **naturepl.com:** Bryan and Cherry Alexander (cr). **90-91 www.meteoblue.com. 91 Alamy Stock Photo:** Reinhold Tscherwitschke (crb). **Getty Images:** Africanway (cr). **Getty Images / iStock:** FrankvandenBergh (cl). **Shutterstock.com:** Kiichiro Sato / AP (br). **93 Alamy Stock Photo:** Johny (bl); RGB Ventures / SuperStock (tl); Travel Pix (br). **95 Alamy Stock Photo:** FALKENSTEINFOTO (tl); Sundry Photography (crb). **Getty Images:** BAY ISMOYO / AFP (c); mikulas1 (cl); Jewel SAMAD / AFP (cr); MR.Cole_Photographer (fclb); JW LTD (clb); bugto (cb). **97 NASA:** Goddard / Katy Mersmann (tl). **98 Alamy Stock Photo:** R.M. Nunes (bl); REUTERS / Amit Dave (clb). **Getty Images:** Matteo Colombo (crb); NurPhoto (bc); Stefan Mokrzecki (cb); Oli Scarff (br).**99 Alamy Stock Photo:** COP21 (crb). **Dreamstime.com:** Andreistanescu (br). **101 123RF.com:** 123bogdan (cl). **Alamy Stock Photo:** Fairgrieve (tl); Ryan McGinnis (tc). **Dorling Kindersley:** Dreamstime.com: Ilfede (tr); Dreamstime.com: Dezzor (cla). **Dreamstime.com:** Anthony Aneese Totah Jr (cra); Dezzor (t); Pozsgaig (cr). **Getty Images:** john finney photography (crb). **Getty Images /iStock:** Spondylolithesis (cb). **104 Alamy Stock Photo:** mauritius images GmbH (br). **105 Alamy Stock Photo:** Euan Cherry (bl); Roger Coulam (ca); REUTERS (cb); redbrickstock.com (crb); REUTERS / Mike Hutchings (br). **Getty Images:** DAVID L. NELSON / AFP (bc). **Getty Images / iStock:** DenisTangneyJr (clb). **NOAA:** NOAA-AOC (tr). **106-107 TurboSquid: Inc.: Dorling Kindersley / broodkovsci (tr). Dorling Kindersley:** Adam Benton / Turbosquid. **107 Shutterstock.com:** Mark Wallheiser / EPA (bc). TurboSquid: Inc.: Dorling Kindersley / Fulip; Inc.: Dorling Kindersley / Pbr Game Ready (cb); Inc.: Dorling Kindersley / Marcos Ninja (crb); Inc.: Dorling Kindersley / zzztonycstech (cla); Inc.: Dorling Kindersley / AssetKit (clb); Inc.: Dorling Kindersley / Verbaska (br). **108-109 Shutterstock.com:** John D Sirlin. **111 Alamy Stock Photo:** dpa picture alliance (cra). **Getty Images:** Warren Faidley (tl). **113 Alamy Stock Photo:** Christina Simons (br); Soma (tr). **Getty Images:** Justin Sullivan (tc). **114 Dorling Kindersley:** Dreamstime.com: Lunamarina (cr). **naturepl.com:** Neil Lucas (cl). **116 Alamy Stock Photo:** Phil Degginger (tc). **Getty Images:** Michele D'Amico supersky77 (crb); Onfokus (tl); Vasilis Karfis (tr); Thomas Roche (cl); Harald von Radebrecht (bl); Yannick Tylle (bc). **Getty Images / iStock:** FilippoBacci (cb). **117 Dreamstime.com:** Nadezhda Bolotina (tl); Viktor Nikitin (ca). **Getty Images:** Georgette Douwma (bc); Jason Edwards (bl); Richard McManus (br). **Shutterstock.com:** Nikolay Karasev (c). **118 Renderosity:** Ken_Gilliland (cl). **Science Photo Library:** Bernhard Edmaier (tr). **119 Getty Images:** VASILY BOGOYAVLENSKY / Stringer (cra). **120 Alamy Stock Photo:** blickwinkel (c); Brian Hartshorn (cra); Zoonar GmbH (ca); Minden Pictures (cl); Robin Weaver (clb); Minden Pictures (cb); Andrew Walmsley (br). **Getty Images / iStock:** Adventure_Photo (tr). **121 Alamy Stock Photo:** Nature Picture Library (br); George Ostertag (bc). **Dorling Kindersley:** Simon Mumford / NSIDC: Sea Ice Index (cla); Simon Mumford / NSIDC: Sea Ice Index (ca). **Getty Images:** John Conrad (tr); Roland Hemmi (cra); Harry M. Walker / DesignPics (cr); Danita Delimont (crb). **122 Alamy Stock Photo:** agefotostock (bl); agefotostock (bc). **Getty Images:** Massimiliano Finzi (cr). **123 Alamy Stock Photo:** AGF Srl (t); Andreas Altenburger (cb). **Getty Images:** Ian Billenness (br); Lars Johansson / EyeEm (crb); Valentina Milkovics / EyeEm (bl); Sieboldianus (clb). **124 Dorling Kindersley:** 123RF.com: alein (br); **iStockphoto.com:** DmitriyKazitsyn (tl); **Dreamstime.com:** Iofoto (cla). **126 naturepl.com:** Chien Lee / Minden (br); Neil Lucas (tl). **127 Dreamstime.com:** Jayanta Chakraborty (tr). **Shutterstock.com:**Thommy TFH (crb). **129 Getty Images:** Anton Petrus (cr). **Science Photo Library:** Steve Gschmeissner (br). **130 Alamy Stock Photo:** Moiz Husein (clb). **Getty Images:** Ayzenstayn (c); Mitchell Krog (tc); Enn Li Photography (cr). **Getty Images / iStock:** shellgrit (bl). **131 Alamy Stock Photo:** John Cancalosi (tr). **Getty Images:** Daniel J Barr (cl); Marius Hepp / EyeEm (tc). **Shutterstock.com:** Wojciech Dziadosz (bl). **132 Alamy Stock Photo:** Stephen Barnes / Namibia (tl). **Shutterstock.com:** SC Gardens (cra). **133 Alamy Stock Photo:** Martin Harvey (tr). **134 Alamy Stock Photo:** Arina Habich (tr). **Shutterstock.com:** Damsea (c); Galina Savina (cb); mariamalaya (br); Gurkan Ozturk (ca); Danita Delimont (cra); Wildnerdpix (cra/stork). **135 naturepl.com:** John Shaw (cra). **Shutterstock.com:** AndreAnita (ca/capybara); Vadim Petrakov (bl); nounours (bc); Artur Bogacki (br); mariamalaya (c); Isarat (cl); Standard store88 (cr); LUC KOHNEN (cr/water plants); SachinSubran (c/anaconda); Kylie Nicholson (cla); Wildnerdpix (cla/jabiru stork); coolrobin2 (ca); Dimitris Timpilis (ca/spoonbill feeding); Split Second Stock (cra/grass); Roberto Tetsuo Okamura (cra/birds); David Watkins (ca/spoonbill); Dimitris Timpilis (tl); Joy Sagar (ftl); Vinicius Bacarin (tl/flying); Leandro Espino (tc). **136 Getty Images:** Robert Brook (cl); M Swiet Productions (tc); Johannes Hulsch / EyeEm (tr); Javier Fernández Sánchez (c); ullstein bild (cr); Alexis Rosenfeld (bc); George Karbus Photography (br). **137 Alamy Stock Photo:** Juniors Bildarchiv GmbH (bl); Michael Patrick O'Neill (cr); Dennis Sabo (crb). **Getty Images:** Sirachai Arunrugstichai (bc); CR Shelare (tl); Ethan Daniels / StocktrekImages (tc); Douglas Klug (tr); Georgettte Douwma (c); imageBROKER / Frank Schneider (cb); Hal Beral (br). **138-139 naturepl.com:** SCOTLAND: The Big Picture. **140 Dorling Kindersley:** Dreamstime.com: Lunamarina(br). **Shutterstock.com:** bluehand (cla); Neirfy (cl); Sakis Lazarides (cb); Islandjems - Jemma Craig (c); JonMilnes (ca); Laura Dts (tc); Michael Waddington (tr); magnusdeepbelow (cra); Jsegalexplore (cr/tuna); Andrea Izzotti (cr/whale shark); Alexey Goosev (cra/shark); Joe Fish Flynn (crb); Dan Olsen (cr). **140-141 Shutterstock.com:** Fuel to your fire (t); Amanda S Walker (ca). **141 Alamy Stock Photo:** Marko Steffensen (tl). **Shutterstock.com:** 3dsam79 (bl); Martin Prochazkacz (clb). **142 Alamy Stock Photo:** PhotoStock-Israel (tr). **Dreamstime.com:** Clint Austin (cra); Volodymyr Byrdyak (b); Robin Van Olderen (c); Smellme (cr). **TurboSquid:** khanir (clb). TurboSquid: Inc.: Dorling Kindersley / khanir (clb). **143 Dorling Kindersley:** Dreamstime.com: Michael Sheehan / Bondsza (crb). **Dreamstime.com:** Andreanita (fr); Puntasit Choksawatdikorn (bc); Volodymyr Byrdyak (c); Javarman (cr); Volodymyr Byrdyak (cl); Marielemerle157 (c/hyena); Volodymyr Byrdyak (tl); Anke Van Wyk (cla/grass); Janina Kubik (tr/zebras); Michael Sheehan (fcr); Henryturner (c/carcass); Isselee (tc); Znm (ca/gazelle); Juni (cl/hyena); Iakov Filimonov (c/hyenas); Ecophoto (cl/vulture); Johannes Gerhardus Swanepoel (ca). **144 Alamy Stock Photo:** Worldwide Picture Library (cla). **Depositphotos Inc:** toa55 (clb). **Dorling Kindersley:** Simon Mumford / data from Global Forest Watch: GLAD Alerts Footprint (ca). **Dreamstime.com:** Fabian Plock (cra). **Shutterstock.com:** Naya Nurindra (c). **145 Alamy Stock Photo:** EggImages (cr); Tor Eigeland (tc); Morgan Trimble (br); mauritius images GmbH (cl). **Dorling Kindersley:** Dreamstime.com: Ondřej Prosický (c). **Getty Images:** Brandi Mueller (cla). **148 Dreamstime.com:** Dorling Kindersley: Gary Hanna / Tuktop / Dreamstime.com (ca); Dorling Kindersley: Gary Hanna / Colin Young / Dreamstime.com (ca); Dorling Kindersley: Gary Hanna / Vladimir Lukovic / Dreamstime.com (ca/iguana); Dorling Kindersley: Gary Hanna / Kairi Aun / Dreamstime.com (clb); Dorling Kindersley: Gary Hanna / Pardentevamaya / Dreamstime.com (cb); Dorling Kindersley: Gary Hanna / Soren Egeberg / Dreamstime.com (br). **149 Dreamstime.com:** Dorling Kindersley: Gary Hanna / Imogen Warren / Dreamstime.com (cla); Dorling Kindersley: Gary Hanna / Todd Lipsky / Dreamstime.com (bl); Dorling Kindersley: Gary Hanna / Mattscott / Dreamstime.com (cr). **150 Alamy Stock Photo:** MehmetO (cr); dave stamboulis (cl). **153 Alamy Stock Photo:** Bob Daemmrich (crb). **Getty Images:** Grant Faint (clb); Monty Rakusen (cl); The Image Bank (bl); John Keeble (cr). **naturepl.com:** Michael & Patricia Fogden (br). **154 Alamy Stock Photo:** Joerg Boethling (bl); Design Pics Inc (cl). **Getty Images / iStock:** RelaxFoto.de (br). **154-155 plants by Xfrog, www.xfrog.com:** Luc Bianco (cra). **155 Alamy Stock Photo:** Luiz Ribeiro (tr). **Getty Images:** Alexis Rosenfeld (br). **156-157 AirPano images. 158 Alamy Stock Photo:** agefotostock (cra); MehmetO (cr); Trevor Mogg (br). **159 Alamy Stock Photo:** Zoonar GmbH (b). **160 Alamy Stock Photo:** Gonzales Photo (tl). **Getty Images / iStock:** ferrantraite (ca). TurboSquid: Inc.: Dorling Kindersley / 3D SolidWorks (clb); Inc.: Dorling Kindersley / 3dxin (cb). **160-161 Dorling Kindersley:** Jason Harding / Turbosquid/xfrog/cgmood. TurboSquid: Inc.: Dorling Kindersley / RobertKorsantes (metro); Inc.: Dorling Kindersley / Humanoid Animations (b); Inc.: Dorling Kindersley / Good Models (ca). **161 Dreamstime.com:** Radub85 (tl). TurboSquid: Inc.: Dorling Kindersley / Etractorist (bc). **162 Alamy Stock Photo:** David Wall (br); Xinhua (cl). **162-163 Dorling Kindersley:** 123RF.com: Kittipong Jirasukhanont (tc). **163 Alamy Stock Photo:** Arterra Picture Library (bl); Sipa US (cra); Thamrongpat Theerathammakorn (crb). **Dorling Kindersley:**Dreamstime.com: Diana Rich / Talshiar (cla/GPS); Lauren Quinn (cla); Dreamstime.com: Robert Davies (ca). **Getty Images / iStock:**MicrovOne (cb). **Getty Images:** Peathegee Inc (br). **164 Getty Images:** Cristobal Olivares / Bloomberg (tl). **166 Alamy Stock Photo:** Britpix (bl). **Getty Images:** New York Daily News Archive (br). **Shutterstock.com:** Kristof Kovacs (cl). **167 Alamy Stock Photo:** dpa picture alliance (tr); Xinhua (br); Rob Matthews (bl). **168-169 Shutterstock.com:** Sakarin Sawasdinaka. **170 Alamy Stock Photo:** Reynold Sumayku (bl). Living Seawalls: Alex Goad (br). **170-171 CGTrader:** lafleurstudio (c). **171 Alamy Stock Photo:** An Solas Òir (tr). **Dreamstime.com:** Christopher Elwell (br). **172 Alamy Stock Photo:** LowePhoto (cra); Oso Media (br). **173 Alamy Stock Photo:** David Lichtneker (bc); Sipa US (br); dave stamboulis (tr). **Getty Images:** Jingying Zhao (cla). **174 Alamy Stock Photo:** David Ball (c); Antony Nettle (clb); Mathias Rhode (bl). **175 Airlite:** (crb).**Alamy Stock Photo:** Andrey Nekrasov (tc). **Block Solutions Oy:** Kristoffer Trondsen (br). **Getty Images:** Charlie Crowhurst (clb). **Getty Images / iStock:** pcess609 (cra). **The Ocean Cleanup:** (bl). **176 Dorling Kindersley:** CBS Photo Archive (cl). **Getty Images:** Matteo Rossetti / Archivio Matteo Rossetti / Mondadori Portfolio (bc); Bhawan Singh / The The India Today Group (bl). **Shutterstock.com:** Dejan Popovic (br). **177 FSC / Forest Stewardship Council:** (tc). Leaping Bunny: (c). **Marine Stewardship Council:** (tl). **Roundtable on Sustainable Palm Oil:** (ca). **Shutterstock.com:** elenabsl (tr). The Rainforest Alliance. **The Fairtrade Foundation:** (cla).**178 Alamy Stock Photo:** Avalon.red (cr). **Dorling Kindersley:** Dreamstime.com: David Havel (c). **182 Alamy Stock Photo:** Alpineguide (bl).**Getty Images:** DEA / W. BUSS / Contributor (cla); Matt Anderson Photography (tl); Laura Hedien (clb). **183 Alamy Stock Photo:** Louis-Michel DESERT (tl). **Getty Images:** philippe giraud (bl); Aydin Palabiyikoglu / Anadolu Agency (cr). **Getty Images / iStock:** Stocktrek Images (br). **184 Alamy Stock Photo:** Nature Picture Library (c); Pep Roig (br). **Getty Images:** MARTIN BERNETTI / AFP (bl). **naturepl.com:** Nick Garbutt (cl). **185 Alamy Stock Photo:** Martin Harvey (tc); John Michaels (crb); dave stamboulis (tr). naturepl.com: Brandon Cole (cra). **186 Alamy Stock Photo:** Arterra Picture Library (bc); Johner Images (tl); BIOSPHOTO (cla); LOETSCHER CHLAUS (cl). **187 Alamy Stock Photo:** blickwinkel (cb). **Dorling Kindersley:** Simon Mumford / data courtesy Marc Imhoff / NASA GSFC / Christopher Elvidge / NOAA NGDC. Image by Craig Mayhew and Robert Simmon / NASA GSFC (br). **Dreamstime.com:** Gusa Mihai Cristian (bc). **188 Alamy Stock Photo:** Mike Goldwater (c); Jan Wlodarczyk (tr). **Dorling Kindersley:** iStockphoto.com: Marek Stefunko (clb). **Dreamstime.com:** Ecophoto (br); Michael Turner (bl). **189 Dorling Kindersley:** Dreamstime.com: David Havel (br); iStock: guenterguni (tr). **Getty Images / iStock:** guenterguni (cr). **190 Alamy Stock Photo:** Jochen Tack (cla); Tierfotoagentur (cb); Rosanne Tackaberry (br). **Getty Images:** Timothy Allen (ca). **191 Alamy Stock Photo:** Avalon.red (br); robertharding (crb). **Dorling Kindersley:** Dreamstime.com: Dqran96 (tr); iStockphoto.com: Damocean (cra). **192-193 Shutterstock.com:** Serkanyalcinkaya. **194 Alamy Stock Photo:** Garey Lennox (cl). **Dreamstime.com:** Rafael Ben Ari (bl). **naturepl.com:** Tim Laman (tl). **195 Alamy Stock Photo:** Galaxiid (tl); Ingo Oeland (crb). **Getty Images:** Steve Gisselman (bl); Lucas Schifres / Uluru-Kata Tjuta National Park (br). **naturepl.com:** Gary Bell / Oceanwide / Minden (c); Gary Bell / Oceanwide / Minden (cr). **196 Alamy Stock Photo:** Andy Myatt (bl); RP Images (cl). Robert Harding Picture Library: Michael Nolan (tl). **197 Alamy Stock Photo:** Cavan Imagess (cra); Jeffrey Miller (bl). **naturepl.com:** Klein & Hubert (ca). **Science Photo Library:** KARIM AGABI / EURELIOS (br). **198 Dorling Kindersley:** 123RF.com: Juan Gil Raga (c).**Getty Images / iStock:** SeppFriedhuber (bc). **naturepl.com:** Jenny E. Ross (crb). **199 Alamy Stock Photo:** Øyvind Breyholtz (cra); Minden Pictures (crb). **Getty Images:** Carlo Lukassen (br). **Science Photo Library:** Bernhard Edmaier (tc)

Cover images:
All other images © Dorling Kindersley

31901068695933